John Oman 1860-1939

Image produced by Elliott & Fry, London, and in the
possession of Westminster College, Cambridge; reproduced
by permission.

T0385267

John Oman: New Perspectives

John Oman: New Perspectives

Edited by

Adam Hood

First published by Paternoster, 2012

Paternoster is an imprint of Authentic Media
52 Presley Way, Crownhill, Milton Keynes, MK8 0ES
www.authenticmedia.co.uk

British Library Cataloguing in Publication Data
A catalogue record for this book is available from the British Library

ISBN 978-1-84227-731-7

Typeset by Adam Hood.
Printed and bound in Great Britain
for Paternoster

For Katrina

Contents

PREFACE AND ACKNOWLEDGEMENTS

My involvement with John Oman has been lengthy, beginning with the suggestion of my former doctoral supervisor, Professor Keith Ward, that he would be worth a look as a potential conversation partner to John Macmurray. That initial guidance blossomed into a detailed interest in his work, which was incorporated into a thesis and then a book. Since that time I have had a simmering interest in this enigmatic character, boiling up occasionally in essays that drew on his thought. Yet, there remained a bigger idea in mind, which was to arrange a gathering of Oman scholars and so to move the study of his work forward. This thought was nourished in conversations with, amongst others Stephen Bevans, John Hick, George Newlands, Alan Sell, and Keith Ward. Thanks to their encouragement it was finally possible to convene a conference at Westminster College, Cambridge in the autumn of 2009 and the present volume arises largely out of papers given then.

I would wish to thank a number of people who gave practical assistance with the conference and this book. At Westminster College, Margaret Thompson and Principal Susan Durber were always encouraging and helpful in the run up to the gathering. There really was no other place for the conference; it was very meaningful to participants to be meeting in an institution with so many echoes of Oman. Seeing his portrait in the Westminster dining hall at each meal time, with his kindly, wise, smiling face beaming over our gathering, seemed to offer a kind of blessing on our efforts. I am indebted to Karen Durant, Robert Foster and Vincent Manoharan – all students of the Queen's Foundation for Ecumenical Theological Education, Birmingham – for their assistance in arranging and leading the conference. Also to Robert, Karen and Alan Sell for working with me on planning this book and preparing the conference papers for publication. Thanks to the The Grimmett Trust, The Hope Trust and the Queen's Foundation, Birmingham for sponsoring the gathering. Finally, love and thanks to Katrina, Nathan and Abigail for their patient encouragement and support of my interest in Oman.

Adam Hood
Queen's Foundation, Birmingham
July 2010

Introduction

A striking portrait of John Oman hangs prominently in the dining room of Westminster College, Cambridge. In this fine work, the artist has captured very effectively different dimensions of Oman's personality. He is dressed as a Presbyterian minister in a dark, sober suit and clerical collar, but also wears the teaching robe of an academic. Juxtaposed with the air of serious purpose, Oman has his hands in his pockets, suggesting a note of informality. The portrait captures the noble bearing of Oman's greying, balding head, but his face is fixed in a warm, kindly, knowing smile. His eyes, narrowed, seem to be peering into the distance as if to make out some feature on the horizon.

The Westminster portrait reminds one of why Oman's work remains of importance today. First, it depicts Oman, the minister and scholar, who combined rigorous academic enquiry with a commitment to the Gospel of Jesus Christ. Acutely aware of the intellectual challenges to Christianity in his time, he determined neither to give up on the faith, nor to carry on as though nothing had changed. The Church of the future, he thought, could only prosper if it strove to offer a Gospel worked out in an honest engagement with the full range of human experience and thought. Nothing else would carry conviction. She needed to be a visionary church, with her gaze ever forward, not fixed in the past. In this regard, Oman speaks of the prophetic task of the Church; she has the role of clarifying the meaning of faith to each new generation. She is charged to challenge each generation with the call to higher duties, and to the freedom that comes from obedience to God. In these sentiments Oman, expressing a confident and purposeful view of mission, offers a timely corrective to the contemporary Church's obsession with communication at the expense of theology.

Second, the painting shows Oman as a man of human warmth. This, I think, is a reminder of his commitment to a personal view of God and His dealings with humankind. Oman believed that faith is concerned with a God whom we encounter in our everyday lives. Moreover, the God whom we meet is one who supports and nurtures us in our growth in spiritual wisdom. The appropriate metaphor for our dealings with God is that of dialogue. God has spoken and continues to speak both in the Bible and through the full range of human experience, but He allows space for us to listen and respond. The faith and obedience that He looks for is that which emerges from minds, hearts and wills moved by truth and beauty and goodness. This is to say that the song of faith is the converse of the harsh diatribe of compulsion, a lesson that the Church needs to learn again in each generation.

It was the conviction of Oman's continued importance as a Christian thinker, which led a number of people to Westminster College in the autumn of 2009 to celebrate his life and thought and to mark the 70th anniversary of his death. The current volume arises out of the papers that were given at the conference. The first four essays offer perspectives on the historical background of Oman's work. Sell sets the scene with an account of Oman's cultural, ecclesial and intellectual context, and his interaction with this. One important point is Oman's rootedness within the tradition of the United Presbyterian Church, with its emphasis on moderate Calvinism, a liberal approach to the Creeds, and the responsibility of the individual for their faith. Houston, takes up the story with particular attention to the influence of the William Robertson Smith heresy trial on Oman's theological development. When a student in Edinburgh, Oman's encounter with the trial propelled him into the ministry and shaped his thinking on the key issues of theological truth and authority, and the role of the Church in adjudicating these. In chapter three, Thompson discusses Oman's involvement with Westminster College and the University of Cambridge. The influence of the Great War on Oman's theology is particularly noted; Oman found that the experience of the Great War led him to question the ecclesiology of the day and gave shape to his thinking on theological education. McKimmon concludes the historical section with a ground-breaking analysis of the influence of Scottish Realism and Scottish Personal Idealism on Oman's thinking. McKimmon is somewhat hindered by Oman's reluctance to recognise dependence, but shows with varying degrees of certainty the impact of Calderwood, Fraser, Veitch, Sorley and Pringle Pattison on Oman's writing. There is, for instance in Calderwood's work the rudiments of Oman's understanding of personality; in Fraser we find the distinction between the 'natural' and the 'supernatural'; and in Sorley there is the emphasis on the personal character of grace.

The second section considers some of Oman's fundamental theological commitments. Bevans looks at his theological method, arguing that theology, whilst rational and historically informed, is profoundly personal and involving – that is contextual. Hood discusses Oman's preaching and shows, perhaps surprisingly, that a functional Christology is central to his perception of the Gospel. Finally Hick, in a reflection with personal resonances, comments on the ways in which Oman has shaped his own work, not least in his formulation of our knowledge of God being 'experiencing as'. Hick argues that Oman's approach to Christology (Degree Christology) and other doctrinal tenets are those appropriate to the modern world, but is pessimistic about their reception in the light of the 'drift … to pre-critical orthodoxy'.

The final section includes four chapters picking up issues in Oman's thought or following through on some implications. Hood and Chaudari look at aspects of Oman's work. Hood discusses the role of the evolutionary motif, arguing that Oman adopted a form of evolutionary theism somewhat more radical than that of Rainy, but more conservative than Drummond. Oman was chary of the inclusion of 'mind' in a naturalistic nexus, but adopted an evolutionary framework in his understanding of the development of religion as a set of phenomena. Chaudari, drawing on primary research into a lecture trip Oman made to Auburn Seminary, USA, seeks to clarify his understanding of pastoral authority. Chaudari elegantly unfolds Oman's view that the only true authority given to the faith is its capacity to elicit the willing obedience of men and women to the Father, which is also its liberating quality. In this regard, Chaudary emphasises the centrality of personal experience in Oman's thinking.

Bevans and Nightingale discuss some of the possible implications of Oman's writings for contemporary ministry. Bevans finds in Oman's idea of a gracious God, a powerful underpinning for a vision of mission as participating in God's endeavour understood as non-coercive, concerned with living out the faith, focussed on human beings in their particularity, and prophetic. Nightingale, in an analogous way finds Oman's work potentially rich as a theological framework for adult education. He focuses especially on how Oman's thinking is consistent with and fruitfully enhances our understanding of the approach to adult, theological education associated with the 'pastoral cycle'. He concludes that Oman encourages a view of education that is undertaken with the intent of seeking growth in insight into the will of God, through reflection on concrete personal experience, supported and informed by others, and leading to free choice.

It was noted, some years ago, that there had been 'glimmerings of a renewed interest' in Oman.[1] One outcome of the 'Oman conference' in 2009 was a confirmation that there is indeed a small cloud on the horizon. The hope is, that this volume may introduce Oman to a broader constituency and so contribute in a modest way to a growing, critical dialogue with a man noted as 'one of the most original, independent, and impressive theologians of his generation and of his country'.[2] Certainly, as several of the contributions in this book point out, what he has to say has contemporary resonance.

Adam Hood
Queen's Foundation, Birmingham
July 2010

---

[1] Adam Hood, *Baillie, Oman and Macmurray* (Aldershot: Ashgate, 2003), p. 2.
[2] F. R. Tennant, *John Wood Oman* (London: Proceedings of the British Academy, Vol. XXV), p. 5.

Notes on Contributors

Stephen Bevans is a priest in the Roman Catholic Society of the Divine Word (SVD) and is currently Louis J. Luzbetak, SVD Professor of Mission and Culture at Catholic Theological Union in Chicago, USA. His publications include *John Oman's Doctrine of a Personal God* (1992), *Models of Contextual Theology* (1992 and 2002), *Constants in Context: A Theology of Mission for Today* (with Roger Schroeder, 2004), *Evangelization and Human Freedom* (with Jeffrey Gros, 2009).

Ashok Chaudhary is a Candidate for Minister of Word and Sacrament in the Presbyterian Church USA (PCUSA). He holds the Master of Divinity Degree (MDIV) from Union Theological Seminary in New York City, the MA in religious studies from Stanford University, and the BA in philosophy from Colgate University.

John Hick has worked in the philosophy of religion and theology for many years, some of his most important books being *Evil and the God of Love*, *An Interpretation of Religion*, *The Fifth Dimension* and most recently *Between Faith and Doubt*. Between them his books have been translated into sixteen languages. Hick has taught in the UK at Cambridge and Birmingham, and in the USA at Cornell, Princeton Theological Seminary, and the Claremont Graduate University in California

Adam Hood is Director of Research at the Queen's Foundation for Ecumenical Theological Education; a minister of the Church of Scotland and author of *Ballie, Oman and Macmurray: experience and religious belief* (Aldershot: Ashgate, 2003).

Fleur Houston holds degrees from the Universities of Aberdeen, Oxford, and Cambridge. She taught in the Universities of Belfast and Manchester. She is a minister of the United Reformed Church for which she was trained at Westminster College. She exercised her ministry in pastorates in Sheffield and Blackbird Leys.

Eric McKimmon is a PhD student in the University of Edinburgh working on the contextual aspects of Oman's thought. He studied theology at New College, Edinburgh and was ordained to the ministry in the Presbyterian Church in Ireland. He has ministered in Ireland, and in the Church of Scotland.

John Nightingale is a research Associate of the Queen's Foundation, Birmingham. He has served as a parish priest, adult educator and mission partner in the Anglican Church in England and Nigeria.

Alan P.F. Sell is a minister of the United Reformed Church and is employed in full-time research and writing, and in lecturing at home and abroad on the history of Christian thought, philosophy of religion and theology. His most recent books are, *Philosophy, Dissent and Nonconformity 1689-1920* (2004), *Mill on God: The Pervasiveness and Elusiveness of Mill's Religious Thought* (2004), *Testimony and Tradition: Studies in Reformed and Dissenting Thought,* (2005), *Enlightenment, Ecumenism, Evangel: Theological Themes and Thinkers 1550-2000* (2005), *Nonconformist Theology in the Twentieth Century* (2006) and *Hinterland Theology. A Stimulus to Theological Construction* (2008).

David Thompson has spent his teaching career at the University of Cambridge, where he was Professor of Modern Church History and a Fellow of Fitzwilliam College. He is a former President of the Ecclesiastical History Society. He has also been active in the Ecumenical Movement at the local, regional, national and international level, being currently Ecumenical Officer for the Eastern Synod of the United Reformed Church, Co-Chairman of the United Reformed Church-Roman Catholic Church Conversations, and a member of the International Dialogue between Disciples of Christ and the Roman Catholics.

PART ONE

HISTORICAL PERSPECTIVES

CHAPTER 1

Living in the Half Lights: John Oman in Context

Alan P. F. Sell

The guide books will tell you that the county of Orkney lies some twenty miles to the north of the Scottish mainland, and that it comprises sixty-seven islands. The largest of these, known as Orkney's mainland, covers an area larger than all of the other islands put together. John Wood Oman was born on Orkney's mainland on 23 July 1860. To be precise, he was born at Biggins Farm in the parish of Stenness; and in those names there resides a clue to Orkney's history. For *bygging*, meaning a "building", comes from the Norse verb *byggia*, to build, while *Stenness* is Norse for "stone point". These names remind us, therefore, that in the wake of the Scots Celtic Church of the sixth and seventh centuries, and of Orkney's absorption into the Kingdom of the Picts in the early eighth century came the Viking raids of the late eighth century, and rule by the Norsemen. Thus matters stood until 1472, when the Scottish parliament annexed Orkney and its more northerly neighbour, Shetland, at a cost of 50,000 florins for Orkney and 8,000 florins for Shetland. The financial beneficiary was King Christian I of Denmark, who needed the money towards the dowry required on the marriage of his daughter, Margaret, to King James III of Scotland. But the name Stenness, stone point, suggests an even earlier history, for the community is home to some prize examples of prehistoric megaliths, notably the Ring of Brodgar and the Stones of Stenness, the tallest of which rises to seventeen feet. These stones brooded over ritual activity until the sixth century.[1] Also in the vicinity is the neolithic village of Barnhouse, and the sizeable chambered cairn, Maeshowe, in which prominent individuals were buried some 5,000 years ago. In the midst of all this history, not to mention a rather bloodthirsty legend,[2] with Biggins Farm situated on flat land overlooking the sound, and with a view of distant hills, John Oman was born, the second of four sons of Simon Rust Oman and his wife Isabella Irvine Rendall. Their

---

[1] F.D. Bardgett, *Two Millennia of Church and Community in Orkney*, 18, referring to Anna Ritchie, 'Birsay around AD 800', in *Orkney Heritage*, II (Kirkwall: Orkney Heritage Society, 1983), p. 56.

[2] See William P.L. Thompson *The New History of Orkney* (Edinburgh: Mercat Press, 2001), p. 58. It tells of Ragnhild, who secured the deaths of a succession of husbands by promising to marry their murderers.

family was completed by two daughters.

The nearest town to Stenness is the harbour town of Stromness ('headland of the current'), which was a whaling centre in the nineteenth century. In his younger days Simon Oman had risen to become master of a sailing vessel, but by now he was farming at Biggins. The remains of Pictish dykes made of turf with stone footings have been found in Stenness, and in the eighteenth century farmland was enclosed by turf dykes six feet in height.[3] There was a flourishing peat trade between Orkney and Edinburgh[4]; corn was grown and carefully threshed so that the stalks could be used either for thatching, or by young girl home-workers who plaited them for use by the makers of Orkney straw-backed chairs.[5] Cheese-making was widespread, and the export of salt geese and goose feathers brought further income to the area. Fenton relates that 'A visitor saw a bare-headed, shoeless boy herding a flock of geese in Stenness in 1842.'[6]

John Oman loved his homeland, and later in life he wrote two accounts of it.[7] He describes the sometimes hazardous route by which Orkney was reached in his day; he describes the land and the sea; he recounts the history of the islands and has a good deal to say about life as it was lived. In this last connection he does not shun the anecdote, least of all when the tale concerns ministers. He recalls a man whose wife and cow were blown off a cliff in a gale and fell to their deaths. Some months later the man met the minister, who consoled him in his loss.

'Deed Sir', was the disconcerting reply, 'as ye hae often said, but I never understood it as well before, the ways of Providence are wonerfu. When the wife and the coo were blown off the cliff I thought I had a sair, sair, loss, but I gaed ower tae Graemsay and there I got a far bonnier wife and a far better coo.'[8]

We learn of the minister of Sanday who neatly accommodated the alternatives within a prayer thus: 'Keep thy protecting hand around all who travel by sea and bring them safely to their desired haven. But if in thine inscrutable providence it be thy will that helpless ships should be cast upon the

---

[3] See Alexander Fenton, *The Northern Isles. Orkney and Shetland* (East Linton: Tuckwell Press, 1997), pp. 13, 91.

[4] Fenton, *Northern Isles*, ch. 26.

[5] Fenton, *Northern Isles*, pp. 358, 271.

[6] Fenton, *Northern Isles*, p. 507.

[7] The manuscripts are among the Oman papers at Westminster College, Cambridge. I refer here to the longer of the two. I am most grateful to Mrs. Margaret Thompson for making the Oman papers available to me, and also for supplying photocopies of a number of articles and reviews at a time when unaccustomed quantities of snow prevented ready access to Cambridge.

[8] John Oman, 'The Orkneys', ms., 7.

shore, dinna forget the pair island of Sanday.'[9] Mingling church, school and family, Oman writes,

> Before the days of the Secession the minister was often a very original character who did not believe in making too many new sermons. Mr. Clouston of Stromness ... had but four which he gave in rotation, so that each of them appeared like the quarters of the moon. My great-grandfather, whose name John Wood has come down till I am the fourth to bear it, was about the last man in Stromness to wear a long waistcoat and silver buckles on his shoes and was a strong supporter of the parish minister, but his son, the second John, who afterwards taught the youth of Stromness with such a strong hand that it is said he could send an offender off with one cuff from the far side of the room into the fireplace, made these stale productions more stale by repeating them, when well out of reach of his father's ears, word for word, well garnished with portentous coughs.[10]

Oman's early education was in the hands of a tutor who had been engaged by a neighbour to the family, to whose classes a few other boys were welcomed. But however much Oman may have learned from the tutor, it is not fanciful to suppose that two things impressed his young mind more than anything else. The first was the sense of permanence inspired by the history around him and by the solidity of his home life in a farmhouse in which his family had lived for generations. It is not without significance that he dedicated his Kerr Lectures on *The Problem of Faith and Freedom in the Last Two Centuries* to the memory of his father, 'A scholar only of life and action, but my best teacher.' The second decisive impression was that of his personal solitariness (which is not the same as loneliness). This, as he tells us in his most learned work, *The Natural and the Supernatural*, he gained from his childish yet intense contemplation of the natural world around him:

> Nothing moves simple folk and children like the idea of aloneness in the ever-moving vastness of time, if this be filled with concrete individual forms on the one hand, and invested with ... the feeling of the undifferentiated holy on the other. ...
> [A]n average sort of child, living under the conditions in which man had developed his powers of perception, with nature's work much in evidence around him and man's little, often alone under the open sky, and about as much on the sea as on the land, among simple stay-at-home people and some far-travelled folk and wandering gypsies, is at least as near the conditions in which man's perception developed as this Western

---

[9] Oman, 'Orkneys', p. 27.
[10] Oman, 'Orkneys', p. 27.

modern world affords.

The most noticeable feature of my earliest view of the world is of how minutely, definitely, decisively everything in it was individual.

While my apprehensions of the countryside continually varied with sunshine and shadow, day and night, summer and winter, my general awareness of it was neither of a changing scene, nor of the aspect I preferred, nor was it of an average impression or a composite picture, but of something one in all its moods and aspects, much like awareness of a friend.

To the very long sight of one who constantly looked from horizon to horizon, the depth of the sky was overwhelmingly impressive, and was the first object I think ever to hold my attention immovably ... [T]hough space was ... the illustration, the real impressiveness was in time ... Through this first came the idea that I was alone. I had been to church. I think the preacher had been expressing the absolute difference between good and evil under the material forms of heaven and hell. I went down to the edge of the water alone, and stood, a very small child, with the full tide at my feet. ... It flashed upon me that, if I dropped in and floated out, with endless sea around, I should be alone for ever and ever.[11]

It is perhaps not surprising that at the age of fourteen Oman had no higher aspiration than 'to ride a horse bare-backed and steer a boat in a gale';[12] or that an unnamed Cambridge Professor should later have remarked of Oman, 'When I think of the great man, heather, and salt winds, and mountain mists come to mind rather than a gown and lecturer's desk.'[13] From Oxford there came similar testimony when, in the course of reviewing what he described as Oman's epoch-making work, *The Natural and the Supernatural*, Nathaniel Micklem declared,

It has been said to me that no one can understand Dr. Oman aright who does not see him standing on the prow of a Viking ship with the wind and the salt spray blown around him; certainly there is in his thought a robustness, a freshness, a virility and venture which smack of the sea and of heroic enterprises; there is breadth, a wholesomeness, a common sense which is infinitely refreshing to readers of ordinary theological and

---

[11] John Oman, *The Natural and the Supernatural* (Cambridge: Cambridge University Press, 1931), pp. 132, 133, 135, 136-7. It is interesting to note that Oman contributed the article on 'Individualism, Individual, and Individuality' to James Hastings, ed., *Dictionary of Christ and the Gospels*, I, 1908, pp. 814-21.

[12] John Oman, *Honest Religion*, (London: The Religious Book Club), 1941, p. 36.

[13] Quoted by George Alexander, 'Memoir', in *Honest Religion*, xxxi.

devotional literature.[14]

I

So much for Oman's geographical, historical and home context; but what of the ecclesiastical? In late medieval Orkney the parishes were grouped so that, for example, Firth, Orphir and Stenness had the services of one priest, Sandwick and Stromness, of another.[15] The Reformation in Orkney seems to have been more a matter of ecclesiastical reorganization than of doctrine, and a good deal of the reorganization had to do with the reapportionment of land. Thus in 1563 Patrick Bellenden

> received the Stenness lands which had provided the endowments of the Precentor (Magnus Halcro) [of Kirkwall Cathedral]. On this property the Bellendens had their principal residence, the Palace of Stenness, which according to popular tradition stood so high that it was possible to see ships in Hoy Sound from the upper windows.[16]

Alexander Dick, who conformed in 1574, was the only Cathedral dignitary to serve the Reformed Church;[17] of the others, the Precentor was accused by the Reformed of adultery.[18] In the 1560s the parish of Stenness continued to be linked with those of Firth and Orphir, with Thomas Stevenson as minister.[19] Stromness was now partnered with Sandwick and Graemsay and served by a minister, Jerome Tulloch and a reader, William Smith.[20] There is no suggestion in the literature that the priests who came over from Rome were committed to, or even well versed in, Reformed doctrine, while others subsequently appointed were beset by unwieldy charges covering sometimes inhospitable terrain. Without question Harry Colville, minister of Orphir, Stenness and Firth, stepped outside the *Book of Discipline* in the 1590s. His objective was to find evidence against Earl Patrick Stewart's brother and rival, John Stewart. To this end he 'led the prosecution against Thomas Paplay and Alison Balfour [who were] accused of plotting Patrick's death by poison. The minister supervised the questioning of the suspects by torture - which was extended to Balfour's husband, son and seven-year-old daughter. Followers of John Stewart

---

[14] N. Micklem, *The Christian World*, 22 October, 1931. Micklem further judges that the book is 'devastatingly Protestant and profoundly evangelical in termper and in thought.'

[15] Bardgett, *Two Millennia*, p. 52.

[16] Thompson, *New History of Orkney*, p. 259. This is from ch. 18, the whole of which concerns the Reformation in Orkney.

[17] Bardgett, *Two Millennia*, p. 64.

[18] Bardgett, *Two Millennia*, p. 63.

[19] Bardgett, *Two Millennia*, p. 61; cf. p. 98.

[20] Bardgett, *Two Millennia*, p. 62.

successfully murdered Colville in 1596',[21] whereupon there ensued a pastoral vacancy.

Meanwhile the General Assembly had, during the 1570s sanctioned a church order which had no place for bishops, but bishops remained *in situ*, with the result that during the seventeenth century, turmoil over the relative authority of bishops and presbytery continued, with episcopal lands frequently being a neuralgic factor. The Stuart Kings strove to enforce episcopalianism upon the Scottish Church, and it was not until the accession of William and Mary that, from 1690 Presbyterianism became the established religion across the whole of Scotland. Toleration was extended to episcopalians by the Act of 1712, but in Orkney a number of clergymen and lairds remained sometimes vociferously loyal to the Jacobite cause, and for this they were punished. In the wake of civil and ecclesiastical struggles the turn to the restraint of Moderatism, and the desire for ministerial respectability is not hard to understand. Not, indeed that all ministers were as respectable as they might have been. One lived in 'open concubinage' with another man's wife both before and after his marriage. The Synod gave him four months to break with the woman, but in the meantime the Court of Justiciary tried the minister, found him guilty, and banished him to the plantations for life.[22] Among further deficiencies were that on some islands the people had received the Lord's Supper on only one or two occasions in fifty years; and the intrusion of unwanted ministers under the patronage system caused real concern in some quarters. In one such case, at Orphir, a minister was to be ordained but the people secured the church so that nothing could be done. Nine months later the Presbytery sent troops from Caithness in order to ensure that the ordination went ahead, and during the ensuing struggle one woman was killed and several people were wounded.[23]

But some church members, not least because they heard of religious revivals in parts of mainland Scotland, became restive under the moralistic perorations of Moderate ministers, the perceived evil of patronage, and the general low state of religion in the county. Orkney which, unlike the Western Isles, had not imbibed a solid, still less a scholastic, version of Calvinism, was ready to receive a more evangelically open version of the Reformed faith.

In 1797 the godfather of Scottish revivalism, James Haldane, paid his first visit to Orkney. According to his biographer he 'brought to the inhabitants a

---

[21] Bardgett, *Two Millennia*, p. 73, referring to Peter D. Anderson, *Black Pattie: the Life and Times of Patrick Steward, Earl of Orkney, Lord of Shetland* (Edinburgh: John Donald, 1992), pp. 49, 50; and James B. Craven, *History of the Church in Orkney: From the Introduction of Christianity to 1558* (Kirkwall: Peace, 1901), pp. 66-70.

[22] See David Small, *History of the Congregations of the United Presbyterian Church from 1733 to 1900* (Edinburgh: David M. Small, 1900), II, p. 482.

[23] Small, *History of the Congregations*.

large outpouring of spiritual blessings'.[24] Haldane's observations led him to the conclusion that, with very few exceptions, the islands of Orkney were 'as much in need of the true Gospel of Jesus Christ, so far as respects the preaching of it, as any of the islands of the Pacific Ocean'.[25] He preached in Stromness, where the minister, Mr. Hamilton and his wife received him kindly; while in Kirkwall, where the fair was in progress, his hearers numbered from three to four thousand on weekdays and six thousand on Sundays. In his *Journal* Haldane notes with pleasure the seeds of the Gospel sown by an Orkney man who had been apprenticed to a 'pious tradesman' in Kirkwall. This man went to Newcastle on business, and there he much appreciated the ministry of the Antiburgher minister, William Graham. On his return he gathered for prayer with others, and after a time they appealed to the Antiburgher Synod for a preacher.

This Orkney tradesman was John Rusland or Russell. By August 1795 a church building to seat eight hundred was in progress, and in the following year the work was completed. The Edinburgh Presbytery of the Antiburgher Synod sent two supplies to Kirkwall: Chalmers of Haddington served in June and July 1796 and Culbertson of Leith in August and September. Chalmers presided over the opening of the church on 1 July. Six elders, who were nominated and unanimously elected by the members of the congregation, were ordained on 14 August. On 16 July 1797 the first communion service was held in the open air, with Stuart of Falkirk presiding. By now the membership stood at 196. The first minister, William Broadfoot, arrived in 1798, and by 1814 he could report that 1250 persons were attending Sunday worship, of whom at least three quarters were church members.[26]

News of this new venture spread around Orkney, and although their town was fourteen miles from Kirkwall, people from Stromness began making the journey to worship there. In 1802 the Synod provided a catechist for Stromness, and in 1803 money was collected towards a church of their own. In 1806 thirty communicants, including two elders, were disjoined from the Kirkwall church and constituted as a separate congregation. Their building, seating 643, cost £600. This was the church which John Oman and his family attended from nearby Stenness. Oman was born during the ministry of William Stobbs, the second minister, who had arrived in 1829 and remained until his death in 1863. In 1837 he reported that there were 544 communicants, that he conducted a two-hour Sabbath-evening school with an attendance of 310, and that between 200 and 300 people attended his monthly prayer meeting. Stobbs was followed by James S. Nisbet (1865-1874), and who was followed by Thomas Kirkwood

---

[24] Alexander Haldane, *The Lives of Robert and James Haldane*, (1852) (Edinburgh: The Banner of Truth Trust, 1990), p. 167.

[25] Haldane, *Lives of Robert and James Haldane*, p. 169, from Haldane's *Journal*, 12 August 1797.

[26] Small, *History of the Congregations*, pp. 482-3.

(1876-1880).[27] Nisbet and Kirkwood were the ministers John Oman would remember.

I have already said that Orkney, though ecclesiastically impoverished by the end of the eighteenth century, did not have a legacy of staunch Calvinism, and was therefore open to a more evangelical version of the Reformed faith. Indeed, one of the historians of the Secession Church declared that 'In no part of Scotland perhaps has [the Secession Church's] beneficial influence been more extensively felt or visibly displayed, than in the interesting group of the Orkney isles.'[28] Another concurs: 'In no part of the British dominions has the Secession prospered more than in Orkney. It has planted congregations in almost all the islands; and exercised an influence peculiarly favourable to the moral and religious improvement of the islanders.'[29] It is not too much to say that this Church became the folk church in many parts of Orkney during the nineteenth century. We need to understand the testimony of his Church if we are to understand Oman's developed ecclesiological positions and attitudes.

In 1733 Ebenezer Erskine, William Wilson, Alexander Moncrieff and James Fisher, who had been deposed from their ministerial charges by the General Assembly of the Church of Scotland, joined with Ralph Erskine and Thomas Mair in constituting themselves an Associate Presbytery. There were two neuralgic issues. The first was doctrinal. In 1722 Ebenezer and Ralph Erskine, together with eleven others, had presented a representation to the General Assembly of the Church of Scotland against the Assembly's repudiation of the book, *The Marrow of Modern Divinity*. The Assembly construed the book as teaching antinomianism and universalism, whereas Erskine and his friends, who staunchly upheld particular redemption, construed it as endorsing the free offer of the Gospel to all, for all have the warrant to believe. Here are the seeds of evangelical Calvinism.[30] The second issue, or constellation of issues,

---

[27] For a full account of the Stromness church see Small, *History of the Congregations*, pp. 490-492. Cf. William MacKelvie, *Annals and Statistics of the United Presbyterian Church* (Edinburgh: Oliphant, and Andrew Elliott, and Glasgow: David Robertson, 1873), p. 554.

[28] Andrew Thompson, *Historical Sketch of the Origin of the Secession Church* (Edinburgh: A. Fullerton, 1848), p. 146.

[29] John M'Kerrow, *History of the Secession Church* (Edinburgh: A. Fullerton, 1847), p. 392.

[30] For the complicated tale of which this is an all too brief summary, see C.G. McCrie, ed., *The Marrow of Modern Divinity* (Glasgow: D. Boyce, 1902); *Testimony of the United Associate Synod of the Secession Church*, Edinburgh: for the Synod, n.d.; John McKerrow, *History of the Secession Church* (Edinburgh: Fullerton, 1847); Henry F. Henderson, *The Religious Controversies of Scotland* (Edinburgh: T & T Clark, 1905); David C. Lachman, *The Marrow Controversy, 1718-1732: An Historical and Theological Analysis* (Edinburgh: Rutherford House, 1988); Alan P.F. Sell, *The Great Debate: Calvinism, Arminianism and Salvation*, (1982) (Eugene, OR: Wipf & Stock, 1998), pp. 55-7.

concerned polity and church order, and arose in part from the manner of their treatment by the Assembly. In 1734 they published *A Testimony to the Doctrine, Worship, Government, and Discipline of the Church of Scotland: or, Reasons for their Protestation entered before the Commission of the General Assembly, November 1733*. Among other things they opposed the intrusion of unwanted ministers upon congregations and the exclusion from communion of those who opposed the ministers thus appointed; the conferring of *quasi-presbyteral* power upon the Commission and Sub-commissions; the 'prosecution of such measures as corrupted, or had a direct tendency to corrupt, the doctrines contained in our excellent Confession of Faith';[31] and the refusal to censure those who departed from it.

In 1747 we come to the Breach within the Associate Presbytery, and the formation of the General, or Antiburgher, Associate Synod. From 1744 onwards the citizens of Edinburgh, Glasgow and Perth were required to take the Burgess Oath if they wished to work in commerce, join a trade guild or be enfranchised. The terms of the Oath were: 'Here I protest before God and your Lordships, that I profess, and allow with my heart, the true religion presently professed within this realm, and authorized by the laws thereof: I shall abide thereat, and defend the same to my life's end; renouncing the Roman religion called papistry.'[32] To the Antiburghers this struck at the principle of the Church's spiritual freedom and independence of other authorities. Over the next half century the Antiburghers toiled through one theological dispute after another, but they also engaged in productive overseas missionary work, and denounced the slave trade in 1788. The next excitement of importance from our point of view followed in 1804, when some in the Antiburgher Synod embraced New Light principles and published them in its *New Testimony*. That is to say it formally affirmed that the power of worldly kingdoms was limited to secular matters only. Interestingly, a formative work which encouraged the Synod to this conclusion was entitled, *A Review of Ecclesiastical Establishments in Europe. An Attempt to Prove that every Species of Patronage is Foreign to the Nature of the Church, and that any modifications which have ever been, or ever can be, proposed, are insufficient to regain and secure her in the possession of the liberty wherewith Christ has made her free.* The work appeared anonymously in 1792, but in his *Candid Vindication of the Secession Church* the author unmasked himself. He was none other than the William Graham of Newcastle whose preaching, heard by John Rusland/Russell of Kirkwall had been instrumental in securing the presence of the Antiburghers in Orkney.[33]

---

[31] *Testimony of the United Associate Synod*, p. 45.

[32] Quoted by J. M'Kerrow, *History of the Secession Church*, p. 210.

[33] Graham also published a handful of sermons. We further learn that he 'was an excellent mathematician, and bestowed great labour and spent much money in endeavouring to discover an exact method of finding the longitude at sea.' See MacKelvie, *Annals and Statistics*, p. 524.

With this the New Light Antiburghers became voluntaryists, and on this basis they were able to unite with the New Light Burghers in 1820 to form the United Secession Church.

The final piece of the jigsaw concerns the Relief Church. The Relief Presbytery was constituted in 1761, and, once again, patronage as applied by Moderate churchmen was a principal cause of the secession. The seceders were led by Thomas Gillespie, who was deposed from his Dunfermline parish in 1752; Thomas Boston of Jedburgh, who left his charge in 1757; and Thomas Colier/Collier, a native of Fife.[34] In view of the polity of the Relief Church it is perhaps not insignificant that both Gillespie and Colier had sojourned amongst English Dissenters. Indeed, Gillespie, having left the Divinity Hall of the Church of Scotland in Edinburgh at the suggestion of his mother, who had become a keen supporter of Erskine and the Secession Church, found that Church's Theological Hall in Perth not to his liking and left it after only ten days, and went on to the Independent/Congregational academy conducted by Philip Doddridge at Northampton.[35] 'There', says J.H. Leckie, 'he learned a "Voluntary" doctrine of the relation between Church and State, being taught that "the Civil Magistrate" had nothing to do with the religious opinions of citizens, nor had any right to confine the minds of men within the bounds of established creeds'.[36] From there he proceeded to Hartbarrow, Westmorland,[37] as is clear from John Birkett's letter written from Kendal to Doddridge on 8 November 1740. Birkett informs Doddridge that the latter's suggestion that Gillespie serve at Hartbarrow for six months 'on Mutual Trial' has been accepted, notwithstanding that 'the Presbyterian Ministers of this North Class of Westmorland and Cumberland are extremely prejudiced against Scotch

---

[34] Not therefore 'an English dissenting minister', as stated by N.R. Needham in 'Relief Church', *Dictionary of Scottish Church History and Theology*, ed. N.M. deS. Cameron, *et al.* (Edinburgh: T & T Clark, 1993), p. 702(ii).

[35] James Barr, *The United Free Church of Scotland* (London: Allenson, 1934), p. 67, writes, 'It is not generally known that the famous Dr Philip Doddridge ... was ordained a Presbyterian ere he became an Independent.' This is just as well, for it is not the case. In evidence Barr reproduces Doddridge's ordination certificate which does indeed show that he was ordained a 'presbyter', and that five of the eight ministerial signatories were Presbyterians. But (a) in the eighteenth-century there was a good deal of ministerial co-operation across what would later become regarded as 'denominational lines' (denominations as we know them being creatures of the nineteenth century); (b) generally more than one English Presbyterian minister would be ordained at a time, and not always in the pastorate of any of them; (c) there is no question that Castle Hill, Northampton was an Independent/Congregational church, or that the practice in that tradition was that ministers were ordained in the pastorates they were called to serve.

[36] J.H. Leckie, *Secession Memories. The United Presbyterian Contribution to the Scottish Church* (Edinburgh: T. & T. Clark, 1926), p. 71.

[37] Barr, *United Free Church*, p. 68, says that efforts to determine the place in *Lancashire* to which Gillespie went have proved unsuccessful.

ministers in general' because of the Scots' 'unwillingness to embrace every Wanton, Wild, Novel Notion, that is broach'd now-a-days'.[38] The reference here is to the disquiet caused in some northern circles by the drift into 'Arianism' of a number of English Presbyterian ministers. Gillespie was licensed by Doddridge and others on 30 October 1740, ordained in northern England on 22 January 1741, and received into the Presbytery of Dunfermline in March of that year, on the recommendation of Doddridge, Job Orton and thirteen other ministers.

Thomas Colier had served the pastorate of Ravenstonedale, also in Westmorland, for an unspecified period until 1761.[39] Originally Presbyterian, the theology of its ministers oscillated during the eighteenth century. John Magee, who served from 1714 to 1733, was the first Ravenstonedale minister to be supported by the Independent Fund, and he must therefore be deemed to have been orthodox. Indeed, during his ministry some more radical Presbyterians seceded from the church. His successor, James Ritchie, a Glasgow University graduate, declined to subscribe to the Westminster Confession of Faith with the result that the church members 'could not in conscience take the Lord's Supper at his hands'.[40] There followed a fourteen-year-long legal battle which concluded in 1747 in favour of Ritchie, who by then had moved on; he and his supporters did, however, pay half of the costs of £820/0/0 incurred by the church. By 1753 Ritchie was an 'Arian'.[41] The trustees of the church continued to exercise authority, until James Muscutt made it a condition of his accepting the call to the pastorate in 1811 that 'the Church be re-organised and put upon the Independent or Congregational plan'.[42] Thomas Colier was clearly not heterodox, or he would not have been welcomed as a coadjutor by Gillespie and Boston. Moreover, he was sympathetic to the Congregational church order, for he was called to the pastorate of the Colinsburgh Independent church 'by the congregation in the presence of the great Head of the church. ... As Mr. Colier was from among the

---

[38] See LNC MS L1/4/101 at Dr. Williams's Library, London; Geoffrey F. Nuttall, *Calendar of the Correspondence of Philip Doddridge, DD (1702-1751)* (London: HMSO, 1979), no. 652; Alan P.F. Sell, *Church Planting. A Study of Westmorland Nonconformity*, (1986) (Eugene, OR: Wipf & Stock, 1998), pp. 116-17.

[39] Though there is no reference to him in Francis Nicholson and Ernest Axon, *The Older Nonconformity in Kendal* (Kendal: Titus Wilson, 1915), or Thomas Whitehead, *History of the Dales Congregational Churches* (Keighley: Feather, 1930). However, Phyllis L. Woodger and Jessie E. Hunter, *The High Chapel. The Story of Ravenstonedale Congregational Church* (Kendal: Titus Wilson, [1962]) include a table of ministers in their front pages, in which Thomas Collier's date of arrival is not known, but his date of departure is given as 1761.

[40] See Whitehead, *History*, p. 95; Woodger and Hunter, *High Chapel*, p. 5, Nicholson and Axon, *Older Nonconformity*, pp. 288-9.

[41] See Nicholson and Axon, p. 289.

[42] See Whitehead, p. 97; Woodger and Hunter, p. 8.

dissenters in England, this mode of forming a ministerial engagement with a Christian society would be perfectly familiar to him, and was in all probability accepted by himself.'[43] This church owed its origin to a secession from the Church of Scotland in 1760, prompted by the intrusion of Dr. John Chalmers upon the people as minister. The majority of the congregation left the Parish Kirk and built a large church for themselves. Gillespie, himself out of charge, preached there and encouraged the flock in the direction of Relief, and was instrumental in securing the services of Colier. On the day prior to his induction Colier and the church members 'observed a solemn fast; accommodating themselves also, in this matter, rather to the English Congregational than to the Scotch Presbyterian model'.[44] The induction took place on 22 October 1761, with Boston delivering the admission sermon on I Corinthians 2: 2, 'For I am determined not to know any thing among you, save Jesus Christ and him crucified.'[45] On the same day Gillespie, Boston and Colier, together with one elder from each of their congregations, constituted 'a presbytery for the relief of Christians oppressed in their Christian privileges'.[46]

Among the principles of the Relief Church were the following:

The calls, commands, and invitations of the word, are the ground of faith, and they are directed to mankind, as lost and perishing sinners of Adam's family.

The Israelitish church, established in Palestine, was not a *voluntary* society, but the Christian church *is*.

As [Christians] are *members* of the church of Christ they *belong* to a community entirely *different* from the civil state.

In regard to other churches around them, the Relief held it unlawful to hear legal and unsound preachers who overturned in their discourses the doctrines of grace, - and also to hear intruders who had violently thrust themselves into particular charges in the church of Christ, and who by so doing had robbed Christ of his *authority*, and his people of their *liberty*.

[I]t is *real saintship* that entitles men to the sacred supper, *in the sight*

---

[43] Gavin Struthers, *The History of the Rise of the Relief Church*, bound with A. Thompson's *Historical Sketch* and paginated consecutively, p. 284. See also Small, *History of the Congregations*, pp. 376-9. Neither Colin's name nor that of the Colinsburgh church appears in William D. McNaughton's works: *The Scottish Congregational Ministry 1794-1993* (Glasgow: The Congregational Union of Scotland, 1993), and *Early Congregational Independency in Lowland Scotland*, I (Glasgow: The Congregational Federation, 2005). This suggests that the cause had but a brief independent life prior to its reception into the Relief Presbytery.

[44] Struthers, *History*, p. 284.

[45] Struthers, *History*, p. 285. It is therefore odd that Leckie should say that nether Gillespie nor Boston 'seem to have addressed the gathering or to have taken any part in the proceedings.' See *Secession Memories*, pp. 90-91.

[46] Struthers, *History*, p. 287.

of God ... it is the *visibility* of saintship *before the world*, that entitles men to communion in the *eye of the Church*.[47]

It should be added in connection with the last point here that the Relief Church, unlike the Antiburghers, advocated a communion table open to all saints, whether or not they held to the National Covenant of 1638 and the Solemn League and Covenant of 1643; such adherence, they felt, should not be made a term of communion.

In 1821, as if in demonstration of its relative openness of spirit, the Relief Church made overtures to the recently-united Associate Churches; thirteen years later the United Secession Church, having by now become more generally voluntaryist in attitude, reciprocated; and in 1847, after protracted negotiations, the United Presbyterian Church came into being – a church comprising 518 congregations; and this was Oman's Church. On the occasion of the Church's Jubilee in 1897 Dr. Henderson neatly summed up the situation. With reference to the Secession and Relief strands he said,

Both sections ... proclaimed the same gospel of Jesus Christ; both stood for relief from the evils which were dominant in the Establishment; but to the one it was given to work out the problem of the relation in which Church and State should stand to each other; for in all its contending and testimonies, in all its breaches and divisions of Burgher and Anti-Burgher, of Old Light and New Light, this question was ever coming up. To the other was given the task of showing that a Church of Christ can look beyond its own narrow limits, recognise the brotherhood of all true believers, and hold fellowship with them, thought in many points of doctrine and practice they may differ from itself. In the end, the time came when the one was more or less permeated by the spirit of the other, so that a union between them became possible.[48]

But a Church is more than its statements of belief and practices; it has an ethos too; and perhaps Professor James Orr captured this in his remarks on the Jubilee occasion. He suggested that the 'spiritual movement' underlying both Secession and Relief 'was at bottom one':

No name was more savoury in the cottage homes of Scotland than that of Boston of Ettrick, and where did Boston get his light? He was converted by Ebenezer Erskine's father. And where did Gillespie, the founder of the Relief, get his religious impressions? From conversations with Boston of

---

[47] Struthers, *History*, pp. 301, 309, 311, 317.
[48] Dr. Henderson, 'The Divine leading in the origin and progress of the Secession and Relief Churches', in *Memorial of the Jubilee Synod of the United Presbyterian Church May 1897* (Edinburgh: Publications Office, 1897), p. 233.

Ettrick. And who was Gillespie's mother? A good Seceder woman ... And whose was the second great name in the history of the Relief? – Thomas Boston of Jedburgh, the Ettrick Boston's son.[49]

Around the newly united Church there soon began to swirl the tides of modern biblical criticism, the challenge of evolutionary thought, and the doctrinal implications of these. Forward-looking in attitude, the United Presbyterians were the first to reflect on the doctrinal spirit of the times in relation to their formal standards of belief and practice. In 1879 they unanimously adopted a Declaratory Act according to which there would be liberty of opinion 'on such points in the Standards not entering into the substance of the faith.' That the result was so resoundingly affirmative was in no small measure due to the sincerity and skill of the highly regarded and greatly loved Principal of the Theological College, John Cairns, under whom Oman was shortly to sit.[50] In 1892, though after more of a struggle and at the risk of a secession which materialized in 1893, the Free Church followed suit in almost identical words. Evincing an almost English ability to sanctify muddle in a good cause, these Scots omitted to specify which were the points that did not enter into the substance of the faith. Nevertheless, the way was thus clear for the union of the United Presbyterian Church with the Free Church in 1900. Thus was constituted the United Free Church.

That John Oman imbibed the spirit of the United Presbyterian Church and never repudiated it is easily demonstrated from his writings. Let us take the main points one by one. First, a generous interpretation of Calvinism allowing for the free offer of the Gospel. Oman writes,

Extreme Calvinism I never came across, for I knew it only among a race who, whether for thought or action, divided humanity into men who went to sea and muffs who stayed at home, and for whom the sovereignty of God meant the assurance of being able to face all storms, and seek no harbour of refuge. Nor had they any idea of having to work up the salvation of their souls. The real opposite of Divine Sovereignty is striving and crying instead of turning in simplicity and trust to God.[51]

Secondly, the Church is 'a religious, a Divine society, not to be identified with the civil society, and yet with a national significance on better justification

[49] J. Orr, 'The contribution of the United Presbyterian Church to religious thought and life', *Memorial of the Jubilee Synod*, p. 97.

[50] See Alexander R. MacEwen, *Life and Letters of John Cairns, CC, LL.D* (London: Hodder and Stoughton, 1895), ch. 24; John Cairns, *Principal Cairns* (Edinburgh: Oliphant Anderson & Ferrier, [1903]), pp. 131-33.

[51] Oman, *Honest Religion*, p. 165, cf. p. 38.

than mere recognition by the State'.[52] Again, 'To join the Church ... is not bondage, it is freedom wherewith Christ has set His people free, the freedom to obey God only, to make His glory your one end in life, to do His will not your own.'[53]

Thirdly, the obligation of fellowship with all the saints:

> This is the true and practical expression of a belief in the Holy Catholic Church. It is nothing less than a denial of any rejection of any brother for whom Christ died, which is nothing less in the end than a denial or contempt for any man. The heart which prays continually for grace to recognize all who truly name the name of Christ despises no one.[54]

Fourthly, the protest against the elevation of ecclesiastical formulae above the Gospel:

> How often has the Church given way to this temptation, ceasing to strive for a unity in which, through the good-news of God in Jesus Christ, each one sees the same reality, drinks of the same spirit and gladly accepts as his own the same Divine rule, and seeing it instead by fixed creed, uniform organisation, and even by an ordering of recognised duties, all imposed purely from without to conserve what seems already won![55]
>
> From day to day life must be faced with a creed falling far short of omniscience. It is less an illumination than points of light in the darkness, rather lighthouses to direct the course than sun or moon to display the prospect. Except when satisfied with tradition or theory, none question the Apostle's description of our knowledge, as 'seeing in a glass darkly'.[56]

These principles Oman carried with him to the end of his days. They came to him not so much through the books he read as through the air he breathed in the ecclesiastical context in which he was reared. Devoted to that context as he was, Oman spent his working life as one who lived in a diaspora. Passing over for the moment his higher education, I shall briefly sketch his cross-border ecclesiastical context, for his working life was spent as a minister on the roll of the Presbyterian Church of England.

The name of the Church seems innocuous enough, but it hides a rather

---

[52] John Oman, *The Church and the Divine Order* (London: Hodder and Stoughton, [1911]), p. 303.

[53] John Oman, *A Dialogue with God and Other Sermons and Addresses* (London: James Clarke, [1950]).

[54] John Oman, *Vision and Authority, or The Throne of St. Peter* (London: Hodder and Stoughton, 2nd edn, 1928), p. 170.

[55] John Oman, *The Paradox of the World. Sermons* (Cambridge: Cambridge University Press, 1921), p. 277.

[56] Oman, *Vision and Authority*, p. 217.

complicated pre-history, which I shall try to break down into a few concise points. First, following the union of the Scottish and English crowns in 1707 a considerable number of Scots moved to England in quest of work and education. Presbyterian churches were constituted on English soil at Wooler in 1729, Newcastle in 1749, Maryport in 1776, and it was not long before the Scottish Presbyterian presence was felt in Liverpool and London. Most of those who joined such churches regarded the Church of Scotland as their home, though some had been raised in one or another of the Scottish dissenting churches. Secondly, for a complex of intriguing reasons which I cannot stay to elucidate,[57] the vast majority of the English Presbyterians of Old Dissent had become either Congregational or Unitarian by the end of the eighteenth century. Thirdly, the expatriate churches in England were organized into presbyteries, and at first it was thought that an English Synod of the Church of Scotland might be constituted. Questions were raised, however, concerning the propriety and legality of a Scottish established Church having jurisdiction in what the General Assembly called a 'foreign country' which had its own Anglican establishment. In the end the Presbyterian Church *in* England was constituted in 1842. It comprised the new Scottish churches on English soil, together with the orthodox minority of English Presbyterian causes which had not turned Congregational or Unitarian during the eighteenth century. By 1876 it numbered 153 congregations. Fourthly, in Scotland during the 1830s the Ten Year Conflict erupted, and once again the issue was patronage, and the intrusion, or attempted intrusion, of non-evangelical ministers into charges which did not wish to receive them. This led to the Disruption of 1843 and to the formation, under the leadership of Thomas Chalmers and others, of the Free Church of Scotland – or, as its members regarded themselves, the Church of Scotland (Free). Many members of the Presbyterian Church in England sympathised with the Disruption Church, and in 1844 the English church declared independence from the Church of Scotland, regarded the Free Church as a sister Church, accused the Church of Scotland of having compromised sacred principles, and prayed that it might see the error of its ways and repent. A minority of congregations within the English Church, including Crown Court in London, remained faithful to the Church of Scotland, left the English Church and became members of Scottish presbyteries. In the same year, 1844, the Presbyterian Church in England opened its theological college in London, and it is significant that all of its original teachers were drawn from the Free or Secession Churches; and this brings me to the fifth point. An increasing number of Scots were arriving in England, as well as immigrants from Wales and Ireland, and by now a sizeable number of the Scots among them belonged to the Secession Churches which, as we saw, had united in 1847 to form the United Presbyterian Church. It was not long before the United Presbyterian

---

[57] But see Alan P.F. Sell, *Dissenting Thought and the Life of the Churches. Studies in an English Tradition* (Lewiston, NY: Edwin Mellen Press, 1990), ch. 5.

Church had four presbyteries comprising 58 congregations on English soil, and these were formed into a Synod in 1863. They, as we know, were voluntaryists, and, of course, the Presbyterian Church in England had no option but to adopt the same position and throw its lot in with English Nonconformists. This facilitated the union in 1876 of the United Presbyterian Synod with the Presbyterian Church *in* England to form the Presbyterian Church *of* England. At the time of the union the Church had 259 congregations and 46,540 members. The considerable sacrifice, both in terms of fellowship and finance, willingly borne by the United Presbyterian Church as it dismissed 109 congregations should not go unremarked.

On completion of his higher education Oman was licensed as a probationer by the United Presbyterian Synod. For a few months he served the preaching station at Makerstown near Kelso, and whilst there he was able once again to meet his former minister at Stromness, Thomas Kirkwood. From Makerstown he became assistant to Dr. James Brown of St. James's Church Paisley, and from that base he preached at a number of vacant churches, but no call came. It may be that Oman did not have the gifts of pulpit oratory that some congregations expected: he was a preacher of the thoughtful, rather than the histrionic, sort; and there is evidence that he suffered from vocal problems.[58] It is also the case that at that time the number of available ministerial candidates exceeded the number of vacant charges. Whatever the reason, after four years of disappointment, Oman entered the ministry of the Presbyterian Church of England in 1890, on receiving a call to Clayport Street Church, Alnwick.[59] Brown of Paisley, though far from well, attended the welcoming celebrations.

---

[58] Stephen Bevans, *John Oman and his Doctrine of God* (Cambridge: Cambridge University Press, 1992), p. 123, cites a letter which relates that Oman was diagnosed as having a 'corn' in his throat, and an observation of F.G. Healey to the effect that Oman 'reckoned his vocal chords had been damaged by faulty elocution training.' If the latter were the case Oman, sadly, was not alone. He writes, 'As I was obviously in need of help, the advice of my friends was frequent and free; and I learned too late that it was uniformly mistaken,' with the consequent 'ruining of my vocal chords.' See *Concerning the Ministry* (London: SCM Press, 1936), p. 110. Classes in elocution were, and still are, provided for ministerial students in many theological colleges, but all too often they are more concerned with how voices sound (accents, volume, light and shade) than with how they are produced. It is quite conceivable that Oman, and before him Principals Henry Rogers of Spring Hill College and Henry Roberts Reynolds of Cheshunt College, both of whom withdrew from preaching owing to vocal problems, could have been helped had competent guidance been available. For a specialist discussion of voice production and related matters see Karen Sell, *The Disciplines of Vocal Pedagogy. Towards an Holistic Approach* (Aldershot: Ashgate, 2005).

[59] The churches of Alnwick would seem to have had a facility for calling scholarly ministers to their pastorates. F.J. Powicke (for whom see Alan P.F. Sell, *Enlightenment, Ecumenism, Evangel. Theological Themes and Thinkers 1550-2000* (Milton Keynes: Paternoster, 2005) ch. 1), was at the Congregational Church there from 1879-1886.

The Alnwick church had been founded in 1753 by the Associate Burgher Synod. In November of that year John Brown of Haddington ordained three elders who had been called by the congregation. At first meetings were held in a room at the top of Canongate, then in another house, and from 1761 in their own building seating 300. The first regular minister, John Marshall, was ordained and inducted in 1766. The cause prospered and outgrew its premises, so that in 1803 a new meeting house was erected on the south side of Green Batt, with seating for 550. In 1845 John Ker, who went on to teach at the theological college, was inducted, and there was further church growth. The Duke of Northumberland's agent refused to renew the church's forty-year lease on the land, which was passed to the Church of Scotland for the erection of St. Paul's Church. Meanwhile Ker's congregation had a 700-seater church built, and there the distinguished preacher, whom Oman later commended to his students as exemplifying homiletic pathos,[60] held forth. In 1851 William Limont assumed the charge and remained there for forty-seven years. It was he to whom Oman came first as assistant and then as successor. Though by no means an example of 'ecclesiastical man', Oman took his preaching, teaching and pastoral duties seriously. 'This was his extraordinary merit,' wrote one, 'that a man of such brilliant intellect, whose sermons were often hard to follow, could yet create this strong bond of affection and trust between himself and the humblest of his flock.'[61] To his pastoral duties Oman added consistent study. He translated Schleiermacher's *On Religion. Speeches to its Cultured Despisers* (1893), and to the third edition of this book Rudolf Otto contributed the Introduction. In a letter Oman wrote, 'I did Schleiermacher during the first years I was in Alnwick from sheer loneliness.'[62] But after a few years he was lonely no longer, for in 1897 he married Mary, one of four daughters of Hunter Blair, J.P., of Gosforth, an elder in the church and a prominent boot manufacturer in Newcastle-upon-Tyne. In due time the Omans had four daughters, and John and Mary remained happily married until her death in 1936. A theological vacancy at New College, Edinburgh, for which Oman was considered, was filled in 1904 by H.R. Mackintosh, who secured a large majority at the General Assembly.[63] Oman's Kerr Lectures were prepared and delivered, and in the winter of 1907 he gave lectures at Syracuse University and

---

[60] Oman, *Concerning the Ministry*, p. 142.

[61] Jane Staker, *A History of St. James' United Reformed Church, Alnwick. Incorporating Lisburn Street and Clayport Street Presbyterian Churches* (Newcastle-upon-Tyne, [1989]), p. 30. Much of the information in this paragraph is drawn from this tercentenary booklet. Among the church members was the chemist, J.L. Newbigin, for more than forty years the secretary of Alnwick Missionary Society. He was the grandfather of J.E. Lesslie Newbigin, to whom further reference shall be made.

[62] Quoted by F.G. Healey, *Religion and Reality. The Theology of John Oman* (Edinburgh: Oliver and Boyd, 1965), p. 159.

[63] See George M. Reith, *Reminiscences of the United Free Church General Assembly (1900-1929)* (Edinburgh: The Moray Press, 1933), p. 47.

Auburn Theological Seminary on 'The foundations of belief'. He was invited to take professorial positions in the United States and Melbourne, but he declined. In 1907, however, Oman accepted the Chair of Systematic Theology and Apologetics at Westminster College, Cambridge, and there he served for the next twenty-eight years. With this I come to Oman's intellectual context.

II

However competent Oman's Stenness tutor may have been in imparting the basics of education, it would seem that prescience was not among his gifts, for F. G. Healey relates that 'When Oman's parents told the tutor that they thought of sending their boy to Edinburgh, the tutor replied, according to a contemporary of Oman's at Stenness, 'that he saw no promise "to justify such an effort."'[64] Undaunted, the Omans sent John to Edinburgh University when he was seventeen with the idea that he should in due course enter the medical profession. First, however, in 1882 he gained the degree of MA with first class honours in philosophy, and in addition he won the Gray and Rhind scholarships. His Professor of Logic was Alexander Campbell Fraser of the Free Church of Scotland,[65] while Henry Calderwood of the United Presbyterian Church held the Chair of Moral Philosophy.[66] While their names do not appear in the indices to Oman's major works we may not unreasonably suppose that from these two, both of whom stood broadly in the tradition of Scottish common sense realism flowing down from Thomas Reid, he learned cautions against the absolute idealism which was currently being propounded by John and Edward Caird in Glasgow University. Fraser disliked absolutism's pantheizing tendencies, and its 'Gnostic' confidence that we could comprehend the reasonableness of the universe – a claim against which Fraser pitted the undeniable obstacle of moral evil. He was always aware of the limits of our knowledge and hence of the need to exercise prudence in assertion – a marked characteristic of the articulated thought of John Oman. His realistic caution did not, however, prevent Fraser from arguing that from the generally trustworthy natural order we might legitimately infer a morally good Divine creator. He accompanied this claim with an argument to the effect that a universe which includes sin and suffering is preferable to a non-moral universe, not least because it affords a training ground for moral agents. Calderwood likewise exercised scholarly caution. Perceiving atheistic tendencies in his teacher

---

[64] Healey, *Religion and Reality*, p. 158.

[65] For Fraser (1819-1914) see chapter 4 for fuller discussion; see also ODNB; W.J. Mander and Alan P.F. Sell, eds., *Dictionary of Nineteenth-Century British Philosophers* (Bristol: Thoemmes Press, 2002); Alan P. F. Sell, *Commemorations. Studies in Christian Thought and History*, (1993) (Eugene, OR: Wipf & Stock, 1998), ch. 10.

[66] For Calderwood (1830-1897) see chapter 4 for fuller discussion; see also ODNB; *Dictionary of Nineteenth-Century British Philosophers*.

William Hamilton's writings, he defended the view that human beings may have genuine, albeit partial, knowledge of the divine. He countered materialism, Hegelianism and, on the ground of the transcendent intelligence which informs every human mind, physicalism. A. S. Pringle-Pattison (then Andrew Seth) was at the beginning of his career when Oman was a student. Oman was not uninfluenced by the personal idealism of which Pringle-Pattison was a pioneer, and years afterwards he reviewed his old teacher's Gifford Lectures which, owing to the intervention of War between their delivery in 1913 and their publication in 1917, appeared to him as a period piece, albeit a lucid one marked by literary grace.[67]

Even more important than the instruction of his philosophical mentors was Oman's reaction to the *cause célèbre* of the day: the heresy trial of William Robertson Smith,[68] who held the Old Testament Chair at the Free Church College, Aberdeen. Influenced by the documentary hypothesis of his teacher, Wellhausen, Smith contributed articles to the ninth edition of *Encyclopaedia Britannica* which prompted many in his own Church and elsewhere to question his view of the inspiration of Scripture. The case rumbled on for five years, and in 1881 Smith was deposed from his Chair, though not expelled from the ministry, whereupon he repaired to Cambridge where he pursued his studies until his early death. We have no need to speculate upon the influence the trial had on Oman: we have it from his own mouth:

> When I went to the university, a raw lad from the ends of the earth, with little equipment except a vast responsiveness to the intellectual environment, the Robertson Smith case was shaking the whole land. I had no notion, in those days, of ever being interested in theology, and my ignorance of the matters in dispute was profound. But I read [Smith's] speeches, and, on one occasion, heard him. I seemed to find the same kind of knowledge as was making the world a place for me of incessant discovery and the same passion for reality as seemed at the moment life's supreme concern. At the same time I heard people who, not only did not know, but did not want to know, condemning him for vanity, because of this very loyalty to the results of investigation. Again and again I heard people declare that, even if all he said were true, regard for useful tradition and the ecclesiastical amenities should have kept him from

---

[67] John Oman, review of *The Idea of God in the Light of Recent Philosophy*, in *The Journal of Theological Studies*, XIX, 1918, 278-9. For Pringle-Pattison (1856-1931) see ODNB; *Dictionary of Nineteenth-Century British Philosophers*; Alan P.F. Sell, *Philosophical Idealism and Christian Belief* (Cardiff: University of Wales Press, 1995, reprinted Eugene, OR: Wipf & Stock, 2006), pp. 83-92 and *passim*.

[68] For a fuller discussion of the Robertson Smith case, see chapter 2.

saying it.[69]

Oman was appalled by this anti-intellectual, obscurantist stance, was deeply concerned that ordinary folk would reach, or be confirmed in, the belief that religion was 'a kind of trade-union to impose upon mankind merely traditional beliefs',[70] and was disgusted by the sanction the position received from ecclesiastical leaders. As he later put it, they were 'more exercised about unity than veracity'.[71] He was 'shocked' when a lawyer and Free Church elder said to him,

> Granted that Robertson Smith is right, if it is truth, it is dangerous truth, and he has no right, as a professor of the Church, to upset the Church by declaring it. I hope I have not since weakened in my loyalty to truth, but in those days I thought intellectual truth the one worthy pursuit in life: and this suggested that the Church was not interested in it. Had I been intending the ministry probably I should have been put off it, but this affected me somewhat as a call to my life's work.[72]

Accordingly, he entered the United Presbyterian Theological Hall, where the staff included John Ker, to whom reference has already been made, and the greatly loved ecclesiastical statesman and collector of languages, Principal John Cairns. Cairns was the right kind of Principal; that is to say, he was one of whom anecdotes could lovingly be rehearsed. Thus J.H. Leckie, who entered the College two years after Oman left it, recalled that on entering the classroom one day the students found that Cairns had inscribed an Assyrian inscription on the blackboard: 'For two days he lectured on this inscription with the most assured belief that we were following every word, and there was deep regret in his face and in his voice when he said: "And now, gentlemen, I am afraid we must return to our theology."'[73] More to our present purpose are Oman's recollections on his Principal. '[A] great man has departed', he wrote on learning of Cairns's death, 'for myself I would say the greatest man I have ever met.' An accomplished linguist, Cairns would apologize for his poor Hebrew – 'Hebrew in my day was very imperfectly taught', and then close his eyes and recite pages of the Hebrew Old Testament flawlessly. He was a humble man; he knew all the theologians of note in Germany; and

his mere presence in the world was a benediction. ... Of all things his

---

[69] John Oman, 'Method in theology. An inaugural lecture', *The Expositor*, 8th series, XXVI, June 1923, pp. 82-3.
[70] Oman, 'Method in theology', p. 85.
[71] Oman, 'Method in theology', p. 82.
[72] Oman, *Vision and Authority*, Preface to the 2nd edn, 1928, pp. 9-10.
[73] MacEwen, *Life and Letters*, p. 743; cf. John Cairns, *Principal Cairns*, p. 138.

laugh was most wonderful. It was like a mountain enjoying an earthquake. ... He was so careful not to hurt that sometimes he was not bold enough to criticise. ... He never seemed to perceive any evil in any mortal ... The many things that make men little he did not perceive for a man only perceives that into which his own heart opens a window. ... While here he lived the eternal life.[74]

If the Robertson Smith case had, as Oman said, shaken the whole land, the need to adjust to modern biblical criticism was by no means the only intellectual challenge facing Christians at that time. There was evolutionary thought and a bundle of 'isms' including agnosticism, materialism, pantheism – all of which were slain by Robert Flint, the most learned apologist of the day; but he was by no means alone in defending the faith against attack. On the contrary, this was the golden age of Scottish apologetics.[75] Such writers as John Stuart Mill and Herbert Spencer came under regular scrutiny. Under the title, *Unbelief in the Eighteenth Century as contrasted with its Earlier and Later History*,[76] Principal Cairns had judiciously discoursed upon rationalistic trends in his Cunningham Lectures of 1880. As for Oman himself, he was particularly opposed to the post-Hegelian immanentist idealism being promulgated in Glasgow by the Cairds. For thinkers of this type, 'The final word was immanent cosmic process, and rational man is but its highest vehicle and most conscious mirror. This is predestinarianism in a way to have taken away even Calvin's breath.'[77] Later, in the midst of war, Oman lamented that Germany had constructed a myopic idealism out of Hegel, making the state the Absolute's final organ, to which the individual, lost in the crowd, had to do obeisance.[78] He returned to the theme in his greatest work, in which he complained that Hegelianism 'does not merely dismiss the problem of the individual, but is the profoundest attempt to account for it on a scheme which, nevertheless, derives

---

[74] J. Oman, 'Dr. Cairns. By one of his students', ms. at Westminster College, Cambridge.

[75] See Alan P.F. Sell, *Defending and Declaring the Faith. Some Scottish Examples 1860-1920*; (1987), 2nd edn (Milton Keynes: Paternoster, 2009). For concurrent apologetic efforts in Nonconformity south of the Scottish border see Alan P. F. Sell, *Philosophy, Dissent and Nonconformity 1689-1920* (Cambridge: James Clarke, 2004), ch. 5.

[76] Edinburgh: A. & C. Black, 1881.

[77] John Oman, *Grace and Personality*, (1917), (London: Collins Fontana, 1960), p. 32. He proceeds to argue that this is, nevertheless the logic of Calvin's own position. For immanentism, modern biblical criticism and evolutionary thought see Alan P. F. Sell, *Theology in Turmoil. The Roots, Course and Significance of the Conservative-Liberal Debate in Modern Theology*, (1986) (Eugene, OR: Wipf & Stock, 1998), chs. 1-3; for a fuller discussion of the first see Sell, *Philosophical Idealism*.

[78] John Oman, *The War and its Issues. An Attempt at a Christian Judgment* (Cambridge: CUP, 2nd edn, 1916), p. 91.

all rationality from absorbing him into the process of the Cosmic Reason'.[79] Over and above the excitements surrounding the Declaratory Acts, there was considerable doctrinal and more general theological publication during the second half of the nineteenth century. It is quite remarkable that Scotland could produce sufficient scholars to staff not only the four ancient University departments, but also the three new Free Church colleges required following the Disruption, the Secession Colleges, and still have a number of scholar-pastors in charges across the land. As if that were not enough, theologians from Scotland staffed many colonial institutions, and the Congregationalists were able to despatch Gilbert Wardlaw to Blackburn, A. M. Fairbairn to Bradford, Robert Mackintosh to Manchester, and P.T. Forsyth and A.E. Garvie to London.

Such was the apologetically and theologically vibrant environment in which Oman read for his degree of BD, and subsequently for his D.Phil. of Edinburgh. During his theological course Oman was able to spend two summer terms abroad. In 1883 he, together with his fellow-students James Gardner and B.R. Mein, was at Erlangen University, where he sat under the dogmatician F.H. Frank,[80] the biblical scholar, F.T.R. von Zahn, and the philosophical theologian, G. Class. Two summers later he was at Heidelberg, where he heard Adolph Hausrath on New Testament Introduction and Merx on the Psalms. As well as contributing substantial volumes in his field, the former wrote a number of historical romances under the pseudonym George Taylor – an achievement which, as far as I know, is unmatched by any other devotee of the Tübingen school of criticism. By a happy coincidence Adalbert Merx later studied the Sinaitic Palimpsest which had been discovered in 1892 by Agnes Smith Lewis who, with her twin sister, Mrs. Margaret Dunlop Gibson, was a benefactress of Westminster College, Cambridge. On leaving Erlangen Oman went on to Neuchâtel with a view to mastering French.[81]

In 1907, following his period as a United Presbyterian probationer and minister at Alnwick, Oman assumed the Barbour Chair of Systematic Theology and Apologetics at Westminster College, Cambridge, in succession to James Oswald Dykes, who had just retired from the combined position of professor and principal. Members of the appointing Synod had cast 402 votes in favour of Oman, against 101 for Patrick Carnegie Simpson. Oman's academic colleagues in the College combined academic prowess and ecclesiastical loyalty to a high degree. In 1908 John Skinner became Principal, a position he held until his resignation in 1922, when Oman succeeded him in that office, once again

---

[79] Oman, *Natural and Supernatural*, p. 475.

[80] Whose position Oman outlines in *The Problem of Faith and Freedom in the Last Two Centuries* (London: Hodder and Stoughton, 1906), pp. 346-8.

[81] See G. Alexander, 'Memoir', xviii; J. Oman, 'Reminiscences of continental travel' and 'German student life', unpublished papers at Westminster College, Cambridge.

defeating Simpson, but this time by 'a slight majority'.[82] Skinner had been on the staff since 1890. He held the Chair of Old Testament Literature and Apologetics,[83] and became the first Nonconformist to receive the Degree of Doctor of Divinity of the University of Oxford. Charles Archibald Anderson Scott held the Chair of New Testament Language, Literature and Theology from 1907, and in 1920 he became the first Nonconformist minister to gain Cambridge University's DD. Meanwhile in 1914 he had been nominated for the Chair of Church History, but on this occasion Carnegie Simpson, a distinguished ecclesiastical statesman, was successful. In the same year a rumour was started to the effect that Oman was to be nominated for the Chair at Glasgow United Free Church College which had fallen vacant on the death of Professor James Orr. On 17 February R.C. Gillie, the convenor of the Westminster College Committee wrote a letter for circulation in which he strongly expressed the view that Oman's removal would be a disastrous blow to the College; and the Birmingham Presbytery, on the motion of the Revd J.R. Gillies resolved to resist Oman's removal, and the London North Presbytery did likewise.[84] Oman himself made it clear that he did not wish to leave Cambridge.

In his capacity as Principal, Oman sent a memorandum to a sub-committee established by the Moderator's Committee to review the Presbyterian Church's ministry. Oman wrote on the basis of enquiries he had made into the curriculum of theological colleges. The question was how broad the curriculum should become. 'The strongest opinion' he reported, 'I had from President Wilson. "Stick at all costs to your four central subjects. Our method means utterly superficial knowledge ..."' On this Oman remarked, 'My experience as a teacher has rubbed into me the enormous difference between knowing a subject and knowing about it.'[85] Accordingly he maintained the longstanding policy of focusing upon the Old and New Testaments, Church History and Theology, and this with a view to fostering depth of understanding on the part of his students as courses proceeded from session to session.

When Skinner died in 1921, he was succeeded in the Old Testament Chair by William Alexander Leslie Elmslie, whose father, William Gray Elmslie, had earlier held the post. When Oman retired in 1935, the younger Elmslie succeeded him as Principal, while Oman's former student, H.H. Farmer, was called to the Chair of Systematic Theology.[86] On his retirement, Oman was

---

[82] Report on 11 May 1922 among the Westminster College Oman papers.

[83] Skinner was a native of Aberdeenshire, that nursery of Old Testament professors, of whom two, Skinner and W.G. Elmslie, taught at Westminster College. Others were A.B. Davidson, W. Robertson Smith and George Adam Smith.

[84] See the Oman papers at Westminster College, Cambridge.

[85] Typescript 'Memorandum' at Westminster College, Cambridge.

[86] For sketches of the academic staff see W.A.L. Elmslie, *Westminster College Cambridge 1899-1949* (London: Presbyterian Church of England, [1949]); R.S. Robson, *Our Professors. Brief notes of men who after occupying English Presbyterian pulpits*

promised a copy of Hugh Rivière's portrait of Oman made by the artist himself; and the Omans were given tickets for a fortnight's cruise to the Norwegian fjords.[87] The fact that it was an independent institution notwithstanding, by now Westminster College's contribution to the University of Cambridge was taken as a matter of course. This was in no small part to the distinguished service Oman gave to the Board of the Faculty of Divinity and the Degrees Committee. In addition he lectured in Comparative Religion from 1913-1922, served three terms as Stanton Lecturer in the Philosophy of Religion, was elected an Honorary Fellow of Jesus College in 1928, became an Honorary DD of the University of Oxford in 1928, and a Fellow of the British Academy ten years later – an honour he accepted with some hesitation because he felt he would not be able to make further contributions 'to support the honour'.[88]

Whilst at Cambridge Oman served his Church in a variety of ways. He undertook pulpit supplies in the Birmingham Presbytery on behalf of ministers who were called away during World War I. He visited the troops in France under the auspices of the YMCA and, deeply affected by the War, he published *The War and Issues* in 1915 – a second edition being required the following year. He found during his visits to military camps and hospitals that 'fundamental religious questions were constantly being discussed', and this 'forced upon me the reconsideration of my whole religious position'.[89] Following the cessation of hostilities he toured occupied areas;[90] and he was still reflecting upon the War in his last book, *Honest Religion*, published posthumously in 1941.[91] Though far from being a professional ecclesiastical statesman, he was nevertheless honoured by the call of the Presbyterian Church of England to be Moderator of its General Assembly in 1931. It is characteristic of Oman that he kept in touch with his roots. Thus, for example, he paid return visits to Alnwick. On one such occasion *The British* Weekly reported that 'Dr. Oman's ripe scholarship, combined with a most reverential mind, mark him as an outstanding preacher. The services throughout were very hearty.'[92] On another occasion *The Alnwick Guardian and County* Advertiser devoted almost a full page, including a large photograph of Oman, to one of his return visits.[93] Again, he was present as a distinguished visitor at the General Assembly of the

---

have been appointed to chairs (London: Presbyterian Historical Society of England, 1956). Note that Robson curtails C.A.A. Scott's tenure of his Chair by ten years, 12.

[87] J.L. Cottle and A.S. Cooper, 'Westminster College Bulletin', *The Presbyterian Messenger*, 1935, p. 230.

[88] G. Alexander, 'Memoir,' xxiv.

[89] Oman, *Grace and Personality*, p. 5.

[90] Obituary in *The Times*, 18 May 1939.

[91] See, for example, *Honest Religion*, pp. 5, 16.

[92] *The British Weekly*, 1 April 1909.

[93] *The Alnwick Guardian and County Advertiser*, 21 September 1912.

United Presbyterian Church in 1924.[94] In 1932 he joined William Temple and others in signing a letter to *The Times* urging that aid be sent to China where, during the summer of 1931, an area larger than England had been flooded.[95] Four years later he, together with the Baptist, M.E. Aubrey, the Congregationalists, Sidney M. Berry and A.J. Grieve, the Methodist, J. Scott Lidgett, and others, signed a letter regarding the four hundredth anniversary of the martyrdom of William Tindale. The signatories' objective was to encourage churches, Sunday schools and brotherhoods to mark the occasion, and to commend a commemorative pamphlet published by the British and Foreign Bible Society.[96] Above all, however, during his Cambridge years Oman did the bulk of his writing, most notably his books, *Grace and Personality* (1917) and *The Natural and the Supernatural* (1931). While a full account of these cannot here be provided, we have not finished placing him in his intellectual context until we noted some of the intellectual influences, both positive and negative upon him, certain trends of thought to which he paid no heed, and the way in which the main lines of his own thought were received.

Later in life Oman published his summary impressions of the varieties of continental thought, contemporary with himself that he had encountered.[97] Of the Tübingen way of forcing facts to conform with Hegelian categories he declared that no other school 'has risen to quite this height of glorifying the abstraction as universal oracle ...'; and he elsewhere objected to postulate of the Tübingen authors, namely, that 'As soon as a book is shown to have been written with a purpose, it is to be discounted as an accurate historical report.'[98] In opposition to this, and to a perceived pantheistic and non-moral interpretation of Christianity, the Ritschlians, for all their elevation of the Kingdom of God construed in *quasi*-Kantian terms of 'the progressive moralisation of the race', could not show why 'the mould of moral form – the Pharisee – did not go into this kingdom before the publican and the sinner.' On the other hand, Oman defended Ritschl against the charge that his repudiation of metaphysics entailed the denial of the objectivity of religious knowledge. Ritschl 'had worshipped at [the shrine of the Transcendental Philosophy] only to find the cosmic process instead of God, and he had also been a disciple of the Tübingen school, till he found that its criticism was only subjection to this metaphysical idol'.[99] Ritschl's point, says Oman, was that 'a theoretical truth is one that can be forced upon any intelligent person by argument, and religious

---

[94] See George M. Reith, *Reminiscences of the United Free Church Assembly*, p. 274.

[95] *The Times*, 21 March 1932, p. 10.

[96] *The Times*, 26 September 1936, p. 13.

[97] Oman, 'Author's preface' to *Honest Religion*, xxxiv-xl. Quotations in this paragraph, other than those numbered 97-100, are all drawn from these pages.

[98] Oman, *Faith and Freedom*, p. 300.

[99] John Oman, 'Ritschlianism', *Journal of Theological Studies*, XI, 1910, p. 272.

truth never arrives at that stage;'[100] it requires 'not merely intelligent consideration, but an attitude of the will.' The Ritschlians were 'less Olympian than the Tübingen authors, and their contribution to raising the essential questions about early Christianity was much greater; yet their answers were determined by their outlook, far more than their outlook by their answers.' For all that, Ritschl understood that 'Personality is the prime religious basis. Men do not start from the Absolute and then add personality. They start from personality, and, by discovering that in spite of sin and evil they can ... subject all things to moral and spiritual ends, they arrive at a belief in omnipotent personality.'[101] For their part, the Apocalyptic School 'denied all that was rational in its predecessors' view. But by the spectacles of its theory its vision was even more controlled' and 'it still continued to measure with the old Kantian ethic, if not the old Kantian reason.' Thus, Schweitzer argues that Jesus did not spiritualize, but ethicized the political ideal of late Jewish Messianic expectation in Kantian fashion, whereas Oman is utterly convinced that 'If ... there is anything certain about what Jesus did, it was to work a moral regeneration by a religious one, and that His ethical spirit was not of the Kantian order to be merely poured into anything. The most recent School', he continues (citing Dibelius),

> tests all by 'form' and what it calls 'set in life'. This might seem to show more regard to life and history, but ... it is used just as another category to drill the records and has a great part of its impressiveness from becoming the slogan or battle-cry of a school. ... [T]here is nothing it says but may in certain cases be true: only it is not so universally true that a general ordering of all can be derived from it.

Oman's preference is for Rudolf Otto's view that 'Jesus announced a Kingdom already present in spiritual power but which was to have further manifestation and consummation, yet this was to be of the nature of the prophetic vision of knowing God and having His commandment in the heart.' His difference from Otto lay in the fact that he could not endorse the view that the holy is simply a matter of intense, value-free emotion: 'As mere feeling,' he writes, 'the sense of the holy would be impossible to distinguish from the mere spooky feeling which is magical, at one end, and from the sense of the sublime which is artistic, at the other'.[102] That is to say, Abstracted from moral considerations, the 'awesome holy' characterizes magical, superstitious, belief.[103] In making this point elsewhere Oman draws a delightful illustration

---

[100] Oman, 'Ritschlianism', p. 365.

[101] Oman, 'Ritschlianism', p. 473.

[102] Oman, *Natural and Supernatural*, p. 61.

[103] Oman, *Natural and Supernatural*, pp. 60-63. Oman's point was endorsed by English Nonconformity's most scholarly, and most undeservedly neglected, theologian

from his youthful experience:

> When a boy of fourteen or thereabouts, I was riding through the Standing
> Stones of Stenness on a winter afternoon when dusk was settling into
> darkness. They stand on the top of a lone narrow neck of land between
> two lochs. ... The circle of stones had a look of ancient giants against the
> grey sky, and the gaping mounds which had been opened stood shadowy
> and apart. A More numinous scene, at a more numinous hour, could not
> be found on earth. And the feeling which suddenly struck me is not
> inaptly described as the *mysterium tremendum et fascinans*. But at the
> same moment it struck my old horse at least as vehemently as myself. He
> threw up his head, snorted, set his feet, trembled, and finally bolted at a
> rate I should have thought impossible for his old bones. Now there is little
> doubt that Prof. Otto is right in finding the reason why the early Briton
> erected this circle of stones on that particular spot in the peculiar eerie
> feeling it created rather than in merely intellectual ideas; but, as the
> feeling had probably not yet arrived at being religious for my horse, and
> had ceased to be religious for me, it would be necessary to ask, what was
> the peculiarity which, without disrespect to his intelligence, I may assume
> my horse not to have attained and which, without excessive pride in my
> state of civilization, I may assume I had passed beyond, which made it for
> primitive man religious? ... [Feelings aroused by nature] may stir and pass
> over into the holy ... but are we not then in a new order? And is not the
> essence of it that it is an order of absolute value which, when it escapes
> from its material form, is just the ethical sacred, the sense of the
> requirements of a Spirit in the world which is absolute and of a spirit in
> ourselves in its image which has its worth in accepting as its own these
> absolute requirements and refusing to bring them down to the level of our
> temporal convenience? ... My horse, we may assume, had not reached this
> valuation, and I was at least learning to make it by less material ways.[104]

Apart from this ethical valuation, he continues, we have superstition, not
religion, and we do not have a love which casts out fear. By separating the
rational from the religious Otto 'can do no more than say that they are
connected *a priori*, which is not very satisfactory'.[105] The upshot is that Otto's
work 'does little to satisfy thought', but 'it does a great deal to stimulate

---

of the twentieth century, Robert Franks. See his *The Atonement. The Dale Lectures for
1933* (London: OUP, 1934), p. 21. For Franks see Alan P.F. Sell, *Hinterland Theology.
A Stimulus to Theological Construction* (Milton Keynes: Paternoster, 2008), ch. 10 and
passim.

[104] John Oman, 'The idea of the holy', *The Journal of Theological Studies*, XXV,
1924, pp. 282-3.

[105] Oman, 'The Idea of the holy', p. 286.

enquiry and reflexion'.[106] Integrity prompts the observation that to C.A. Campbell this was nothing other than an unjustified 'attack' on Otto. To him it was the 'incredible', but 'sober truth' that Oman wrote as if all that Otto had said about the *fascinans* aspect of the numinous 'simply did not exist.' He felt that if Oman had paid as much attention to Otto's *fascinans* as he had done to his *tremendum*, his one-sided critique would have been balanced by the recognition that 'The *fascinans* aspect is that in virtue of which the numinous consciousness is enraptured and entranced by the transcendent *worth* or *value* of the numen.'[107] He would therefore have seen that Otto did not banish the moral as charged.

Lying behind Otto as a prominent influence upon Oman is Schleiermacher, with his experiential starting-point for understanding religion. Oman defends Schiermacher against the charges that there was nothing objective in his theology, that by feeling he meant sentiment, and that by absolute dependence he meant 'mere mystical self-surrender'.[108] On the contrary, for Schleiermacher, feeling 'is neither sensation nor emotion, but the contract with reality, which, while it precedes clear intuition, is not a mere cause of it but passes into it. Thus religion and perception are both contacts with reality and united at their source.'[109]

From time to time Oman was called upon to review the work of living theologians. Among the works allotted to him was Hastings Rashdall's *The Idea of Atonement in Christian Theology*. He finds that 'The work is pervaded throughout by the conviction, not only that the study of history is a necessary preliminary to any serious reconstruction, but that, to a large extent, it will supersede the need for any such task.'[110] He wryly remarks that Rashdall does not have much difficulty in selecting authors for discussion, 'seeing he believes that all that is obnoxious to him was maintained only by a few dominating but deluded individuals, beginning with St Paul and culminating in Luther'.[111] Rashdall rejects 'every form of vicarious, substitutionary, or representative theory of atonement'.[112] Anselm left us with a God who cared more for his own honour than for his debt-paying Son, but he did at least call forth Abelard's moral influence theory, with which Rashdall finds himself in general sympathy. Oman agrees with Rashdall that no atonement theory that conflicts with Jesus' teaching can be called Christian, but queries whether Rashdall's idea of God,

---

[106] Oman, 'The Idea of the holy'.

[107] See C.A. Campbell, *On Selfhood and Godhood* (London: Allen & Unwin, 1957), p. 343.

[108] John Oman, 'Schleiermacher', *The Journal of Theological Studies*, XXX, 1929, p. 403.

[109] Oman, 'Schleiermacher', p. 404.

[110] John Oman, review of H. Rashdall, *The Idea of Atonement in Christian Theology*, in *The Journal of Theological Studies*, XXI, 1920, p. 267.

[111] Oman, review of Rashdall.

[112] Oman, review of Rashdall.

namely, that he is a 'kind of moral governor who justifies us as we are just', takes full account of the fact that 'For Jesus there is only one condition of forgiveness – the God to whom we return.'[113] Whereas Paul had a gospel for sinners, Rashdall's treatment of reconciliation is slight. Indeed, 'he does not get very far beyond a morality which is still entangled with the old Pharisaic demand for an equivalence of merit and reward, which any doctrine of atonement that means anything must deny to be the final method of God's rule'.[114]

When he turns to H.R. Mackintosh's book, *The Christian Experience of Forgiveness*, we find Oman diagnosing his response thus: 'disagreement is probably rather from a difference of race and temperament and general outlook than from any clear difference of opinion. ...[T]here is something of a Celtic quality with which the ordinary Briton feels a little overwhelmed.'[115] He proceeds to posit two kinds of mind, the first, exemplified by Mackintosh, 'takes naturally to Otto's awed holy; the other type instinctively shakes it off as a nightmare'.[116] The types vary as to the difficulties they perceive:

> Prof. Mackintosh very easily thinks of God as just doing things; it is an essential part of the [other's] idea of God that God is just another name for the ultimate real. Thus the problem of forgiveness is apt to be, for him, something exceptional that God does, while, for the other type it is something which is just because God is what He is, and we have found it out.[117]

Oman further feels that Mackintosh so dwells on the suffering of the Cross as to minimize the victory of the Cross. To all of which I shall return shortly.

Karl Barth was probably the theologian by whom Oman was least likely to be influenced in a positive direction. Recalling the theological atmosphere he had experienced in Erlangen, Oman remarked that 'if we had to choose between the older orthodoxy of the Erlangen School and the newer of the Barthian, the former has at least the Christian temper'.[118] Oman objects to that way in which Barthians fault Schleiermacher's empiricism for rendering religion anthropocentric:

> It used to be said that Schleiermacher deserved his name, which means veil-maker, but Barth and his disciples deal in thicker and still more

---

[113] Oman, review of Rashdall, p. 272.

[114] Oman, review of Rahsdall, p. 274.

[115] John Oman, review of H.R. Mackintosh, *The Christian Experience of Forgiveness*, in *The Journal of Theological Studies*, XXIX, 1928, p. 297.

[116] Oman, review of Mackintosh.

[117] Oman, review of Mackintosh, pp. 297-8.

[118] Review of A. Chapman, *An Introduction to Schleiermacher*, in *The Journal of Theological Studies*, XXXIV, 1933, p. 214.

opaque material. Much of the criticism of this school is true, and they have done a great deal to clear the ground. I am not very learned in their works and cannot claim to know all that is maintained, but the effect so far seems to leave more of a quagmire than before. Schleiermacher is denounced as a high-priest of error. Ever since his day Protestant theology has wandered in the quagmires of pious emotion and not found objective God-given truth. This is preached with prophetic fire. But when we come to ask what is God-given truth, what is *Das Wort Gottes* which is the supreme truth, and how do we know it is God's word; so far as I have read, the writers clothe themselves in vagueness and become abusive.[119]

Oman cannot see how human beings can do other than measure the universe and do so by using human measures. Even an infallible Scripture or an infallible papacy is humanly measured. But Barth and his followers deny that they are biblical infallibilists and affirm their acceptance of biblical criticism: 'Therefore, it would seem an unavoidable conclusion that we must somewhere find our knowledge anthropocentric, and the question must arise of how it can be anthropocentric in such a way as to be objective knowledge. But apparently we go after strange Gods with Schleiermacher when we make the attempt.'[120]

In view of the foregoing, Stephen Bevans seems wide off the mark when he writes, 'It is rather ironic that Oman had such an antipathy to Barth. While differing radically in terms of theological method, both Barth and Oman would agree on the personal nature of God.'[121] But (a) as between these two method is all, Barth being the disjunctive thinker, Oman the conjunctive; Barth eschewing apologetics, Oman writing *Honest Religion*; and (b) everything turns upon the connotation of 'personal' in the term 'personal God'; for Oman, God was the holy One, but he was never the wholly other One, and God's grace (*pace* Augustinian*ism* and Calvin*ism*) was persuasive not irresistible.[122] It is not inconceivable that Oman would have applied his words of 1923 to Barthianism:

---

[119] Oman, 'Schleiermacher', p. 403.

[120] Oman, 'Schleiermacher', p. 404.

[121] Bevans, *Oman and his Doctrine of God*, p. 121.

[122] See, for example, the exposition of W.M. Horton, *Contemporary English Theology. An American Interpretation* (New York and London: Harper, 1936), p. 135. Horton muses, *ad loc.*, that 'Karl Barth seems to be urging us along that path [of Augustinian irrationalism and immoralism] as the only alternative to Pelagian pride of intellect and moral self-sufficiency.' In fairness it must be granted that many Calvinists construed 'irresistible' in 'irresistible grace' not in terms of sheer omnipotent force, but in the sense that God's overflowing love towards the undeserving is so lovingly attractive that any resistance to it is quelled *ab initio*: the recipient would not wish to resist such grace. In this context they spoke of 'the Father's drawing' - a very different thing from the Father's dragooning or compelling.

Every now and then movements make a great impression by dogmatic assertion, but the sapping of the foundations goes on all the time, and, over a long period, it is always evident that they have not kept serious and thoughtful minds within the Christian Church, but that, what is still worse, they have been stirring doubt regarding the whole reality of a spiritual world.[123]

Even student skits can convey truth, as when Westminster College students produced a booklet entitled 'What I owe to Karl Barth, by John Oman'; the pages in the booklet were blank.[124] When, in his last book, Oman declared that 'there is no worse preparation for profitable dialogue than a mind school-mastering everything by dialectic',[125] the innocent reader cannot help wondering whom he might have had in mind.

It would seem that outside the walls of Westminster College the Cambridge friend whose work Oman most greatly valued was F. R. Tennant. Oman reviewed the two volumes of Tennant's *Philosophical Theology*, welcomed the empiricist basis of the work, but regretted that 'we deal with the environment as meaning', whereas Oman asks 'what is meaning apart from value?' He would have pressed the 'absoluteness of regard for the ideal value as sacred', which was foreign to Tennant's method.[126]

In the broader realm of contemporary philosophy Oman adjusted himself to the thought of a number of writers. For example, he opposed Samuel Alexander's view of space-time as

the matrix of all reality, from which all else in our experienced universe "emerges". In order to make a start at all, [Alexander] has to assume that it has qualities. But this is precisely the all-important step from motion to meaning, which nothing in the mathematical conception of space-time justifies him in taking.[127]

Again, Oman had pertinent things to say concerning Henry Jones's Gifford Lectures, *The Faith that Enquires*. I am sure that Oman writes with utter sincerity, but the line between that and praising with faint damns, or writing

---

[123] Oman, 'Method in theology', pp. 85-6. This was Oman's Inaugural Lecture on assuming the Principalship of Westminster College.

[124] This incident is recalled by P. Carnegie Simpson, *Recollections* (London: Nisbet, 1943), p. 65.

[125] Oman, *Honest Religion*, p. 30.

[126] See the review of *Philosophical Theology*, I, in *The Journal of Theological Studies*, XXXI, 1930, pp. 403-7; and II, *The Journal of Theological Studies*, XXXIII, 1932, 281-3. The quotations are from I, p. 406.Tennant contributed an obituary of Oman to *Proceedings of the British Academy*, XXV, 1939, pp. 332-8.

[127] Oman, *Natural and Supernatural*, p. 184. He refers to Alexander's *Space, Time, and Deity* (London: Macmillan, 1920).

with tongue in cheek, is not always easy to discern:

> Regarding a book which sets out to be philosophy, to say it is great preaching may seem doubtful praise. But there never was any doubt at any time that Prof. Jones's real gift lay in the region of moving appeal rather than in the severer disciplines of thought and reasoning ... and this time ... he has come into his kingdom. ... A superficial judgement might give an impression of something like failure: and in one sense it is a quite correct impression. Yet the interest and value of the book are to be found in that very lack of logical success, because it comes through a faith too vital and strong to be imprisoned in any intellectual form.[128]

The late author triumphed over suffering, and hence there is a 'beautiful and heroic religious element in the book' which will enable theologians 'readily to pardon the neglect of their own labours'.[129] What is clear is that Jones's 'real religion and active experience are no longer able to be contained in [his Hegelianism]'.[130] Jones identified God and the Absolute, and rebuked F.H. Bradley for distinguishing between them, 'But can any one read the book and suppose that the author's God is the name for the sum of the cosmic process?'[131] The strongest part of the book, in Oman's opinion, is Jones's demolition of Bosanquet's system as 'mechanism masquerading as spiritual progress'.[132] The book is also marked by 'a mystical, non-ethical, purely emotional and submissive view of religion ... which makes it easy to realize the long attraction for our author of the false peace of cosmic pantheism'.[133]

Without question, the most devastating of Oman's reviews is that of Whitehead's *Process and Reality*. Having tried unsuccessfully to decline the task and return the book, he starts as he means to go on: 'When Prof. Whitehead was a professional mathematician, thinking as a philosopher, his works interested me profoundly, but now that he is a professional philosopher, thinking and expressing himself as a mathematician, they have become, for me at least, of increasing difficulty with diminishing profit.'[134] He finds many echoes of Hegel in the book, which 'is the only philosophical utterance I ... have ever found to be even more of an achievement in technical jargon than

---

[128] John Oman, review of H. Jones, *A Faith that Enquires*, in *The Journal of Theological Studies*, XXIV, 1923, p. 215.

[129] Oman, review of Jones, p. 215.

[130] Oman, review of Jones, p. 216.

[131] Oman, review of Jones. Cf. Oman, *Natural and Supernatural*, p. 475.

[132] Oman, review of Jones, p. 216.

[133] Oman, review of Jones. See further on Henry Jones, Sell, *Philosophical Idealism*, pp. 73-83 and *passim*.

[134] John Oman, review of A.N. Whitehead, *Process and Reality* in *The Journal of Theological Studies*, XXXIII, 1932, p. 48.

Hegel'.[135] He trounces the view that mind is not an individual centre of activity,
but is part of the production of 'novel togetherness' as being not argument, but
assertion. Moreover, 'if we know the world in proportion as we stand over it
and refuse every impression we do not know as our own meaning, and if only
as we are independent do we find the universe respond to us, we must accept
the fact, however incapable we are of explaining it'.[136] As for God as a process
of becoming in the universe,

> God, to have any meaning, is not merely the sense of process, but the
> power whereby we subordinate process to higher ends. The question of
> God is not what the world is, or by process of nature is becoming, but of
> what can be made of the world, if it has a divine purpose in it by which
> we can at once deny it and possess it.[137]

As for trends of thought with which Oman might conceivably have engaged
in writing but, as far as I can discover, did not, I would mention, to look no
further than Cambridge, the philosophical contributions of G.E. Moore and
Bertrand Russell, the emphasis in C.D. Broad's book, *Perception, Physics and
Reality* (1915), upon the limits of knowledge – a recurrent theme in Oman's
writings; and the amalgam of mathematics, logic and mysticism which was
Wittgenstein's *Tractatus* (ET, 1922). In noting such omissions I do not imply
an adverse judgment upon Oman, for time-lags are endemic in intellectual
history, especially where interdisciplinary activities are in view. There would
be as little point in complaining that the work of Oman and Buber, and those
such as H.H. Farmer who were indebted to them, did not receive the attention
of secular philosophers until the 1950s.[138]

But if he passed by the leading philosophical lights of Cambridge, Oman did
cast an eye towards Oxford when A.J. Ayer launched his manifesto of logical
positivism, *Language, Truth and Logic*, in 1936. Oman approves of Ayer's
clarity of style; he chides Ayer for describing himself as an empiricist in the
style of Berkeley and Hume when those two differed significantly on sensation
and perception; when Ayer follows Hume in disposing of the reality of the ego

---

[135] Oman, review of Whitehead, p. 50.
[136] Oman, review of Whitehead, p. 52.
[137] Oman, review of Whitehead, p. 52.
[138] See Alan P.F. Sell, *The Philosophy of Religion 1875-1980*, (1988) (Bristol:
Thoemmes Press, 1996), pp. 194-5, for a brief account of the criticisms of C.B. Martin
and Ronald W. Hepburn, and of the responses to Hepburn by John Hick and John
McIntyre. With this note I recall with gratitude Ronald Hepburn, who set me on my
doctoral way, and who died on 23 December 2008. I never have regretted seeking out a
university (Nottingham) in which my supervisors would be a no-longer-persuaded
Professor of Philosophy and a Christian philosopher of religion, the late James
Richmond. When Hepburn was succeeded by Jonathan Harrison the challenge was in no
way diminished.

on the ground that 'it is never found keeping house alone', Oman retorts that 'there is never any housekeeping in the mind without it'; he contends that if philosophy is to be restricted to the analysis of scientific ideas 'it would have no right to the name of love of universal wisdom' ('Quite so', I can hear Ayer chirruping); but he refrains from direct assault on the principle of verification as such. He concludes,

> Apparently the whole position is imported from Germany, and what is wrong with Germany at present is seeing what it likes with the spectacles of theory and being able to ignore all the rest; and not seeing it as a whole with the eyed of the intellect enlightened by the imagination. In this it is different from Hume, who was a sceptic dealing with philosophical theories, not a dogmatist about all reality.[139]

What becomes clear from this review of positive and negative influences upon Oman is that in no case did he adopt the views of others without modification. On the contrary, in many accounts of the character of his own work the recurring note is that he was an independent thinker. He did not slavishly follow anyone: as Simpson said, he 'was debtor to no man';[140] nor did he attract a school of disciples, though such alumni of Westminster College as H.H. Farmer, F.G. Healey and John Hick have acknowledged their indebtedness to him. Precisely because of his independence of mind it is hazardous to attach unqualified labels to him. He was neither an out and out empiricist, nor an out and out idealist. He has been called a liberal theologian, and he certainly was no biblical or confessional fundamentalist; but neither was he of the kind of whom P.T. Forsyth complained in a seafaring image that would have appealed to Oman: 'too many are occupied in throwing over precious cargo; they are lightening the ship even of its fuel'.[141] But if Oman was not a liberal who sought to discover how little could be believed whilst remaining in good ecclesiastical standing, neither was he one who sublimated a lack of traditional conviction in a flurry of Social Gospel activism.[142] Oman's liberalism, as we shall see, was characterized by his openness to new ideas, and by a refusal to bow to any authority, whether biblicist or ecclesiastical, which did not commend itself to his reason and conscience.

---

[139] John Oman, review of A.J. Ayer, *Language, Truth and Logic*, in *The British Weekly*, 26 March 1936.

[140] Simpson, *Recollections*, p. 65.

[141] P.T. Forsyth, *The Principle of Authority*, (1913) (London: Independent Press, 1952), p. 261.

[142] For the ambiguity of both 'liberal' and 'conservative' see Sell, *Theology in Turmoil*, chs. 5 and 6.

III

With this I come to the final major issue: having seen what Oman made of others, what did he contribute to the intellectual context in which he lived? First, it would surely be impossible to deny that Oman's writings are marked by utter sincerity. 'Sincerity', he declared, 'must maintain a mind ever open to the truth and ever in pursuit of the truth, and the worst insincerity of all is that which has silenced the truth'.[143] By this motto he lived and wrote; but note that 'True sincerity is not a mere emotional response to impressions, but puts all its mind, as well as its heart, into interpreting signs.'[144] As so often, he proceeds to illustrate from his early experiences:

> Have you ever seen an old fisherman studying the weather before committing his frail barque to the mercy of the sea? I think of one who for seventy years had braved the Atlantic, of how his long-sighted grey eyes used to search the horizon on a doubtful morning, and of the long experience behind them by which he interpreted every wisp of cloud and every shimmer of sunshine. To go out in good weather was a necessity of daily bread; to be out in bad might mean a watery grave. Many he had known who, having misread the signs of the sky, had gone out and never returned. Superficial impressions, therefore, had no weight with him ...[145]

Sincerity takes us beyond what merely impresses 'to the signs of the supreme and final realities by which our futures are ultimately determined'.[146] Moreover, 'no strong, independent, true character ever comes to birth except in solitary wrestling with serious thought and noble aspiration and high resolve'.[147]

The serious thought which ever preoccupied Oman was that flowing down from the Rationalism of the eighteenth century and the Romanticism of the nineteenth. It is characteristic of his method that, far from embracing one and shunning the other, he carefully weighed both, and in each of them found both stimuli and cautions. This was consistent with his conviction that 'There is no breadth of judgment without help from the past, but there is no using the past to good purpose without independent judgment on it of our own conscience of truth and right.'[148] Painting with rather broad brush strokes he summarizes his findings thus: 'The eighteenth century was occupied with the problem of the individual; the nineteenth with the problem of individuality.'[149] He applauded

---

[143] Oman, *Dialogue with God*, p. 71.

[144] Oman, *Paradox of the World*, p. 7.

[145] Oman, *Paradox of the World*, p. 7.

[146] Oman, *Paradox of the World*, p. 14.

[147] Oman, *Concerning the Ministry*, p. 41.

[148] Oman, *Honest Religion*, pp. 13-14.

[149] Oman, *Faith and Freedom*, p. 193.

the eighteenth century's 'earnest love of truth' which 'gave to its enquiries, in spite of their limitations, an abiding value; and [the] idolatry of the mathematical method was the chief cause of these limitations'.[150] Thus,

> Rationalism ... conceived religion mainly as an intellectual affair of evidences about God as the maker of the world, and providence as the direction of it, and immortality as compensation for its injustices and perfections. The reason was not that religion ever seemed anything of the sort to those really interested in it, but that interest in religion was replaced by interest in scientific discussion ...[151]

What particularly impressed Oman was Rationalism's testimony that 'nothing is of real value for truth or beauty or goodness which is not of our own insight, choice and deliberate purpose. ... [I]t achieved a clear understanding of the demand for absolute independence in moral judgment and moral decision, if they are to be truly moral.'[152] Putting Descartes and Pascal together, he declares that 'The ultimate standard is ourselves [Descartes], but it is ourselves in all our reach, in all we feel as well as all we think, in all we have attained, as well as in the bare faculty of following a deduction [Pascal].'[153] I would note in passing that when, nine pages later, Oman contrasts Pascal with the Jesuits, and says that 'It is Christ, not the Church, that is our last court of appeal,'[154] it no longer seems to be 'ourselves in all our reach' either. At various points in Oman's writings the question arises, By what steps does he proceed from the individual's authority to Christ's? Some have suspected him of occasional sleight of hand. But the phrase I wish to focus upon now is 'ourselves in all our reach', for this is Oman's bridge to Romanticism.

Oman welcomed Romanticism's

> recognition of elements in human nature and in life which had been ignored, its attempt to live in a world and not in a vacuum, its thought of the universe no longer as a great machine of which the main problem was to find the driving wheel, but as a great work of art, the more glorious that it is still in the process of creation, its idea of man's mind no more as a mere calculating machine, ... but as ... a copy in finite form of the Eternal Reason, not a mere faculty of abstractions, but a treasure-house of all the variety and individuality of the world.[155]

Such benefits notwithstanding, the Romantic Age missed much of

---

[150] Oman, *Faith and Freedom*, p. 54.

[151] Oman, *Natural and Supernatural*, p. 6.

[152] Oman, *Grace and Personality*, p. 29.

[153] Oman, *Faith and Freedom*, p. 61.

[154] Oman, *Faith and Freedom*, p. 70.

[155] Oman, *Problem of Faith and Freedom*, p. 208.

importance 'precisely because of its high-sniffing superiority to what went immediately before';[156] and, as we have already seen, Oman stoutly repudiated the view that 'The final word was immanent cosmic process,' with 'rational man as but its highest vehicle and most conscious mirror.'[157] In Oman's view the good fruits of both Rationalism and Romanticism are to be harvested, the rest rejected. Between them 'they correspond to the two aspects of [the] problem' with which Oman wrestled throughout his writing life: 'that knowing is meaning for the mind that knows, yet is knowledge of reality existing independently and in its own right'.[158] Kant represents the former aspect, Hegel the latter.

Against the background of the thoughts just sketched, Oman went in utterly sincere quest of truth, and his quest was as ardent as his appreciation of the limitations of human thought was realistic. We saw how the question of truth *vis à vis* conventional convictions had been raised for him in a clamant way by the Robertson Smith case, and to the cause of truth he devoted his life. In his view, the 'Search for Truth and Righteousness is just accepting God's invitation to "Come and let us reason together".'[159] Those who enquire into religion are particularly urged 'to spare no pains in seeking truth'.[160] Why? Because, as the Rationalists taught, 'truth is not true for us, except as we ourselves see it; and that right is not righteous, except as we ourselves determine it; and that to determine our own beliefs by our own reason and our own duty by our own conscience, is man's highest and most personal concern, which he may not delegate with honour'.[161] But what is truth? 'Truth for us', he replies, 'is what we know to be a right interpretation of experience when in perfect freedom we have allowed it to speak to us.'[162] He answers the question, How to proceed?, with a rhetorical question of his own: '[I]s there any other way of finding our true bearings than the spirit of Christ and His reconciliation to all God requires as well as all He appoints, without resentment and without evasion?'[163] This, however, presupposes faith in Christ; and Oman makes no bones about it: 'Truth does not appeal to the heart until it is the faith upon which you cannot but act, and you do not act rightly except upon truth which is at once convincing and challenging.'[164] Furthermore, genuine belief is 'belief in a reality on its own testimony', and hence 'belief in God must be a gift of God'.

It is central to Oman's thought that the quest of truth is and must be the quest

---

[156] Oman, 'Schleiermacher,' p. 402.
[157] Oman, *Grace and Personality*, p. 32. Cf. *The Journal of Theological Studies*, XXXI, 1930, p. 404.
[158] Oman, *Natural and Supernatural*, p. 165.
[159] Oman, *Honest Religion*, p. 1.
[160] Oman, *Natural and Supernatural*, p. 8.
[161] Oman, *Natural and Supernatural*, p. 100.
[162] Oman, *Honest Religion*, p. 91.
[163] Oman, *Honest Religion*, p. 51.
[164] Oman, *Concerning the Ministry*, p. 59.

of a free individual. 'Freedom', he remarks, 'is ... as essential for true faith as faith for effective freedom'.[165] Indeed, 'Freedom is not true freedom unless it is our own spiritual judgment in face of all in us that has merely natural appeal.'[166] More specifically, he writes, 'Christian liberty is nothing else than a sense of higher obligation. Christ has set us free not to please ourselves, not to sin or do right as suits our convenience, but He has set us free by giving us a deeper sense of our obligation to God.'[167] Conversely, 'There can be no freedom in the end without reaching God.'[168] How, then, shall we be reconciled to God? Oman answers,

> Regarding Christianity, the great question will not be its outward credentials, but whether it can place man in such a relation to God that his moral and religious needs shall both be satisfied, that he shall be right with himself and master of his life. ... An Atonement must be its own witness to the hearts that have been atoned, or it is nothing.[169]

Small wonder, therefore, that Oman set his face against external authorities deemed infallible, whether confessional, ecclesiastical or biblicist. Against all such he contended that

> God does not conduct His rivers, like arrows, to the sea. ... The expedition demanded by man's small power and short day produces the canal, but nature, with a beneficent and circumambulancy, the work of a more spacious and less precipitate mind, produces the river. Why should we assume that, in all the rest of His ways, He rejoices in the river, but, in religion, can use no adequate method save the canal? The defence of the infallible is the defence of the canal against the river. ...[170]

From Rationalism Oman had learned that God does not override the freedom of human beings by hurling infallibilities at them. Hence his recognition of the fact that while 'A creed which expresses the living convictions of a church is a spiritual power of the first magnitude; a creed which merely sanctions authorised compromises is not concerned with religion at all, but is a worldly agreement for the legal interest of a corporation.'[171] Indeed, 'The highest creed taught merely from without becomes superstition.'[172] Confessions belong to our 'external heredity', and we have to go beyond them; and we have been learning

---

[165] Oman, *Faith and Freedom*, p. 24.
[166] Oman, *Natural and Supernatural*, p. 306.
[167] Oman, *Dialogue with God*, p. 76.
[168] Oman, *Faith and Freedom*, p. 329.
[169] Oman, *Faith and Freedom*, p. 329.
[170] Oman, *Grace and Personality*, p. 25.
[171] Oman, *Church and Divine Order*, p. 325.
[172] Oman, *Vision and Authority*, p. 24.

that 'great differences in doctrine can be consistent with true fellowship of the Spirit, and if a creed be used to insist on orthodox docility, the end would be no more unity than it would be freedom'.[173] The same applies to the injunctions of the institutional Church and to the alleged deliverances of an infallible Bible. The fact is that 'Christianity has no means left to it whereby to compel consent from the outside.'[174] For 'If the infallibilities have been overthrown by inquiry and reason, they cannot be raised again by affirmation or even by the strongest conviction of their utility. ... But the value, for truth and beauty and goodness, of our own insight, choice, and deliberate purpose, being once seen, can never again be wholly renounced.'[175]

But, to repeat, Oman was ever conscious of the limitations of human knowledge. W.A.L. Elmslie recalled his saying that 'There exists a larger scheme of life than any of us can ever yet know, which we can only serve as we serve the truth amidst the things which we do know.'[176] 'From day to day', said Oman,

> life must be faced with a creed falling far short of omniscience. It is less an illumination than points of light in the darkness, rather lighthouses to direct the course than sun or moon to display the prospect. Except when satisfied with tradition or theory, none question the Apostle's description of our knowledge, as "seeing in a glass darkly".[177]

When one compares Rashdall 'with St. Paul or even with Luther, one realizes how little he cares to live in the half lights, and how all the really creative souls have had to live there all their time'.[178] Happily, our 'dim gropings after truth', failures and misunderstandings, 'witness, not to the Divine failure, but to the Divine patience'.[179]

IV

So much for Oman's objectives and manner. As to his method,[180] Oman's theology is conjunctive, reconciling, harmonizing. With one particularly significant exception, to which I shall come in due course, he brings together ideas that are often perceived as opposites. As his former student, T. W. Manson, observed, such book titles as *Vision and Authority*, *Faith and Freedom*, and *The Natural and the Supernatural* exemplify Oman's

---

[173] Oman, *Honest Religion*, pp. 161, 163.
[174] Oman, *Faith and Freedom*, p. 327
[175] Oman, *Grace and Personality*, p. 22.
[176] Elmslie, *Westminster College*, p. 23.
[177] Oman, *Vision and Authority*, p. 217. Cf. *Honest Religion*, p. 40.
[178] Oman, review of Rashdall, p. 270.
[179] Oman, review of Rashdall, p. 96.
[180] See chapter 5 which discusses Oman's method as experiential.

'fundamental struggle to hold together things that, on the superficial view, seem to be incapable of reconciliation'.[181] We have noted the way in which he related faith and freedom, but now we must consider what may be deemed the central relationship in his thought, namely, that of the natural and the supernatural. In the course of this examination we shall not be able to avoid another relationship, namely, that of religion and morality, for Oman's case is of the cumulative, spiralling kind rather than the linear. It is also necessary, as we proceed, to understand that Oman espouses a more than ordinarily hospitable epistemology. For this he was complimented by A.D. Lindsay, who described Oman's account as

> the best account of knowing I have ever read. He distinguishes four types of knowing: awareness, apprehension, comprehension, explanation. The originality of what he has to say lies mainly in his description of the first two types, consistently neglected by philosophers who are themselves so taken up with comprehension and explanation that they simply cannot see the other forms. ... [T]o know truly we need faithfulness in action and sincerity of feeling, as well as clear intelligence, but no one ordinarily takes account of this in theories of knowledge ...[182]

The four types of knowing suggest that Oman's empiricism is by no means exhausted by the understanding of empiricism espoused by most scientists; and this in turn distinguished his approach from that of Tennant, who was much more in accord with scientific method as generally understood. What Oman was intent upon emphasising, however, was that to suppose that we gain a comprehensive view of reality by applying the scientific method is false. Indeed, he expostulates, 'The notion that science gives the true picture of complete reality was the mere illusion of a dominant interest, which is no longer entertained by serious scientific thinkers.'[183] He does not deny the sensational origin of much of our knowledge, but sensation is not the only avenue to knowledge. By contrast with scientific rigidity, 'true theology leaves out nothing of the concrete varied world that is within the grasp of our finite minds, in the hope of seeing the things unseen manifested in the things which do appear'.[184] Throughout, Oman is concerned with insight into reality as the only reliable ground for faith, and 'no worthy and final goal except freedom in

---

[181] T.W. Manson, 'Introduction' for *Vision and Authority*, 8th edn, 1948, p. 2.

[182] A.D. Lindsay, review of J. Oman, *The Natural and the Supernatural*, *The Journal of Theological Studies*, XXXIII, 1932, pp. 385, 386. For Oman's exposition see op.cit., pp. 120-143.

[183] Oman, 'Method in theology,' p. 90. 'No longer entertained'? Behold those scientists of the positivistic-evolutionary sort who have graced our televisions and press in recent years. By Oman's reckoning they are not 'serious scientific thinkers' – as, indeed, I had myself concluded.

[184] Oman, 'Method in theology', p. 93.

loyalty to its requirements'.[185]

With this we are at the threshold of Oman's account of the natural and the supernatural. 'As the natural world is known by sensation and it varied comparative values, so the supernatural world is known by the sense of the holy and its sacred or absolute values.'[186] He further explains that

> the Supernatural means the world which manifests more than natural values, the world which has values which stir the sense of the holy and demand to be esteemed as sacred. ... [The natural and the supernatural] are not in opposition, but are so constantly interwoven that nothing may be wholly natural and wholly supernatural. ... We know the Supernatural as it reflects itself in the sense of the holy and has for us absolute value directly and without further argument: and the question is not that it exists, but how it exists in its relation to us and our relation to it.[187]

At this point F.R. Tennant demurred. Oman, he says,

> rejects the view that the supernatural is known inferentially, as the assigned cause of the awe; and also the view that it is directly apprehended as to its essence or quality by any faculty akin to sense ... its only 'content' is its capacity to excite emotion and valuation. Yet is the 'sense of' the holy involves immediate, as distinct from interpretative or suppositional, cognition of the invisible and intangible Supernatural, it would seem that there must be in it something so far akin to sensation as to be another instance of the 'absolute positing' which, as Kant taught us, is involved in the existent, as distinct from the ideal essence of which no existence is a predicate.[188]

Behind this criticism lies Tennant's judgment that in writing as he does concerning 'feeling' Oman conflates such elements as cognition, feeling and evaluation that are normally distinguished from one another.[189]

Undeterred by such a possibility, Oman elaborates his doctrine thus:

> The Supernatural must be inquired into, like the Natural, as a world in which we live and move and have our being, if it is to be inquired into with profit. ... [T]here is no embodying the Supernatural apart from the Natural; and ... the Natural is ready to become our possession and unfold its treasures as, in the power of the sacred, we stand over against it and

---

[185] Oman, *Vision and Authority*, p. 11.

[186] Oman, *Natural and Supernatural*, p. 69.

[187] Oman, *Natural and Supernatural*, pp. 71, 72.

[188] F.R. Tennant, review of *The Natural and the Supernatural*, in *Mind*, XLI, April 1932, p. 214.

[189] Tennant, review of *Natural and Supernatural*, p. 213.

above it.[190]

The phrase 'and above it' suggests Oman's view that the natural is transformed by the supernatural: the two are not simply glued together, so to speak; rather, there is a mutual inter-penetration the result of which is a refined environment. Oman further insists that experience of the supernatural is objective in character; it is not a matter of a particular subjective feeling or attitude:[191] reality is in view throughout. He also grants that the validity of the experience turns wholly upon the question whether the 'invisible world' exists or not.[192] How might such an existence be proved? He answers, 'we cannot prove the reality of any environment while omitting the only evidence it ever gives of itself, which is the way in which it environs us'.[193] It should be noted that the context of this remark is that of proving the experience to ourselves, not of making it the basis of an argument designed in the hope of persuading others. It is integral to Oman's standpoint that none of the classical theistic arguments will put anyone in touch with reality. Perhaps we might say that his empiricism is the empiricism of immediate personal experience; the empirical order is not, for him, a bran tub from which we pull arguments and evidences and cobble them together as efficiently as we may. In his own words: 'awareness of the reality of the Supernatural is not something added to the sense of the holy and the judgment of the sacred by some kind of argument, say from the natural world'.[194] By this Tennant was exceedingly perplexed: '[I]f any argument seemed necessary to Dr. Oman,' he declares, 'the validity of religious belief should for him depend on the cogency of reasoning from sacred or moral values to a supersensible world; but even this he deems superfluous. ... It is on this fundamental issue that I find myself most at variance with the author's position.'[195] Oman would reply that the only way reality is known is by an immediate experience of it which renders argumentation superfluous.

The term 'environment' recurs in Oman's writings, and in the present context he means by it the natural environment which is shot through with the supernatural, and *vice versa*. But then he takes a further step when he directly associates the environment with God: 'Environment is not merely what we see with our physical vision,' he writes; 'It is still more that we see with the eyes of our soul – our imagination, our insight, our values, our inspiration, our faith in God's mind in it, and His purpose with man in the midst of it.'[196] He further explains that 'religion must be a large experience in which we grow in

---

[190] Oman, *Natural and Supernatural*, pp. 72, 331.

[191] Oman, *Natural and Supernatural*, p. 23.

[192] Oman, *Natural and Supernatural*, p. 23.

[193] Oman, *Natural and Supernatural*, p. 52.

[194] Oman, *Natural and Supernatural*, p. 72.

[195] Tennant, review of *Natural and Supernatural*, p. 215.

[196] Oman, *Concerning the Ministry*, p. 12.

knowledge as we grow in humility and courage, in which we deal with life and not abstractions, and with God as the environment in which we live and move and have our being and not as an ecclesiastical formula'[197] – there, once more, is the anti-ecclesiastical sting in the tail.

The question arises whether 'the meaning of "reality" is "the personal God"' is a purely stipulative definition? If not, how does Oman make the leap from experienced reality to a personal, purposive, God – indeed, may he legitimately do so? John S. Morris has returned a negative answer to this question. He contends that Oman's way of moving from his religious evaluation of reality to an argument for the world a personal God violates his epistemology of immediacy and lands him in what he wished to avoid – an apologetic stance analogous to that of other proponents of theism. As Morris puts it, 'If Oman cannot logically move from knowledge of a Supernatural environment to assertions about the "universe" and God then his argument becomes another version of the Natural Theology which he condemns.'[198] In short, 'If you start from experience you cannot validly end up with a metaphysical system claiming absolute truth.'[199] As I understand matters, however, it is rather that Oman experiences reality as personal and then testifies to this; the truth, for him, is in the experience, it is not in any metaphysical system which may, or may not, be erected upon it. He is more concerned with the enterprise of the person who reaches out after reality, but this reaching out, he says, 'presupposes a universe which responds to such independence and is only really known by it, which means that it also is in some true sense personal. ... [W]e can speak of God as a person who, if he is not the Supernatural, is manifest through it.'[200] Is the reader wrong to expect a justification of this claim? In the first place, are we not confronted by a *non sequitur*? Oman claims that a person who reaches out after reality and finds it in the universe has found something which is in a true sense personal. But since many of the phenomena of the universe are inanimate, yet no less awe-inspiring for that, has he not smuggled into the universe the idea of personality? Secondly, Oman makes a second leap when he says that God is the manifested person, the qualification, 'if he is not the Supernatural [he] is manifest through it' being swiftly dropped. The problem would seem to be that Oman is so wedded to his experiential, 'from below', starting point that there is not only an absence of theistic argumentation in his writings, but also, at crucial points, a revelation-shaped-blank which makes it appear that he proceeds by assertion only. It would seem that Oman's student, H.H. Farmer, had similar qualms, which he construed in terms of Oman's method (note the respectful third word):

---

[197] Oman, *Natural and Supernatural*, p. 471.

[198] J.S. Morris, 'Oman's conception of the personal God in *The Natural and the Supernatural*', *The Journal of Theological Studies*, N.S. XXIII, April 1972, p. 88.

[199] Morris, 'Oman's conception of the personal God', 89.

[200] Oman, *Natural and Supernatural*, pp. 340, 342.

It is perhaps an unsatisfactory feature of Oman's profound discussion of religion in *The Natural and the Supernatural* that he does not make the personal nature of God and of His activity towards man regulative of his thought. ... In the earlier half of [the book] he speaks of the Supernatural in a way that suggests that it is a merely static environment which man becomes aware of, explores, and gets to know through his sense of sacred values. ... Oman's own principle that in interpreting the Supernatural and its relation to us we should start from the highest that we know might well seem to require that the sense in which God and His approach to men are said to be truly personal should have been more deeply analysed and put more fully in control of the argument from the beginning; if this had been done, it would hardly have been possible to treat the Supernatural in the earliest sections of the book in the way just indicated.[201]

This comment seems to be a tacit request for a starting-point rooted in the revelation of a personal God who comes to us – even a request for a Christology and a soteriology. Another way of making the point would be to say that Oman's method, into which his deepest convictions cannot, I think, be squeezed, is too much that of a seeker of the journey towards faith, as distinct from that of the saint on the journey of faith.[202] It is as if at times he works within the environment of a Supernatural from which the Gospel has been extruded.

Elsewhere, however, Oman proposes that it is, above all, through the experience of forgiveness that we give concreteness to our talk of the personal God: 'if we find forgiveness a real and transforming experience,' Oman writes, 'we shall be able to speak of God as a person with the certainty that we are not merely seeing the reflexion of our own faces, but know that our own forgiveness of others is a reflexion of the highest perfection which is kind to the unthankful and evil'.[203] What is odd here in this connection is Oman's description of the essence of sin as 'estrangement from our true environment'.[204] This seems a somewhat remote way of speaking of the disruption of the very kind of inter-personal relations he has been at such pains to delineate in other writings, not least with reference to the father and the prodigal son in Jesus's parable. It is an attenuation analogous to another to which I shall advert in the next section of this paper.

First, however, we observe that Oman draws out the ethical implications of the individual-God personal relationship. Ever alive to the relations of faith and

---

[201] H.H. Farmer, *Revelation and Religion. Studies in the Theological Interpretation of Religious Types* (London: Nisbet, 1954), p. 28 n.

[202] See *Vision and Authority*, p. 56: 'we can never be coming into the unity of the truth unless we are coming into union with all *seekers* after truth.' My italics.

[203] Oman, *Natural and Supernatural*, p. 342.

[204] Oman, *Natural and Supernatural*.

freedom, he argues that 'absolute moral independence and absolute religious dependence are not opposites but necessarily one and indivisible'.[205] 'We are persons,' he continues, 'and not merely individuals, precisely because we ... attain our independence as we find ourselves in God's world and among His children. ... [O]ur relation to God is personal after such a fashion that our religion is necessarily an ethic, and our ethic necessarily a religion.'[206] (Small wonder that Oman had a particular fondness for the Old Testament prophets). In more picturesque terms, he writes of moral progress that if it

> is in response to higher environment, [the human being's] ability to recognize the manifestation of the high and holy, often in direct opposition to the pleasant and desirable, is no mere painting of imaginary pictures in the blackness on the corridor of his prison, but is a window open towards heaven, illumined by at least the first beam of the morning.[207]

He fully appreciates that 'For mapping out from above God's operations, it must be admitted that we occupy no vantage ground', and that 'Only if we can see grace as it works on earth and understand it as it affects our own experience, can we possibly hope to have either clearness or certainty'.[208] He is persuaded that God is not one preoccupied by his own honour, but one who is concerned to 'succour moral persons' deemed to be autonomous, who, in turn, make a personal response to God's personal grace-full gift of aid, and can do this only because they are truly free.[209] Later, invoking italics for emphasis, he adds the important proviso, 'grace is grace precisely because, *though wholly concerned with moral goodness, it does not at all depend on how moral we are*'.[210]

V

Of Oman's revered Principal, John Cairns, it was said that 'he came increasingly to regard the life of the individual Christian and the collective life of the Church as the most convincing of all witnesses to the Unseen and the Supernatural'.[211] As far as I am aware, Oman never made this ecclesial appeal when expounding the Supernatural. On the contrary, it may fairly be suggested that when he thought of the individual in relation to the Church his passion for

---

[205] Oman, *Grace and Personality*, p. 33; cf. p. 57.
[206] Oman, *Grace and Personality*, pp. 62, 78.
[207] Oman, *Vision and Authority*, p. 27.
[208] Oman, *Grace and Personality*, p. 45.
[209] Oman, *Grace and Personality*, pp. 45-47, 81; cf. pp. 159-60.
[210] Oman, *Grace and Personality*, p. 164.
[211] Cairns, *Principal Cairns*, p. 141.

bringing together themes that are often placed in opposition to one another dried up. To put the point in a nutshell, whereas he values the Reformation insight that every individual believer is a priest before God, needing no intermediary – least of all a sacerdotal one – he does not emphasise the idea of the priesthood of all believers together. In other words, he does not construe the priesthood of all believers as a corporate concept; he does not think in terms of the integral relationship of branches to Vine, or limbs to body. Positively, there runs throughout his writings the idea that the church is the gathering of the two or three in Christ's name. Thus, for example, he declares that

> A Catholic Ecclesia, a Church in its wholeness, we acknowledge wherever two or three are met in the name of Christ. That, and that alone, we acknowledge as fully as our Congregational brethren, both adequately and exclusively constitutes a Church of Christ. ... [T]he fundamental thing about the order of the Church is that it ought to be non-legal, the government of each man by the Spirit of God and organisation through love. ... The unit of it is the two or three freely met in Christ's name, and all wider co-ordination of it must be on the same principle of free association.[212]

Here once more is Oman's characteristic conviction regarding freedom; here, too, is the rather individualistic idea of a gathering of two or three persons with one another, each of whom is independently under the Spirit's government. Believers, or saints, are those who have been brought into a 'relationship of trust and freedom with the God and Father of our Lord Jesus Christ,' and their unity is 'a unity of spirit thorough the one Spirit of God working in the individual members' who have been 'individually reconciled to God'.[213] Elsewhere he lists the 'marks' of the Church as follows: '(1) that it has unity in Jesus Christ as its one true Head; (2) that its one treasure is the gospel; and (3) that its one official is the organ of the priesthood of all believers'.[214] By this last point he means that the official is the organ of, not the substitute for, the priesthood of believers, and that there is 'no religious distinction between clergy and laity'.[215] It will be noted that even though in a footnote he has just adverted to the *Westminster Confession*, Oman does not follow that standard in specifying 'the doctrine of the gospel as taught and embraced, ordinances administered, and public worship performed' as marks of the Church[216] - still

---

[212] J. Oman, 'The Presbyterian Churches', in W.B. Selbie, ed., *Evangelical Christianity, its History and Witness* (London: Hodder and Stoughton, [1911]), pp. 67, 73. Cf. Oman, *Church and Divine Order*, pp. 11, 209; Oman, *The War and its Issues*, pp. 55-6.

[213] Oman, *Church and Divine Order*, p. 59.

[214] Oman, *Church and Divine Order*, p. 210.

[215] Oman, *Church and Divine Order*, p. 211.

[216] *The Westminster Confession*, ch. XXV.4; numerous editions.

less discipline, as specified in the earlier *Scots Confession*.[217]

It will also be observed that Oman does not answer those who contended that whereas the two or three gathered together in Christ's name may well describe a prayer meeting, it does not fully describe a New Testament church ordered under the Gospel, with its several gifted and appointed members, its teaching function, its breaking of bread, and its baptismal practice. He does, however, take pains on more than one occasion to distinguish the Protestant from the Catholic ecclesiological principles in terms of the 'two or three gathered': 'What is the Church in principle? To the Catholic its determining principle is in the institution – its priesthood, bishops, councils, Pope; to the Protestant it is in the fellowship, in all that is involved in the two or three met in the name of Christ, in the succession of believers, in the bond of love.'[218]

How, in practice, do the 'two or three' comport themselves *vis à vis* their life together in fellowship? Are they a democratic assembly? Decidedly not, says Oman, as well he might. His emphasis upon the freedom of individual believers notwithstanding, he proclaims that 'an individual possession is not necessarily individualistic',[219] and that 'Christianity is not individualism tempered by the ballot box.'[220] In elaborating upon this he says the right thing but for an inadequate reason: 'Christianity is "ultra-democratic" not because it counts heads, but because it appeals "to the image of God in all men".'[221] While in no way wishing to deny the truth of that Quakerly utterance, we are landed once more in an attenuated position. The Church is not 'ultra-democratic' because its members appeal to the image of God in all men, but because they seek, not their own will, but the will of the Lord of the Church, and because they discern this, insofar as they do, by the Holy Spirit through the Word within the fellowship.[222] Oman's starting-point seems almost entirely confined to the

---

[217] *The Scottish Confession of Faith*, 1560, ch. XVIII, for which see Arthur C. Cochrane, ed., *Reformed Confessions of the 16th Century* (Philadelphia: Westminster Press, 1966). For the addition see also John Craig's *Catechism* of 1561, in T. F. Torrance, ed., *The School of Faith. The Catechisms of the Reformed Church* (London: James Clarke, 1959), p. 160.

[218] Oman, *Church and Divine Order*, p. 207.

[219] Oman, *Vision and Authority*, p. 54; cf. p. 285.

[220] Oman, *Church and Divine Order*, p. 318.

[221] Oman, *Church and Divine Order*, p. 318.

[222] This is the classical Congregational understanding of Church Meeting. In my favoured way of expressing the point: Church Meeting is a credal assembly in which the Lordship of Christ is confessed over the entire life and service of the church; in this sense it is a continuation of the church's worship, and the one who has been called to lead the saints to the throne of grace (and not someone who is good at 'business meetings') should lead them in seeking the mind of Christ for their mission. In connection with Congregationalism, Oman must be corrected at one point. He says (*Church and Divine Order*, p. 279) that the desire of the Independents to be tolerated 'as [part of the national Church' at the time of the Restoration of the monarchy (1660)

'horizontal', human-to-human relationship to the exclusion of the Father who approaches in the Son by the Spirit.

The question arises, Why is Oman's ecclesiology so tilted towards the individual, rather than to the corporate understanding of the priesthood of all believers? A twofold answer may be offered. First, there is Oman's general intellectual position to the effect that 'the Supernatural is an order of independent persons'.[223] Secondly, there is his deep conviction that 'God will do everything for man, suffer everything for him, give everything for him, but He will not override his will. If He cannot have free service He cares for no other.'[224] Hence Oman's antipathy towards freedom-cramping ecclesiastical authority. Whilst agreeing that the Church 'needs outward forms', he insists that 'they are for the expression and operation of a unity that exists, not for compulsion to bring it into existence';[225] and in any case, although we need not rail at dignitaries or disallow 'their usefulness in due place',[226] 'The Church is not a visible corporation, kept together by outward bonds of office and

---

'shows how much [they] were still attached to the idea of a universal Christianity. Their present position is not the result of their theory of the Church, but a departure from it under what has influenced all Churches in the same direction – rationalism and evangelicalism.' Now, working backwards, (1), Congregationalists were, like others, influenced by rationalism and evangelicalism. Crudely put, the former encouraged them towards a critical approach to the Bible and history, the latter led to a modification or dilution of their scholastic Calvinism and sent them out in mission at home and abroad. But their 'theory of the Church' remained intact and was, indeed, a preservative against the eighteenth-century drift to 'Arianism' and thence to Unitarianism which overtook a number of English and Welsh Presbyterian churches. See further, Sell, *Dissenting Thought*, ch. 5. (2) It is no shame to be attached to a 'universal Christianity' if by that it meant the Church Catholic. Congregationalists (and their heirs in united churches) understand that it is by virtue of their membership that they are members of the Church catholic and, indeed, that there is no other way of belonging to the latter, for Christians are '*visible* saints', and one cannot be a Christian 'in general'. See further Alan P.F. Sell, *Saints: Visible, Orderly and Catholic. The Congregational Idea of the Church* (Geneva: World Alliance of Reformed Churches and Allison Park, PA: Pickwick Publications, 1986). (3) The Independents/Congregationalists began to press for toleration during the Westminster Assembly, of which they were minority members, lest subsequently they should be swamped by Presbyterian order. To the extent that they wished for national comprehension, this would have been according to their church order as specified in the *Savoy Declaration* of 1658 - an order which their compatriots in Massachusetts sought to apply with not entirely happy results. Following the Restoration and the ensuing punitive legislation, they much sooner set that aspiration aside than did the Presbyterians, some of whom entertained the forlorn hope of a state Church on Presbyterian lines in England and Wales until the end of the seventeenth century.

[223] Oman, *Natural and Supernatural*, p. 341.
[224] Oman, *Dialogue with God*, p. 88.
[225] Oman, *Honest Religion*, p. 139.
[226] Oman, *Honest Religion*, p. 140.

ecclesiastical order.'[227] More provocatively still, he declares in connection with infallibilities whether ecclesiastical or biblicist, that 'the old external dogmatic attitude of the Church cannot be maintained. ... Uninquiring submission to external authority is neither God's method with man nor a desirable method of human obedience, but mere exaltation of necessity over freedom'.[228] Moreover, 'A God ... credible only on clerical guarantees is a distressing as well as a worthless faith.'[229] It follows that ecclesiastical machinery must never usurp the place of the fellowship, as has so often happened in Christian history. The fact is, he thunders, that 'Nothing ... has done more to mislead men about Christ than this notion that His Church can consist of officials and that His faith can be taught from the outside, and a man's conduct directed by any other authority than God's spirit in his heart.'[230] Whereas some understand the falling away of many from the churches as requiring a strengthening of the Church's 'external authority', Oman interprets the drift as indicative of the fact that the old external authorities have failed, and that 'we ought rather to thank God that so slavish a method is no longer possible, and to see that the patient way of calling men to the liberty of the children of God is the quickest way after all'.[231]

It is possible to have considerable sympathy with many of the points that Oman makes, and yet to feel that there is another side to the matter. For one who characteristically sought to hold together things that properly belong together, he is, where ecclesiology in concerned, strangely disjunctive, as when he writes concerning his own age, 'Never was there an age which brought men so unavoidably to the issue that the basis of the Church is freedom, not authority, individual faith, not organised constraint, prophetic hope, not priestly tradition.'[232] But there is freedom in the Gospel and the authority of grace. While organised constraint has no place in Christianity, the conjunction of individual faith with corporate witness in the body of Christ is essential, for Christianity, though a personal religion, is not a private one; and while the contrast posited between prophetic hope and what I should call the sacerdotal tradition suggests the forward look which was ever in Oman's eye, the function of mutual witness, encouragement, reproof and love as exercised by the true priesthood of believers is a precious possession – which Oman would not, of course, deny. Furthermore, given that Oman thinks that the gathered two or three cannot avoid having some organisational shape in the world, one could wish that he had been more generous concerning the Church's several ministries and *foci* of life. He hardly has a good word to say for those who devote themselves to things ecclesiastical – except that they may be useful in

---

[227] Oman, *Church and Divine Order*, p. 59.
[228] Oman, *Vision and Authority*, p. 94; cf. p. 182.
[229] Oman, 'Method in theology', p. 86.
[230] Oman, *Dialogue with God*, p. 143.
[231] Oman, *Church and Divine Order*, p. 317.
[232] Oman, *Church and Divine Order*, p. 290.

their place. This, at least, was the feeling of a contributor to *The Presbyterian Messenger*, who regretted Oman's 'often terrible critique' of institutional religion, and diagnosed in him a 'temperamental inability to appreciate the opposite view' with the result that 'Oman now and again tends to put asunder what God has joined,' failing to understand that for 'frail and groping beings such as we it is only through what he would call the "lesser" mysteries that the greater can be appreciated.'[233]

For all that, it is not impossible to discern in Oman's writings a suggestion of that lateral thinking which, I believe, is urgently required if the unity of the Church catholic is to be more fully manifested (I do not say 'created' – it is already given in Christ). Oman fully recognizes that what requires to be

---

[233] Hugh Sinclair, 'Living voices ... Professor Oman', *The Presbyterian Messenger*, 1915, p. 430. Oman, as we have seen, had no patience with those who recommended silence where matters of truth were concerned lest the ecclesiastical boat be unduly rocked. This is a perennial issue in churchly fellowship, and there is something to be said in favour of the 'ecclesiastics'. Ministers sometimes face what W.D. Ross would have called a clash of *prima facie* duties. On the one hand they must state their convictions with integrity (Oman's position); on the other hand they must not needlessly break the fellowship of the church, and they are to lead *the people's* worship. Of Benjamin Fawcett of the Old Meeting, Kidderminster, where Calvinists, Arminians and 'Arians' gathered, it was said that 'he managed so far to conceal his opinions as to be very popular with his hearers, a large chapel being crowded at all the Sabbath-day services.' Thomas Wright Hill, quoted by George Hunsworth, *Baxter's Nonconformist Descendants; or Memorials of the Old Meeting Congregational Church Kidderminster* (Kidderminster: Edward Parry, 1874), p. 41. Fawcett was not necessarily 'trimming', still less guarding his stipend. The high Arian, Micaijah Towgood, was commended by his biographer because 'The main scope and tenor of his preaching was practical. He led not his flock for nourishment to the dry and barren hills of cold and unedifying speculation.' See James Manning, 'A Sketch of the Life and Writings of Micaijah Towgood', 1792, pp. 92-3. When the young Joseph Priestley was at Needham Market , 'though I had made it a rule to myself to introduce nothing that could lead to controversy into the pulpit; yet making no secret of my real opinions in conversations, it was soon found that I was an Arian. From the time of this discovery my hearers fell off apace ...' See J. T. Rutt, ed., *The Theological and Miscellaneous Works of Joseph Priestley*, (1817-1831) (reprinted Bristol: Thoemmes Press, 1999), II 30; cf. ibid., XV, p. 23, XXI, p. 245. Thomas Belsham (one of my predecessors at Angel Street Congregational Church, Worcester) left the pastorate there in 1781 and became a tutor at the Dissenting academy at Daventry. Whilst there he became Unitarian in doctrine, resigned on conscientious grounds in 1789 and removed the academy in Hackney established by Rational Dissenters. He thereby preserved his own integrity, and at the same time recognized that the Trinitarian worshippers served by the Daventry academy had the right to worship and teaching in that style. The underlying point is that the minister is not simply a private person, but a representative one; the moral is that some matters are best aired in discussion groups rather than from the pulpit. See further Sell, *Dissenting Thought*, pp. 152-6; Sell, *Enlightenment, Ecumenism, Evangel*, pp. 101-5, 374.

repudiated is the sectarian spirit which places obstacles in the way of fellowship of those who are saints in the Lord and members of his Church. Nowhere is the problem more acute than at the Lord's table. As Oman writes, 'That in the name of the Carpenter of Nazareth [the Lord's Supper] should be made the basis of a sacerdotal and hierarchical exclusiveness is perhaps as sad a perversion of the original purpose as anything in history.'[234] Indeed,

> from the time when the Church was founded on the bishop, not the prophet, from the time when it became a corporation with ruler and subject, the eucharist could no longer be the festival of the amazing fellowship where all were equally brethren of Christ, all equally kings and priest unto God ... and where all a man was and all he had could be an offering of thanksgiving.[235]

Augustine was responsible for this drastic turn of events. He introduced the 'artificial view' that baptism 'leaves an indelible mark' on the baptized person. This in time led to 'the idea of an indelible mark of ordination upon the person who had power to imprint such a sacramental mark, and then the Church ... was ready for an equally ecclesiastical and artificial view of the eucharist as a rite of priestly not personal sacrifice'.[236] In all of this Oman sees the need to get behind what I have sometimes called 'denominational small print' to that which already holds believers together. But, once again, his approach remains individually-focused, as when he says, 'the greatest champion of the true unity is the man who most ardently seeks the truth and truth only and utterly, and who most uncompromisingly follows righteousness with entire consecration of aim and energy'.[237] My own suggestion is that we go behind the sectarian talk which is enshrined in such propositions as, 'When you submit to our order, or do things in our way, or read the Bible as we do then we will have full fellowship with you', by asking, What has God in Christ done for us all? I believe that he has called Christians into the one Church and therefore we should all accept the one Lord's invitation to his table in an utterly mutually reciprocal way, thereby manifesting the gift of unity we have all received and too frequently obscured in Galatian fashion by our several 'new circumcisions'.[238] It is the Gospel, not the individual's quest of truth, which

---

[234] Oman, *Honest Religion*, p. 176. Cf. Oman, *Vision and Authority*, p. 170.

[235] Oman, *Church and Divine Order*, p. 105.

[236] Oman, *Church and Divine Order*, p. 164.

[237] Oman, *Vision and Authority*, p. 151. Cf. Oman, *Paradox of the World*, p. 177.

[238] I write this after some decades of participation in international dialogues between the Reformed family and others. While the gains in understanding are welcome, and while reunion has been facilitated in some cases, it seems highly unlikely that there will ever be uniformity of belief and practice across the whole Church – nor need there be. If this is so, the only way forward is to ask in the first place not, where do we stand, how do we conduct our churchly life, but what has God in sovereign grace

should take precedence over all the inherited ecclesiastical practices which so rightly distressed Oman. As he said,

> the best means of all for unity of fellowship is not available. Of all ways of showing how the love of the Father in the life without and the Fellowship of the Spirit within is one in the grace of Christ the greatest is the sacrament in which the symbols used sanctify the whole material life and make it transparently radiant with the spiritual.[239]

This is as Christological – indeed, as Trinitarian – a mode of expression of the relation of natural and supernatural that I have found in Oman's writings, and it brings me to the heart of Oman's Gospel.

VI

What, for Oman, is Christianity's central message? In his major works we find his answer by a process of deduction rather than because he first placards it after the manner of a P.T. Forsyth and then proceeds to elucidate its ramifications. What is more, Oman's understanding of the central message is presented in a constellation of ways, some of which appear to be more lukewarm than others. Thus, writing of the Christ's saving work he says, 'Love could do no more to show that it would do everything for man, everything except corrupt his will and replace his freedom, and so deprive him of his best heritage.'[240] This might suggest that the Cross is somehow a display of loving outreach with special reference to Oman's concerns for voluntarism and freedom. On the same page things become a little clearer: 'By the cross Christ has abolished the enmity between man and God, not merely by removing some outward causes of alienation, but by the demonstration of the succour which has nothing of the might which constrains, but is all of the might which persuades. ...'[241] But is sin merely an outward cause of alienation, given that we are urged by Oman to think in terms of the personal divine-human relationship? Is it not rather the wilful abuse of that relationship?[242] Furthermore, if we are to

---

done for us all? He has made us saints by calling, and saints are required to love their brothers and sisters. It is not loving to bar them from the table of the Lord. See further, Sell, *Enlightenment, Ecumenism, Evangel*, ch. 11; Sell, 'Receiving from other Christian traditions, and overcoming the hindrances thereto: some Reformed reflections,' forthcoming.

[239] Oman, *Honest Religion*, p. 176.

[240] Oman, *Vision and Authority*, p. 117; cf. p. 226.

[241] Oman, *Vision and Authority*, p. 117.

[242] There could hardly be a more clinically impersonal sentence than this: 'We can go wrong through unveracity in thinking, sensuality in feeling or unrighteousness of decision, but all are varieties of the lack of true independence and, therefore, of freedom,

understand that the succour that sustained Christ on the Cross is available to us in time of trial, is this all that the Cross signifies? What, for example, of mercy, forgiveness, new life? Later still in the same book we catch more of the note of victory: 'It is the Christ overcoming sin and sorrow and death and defeat, who sets up God's will of love in the freedom with which it rules in Heaven, and so delivers us from the self-pity and self-love which is caused by the fear and the favour of the world.'[243] The experience of many is that the Cross does more than this. Further puzzlement is caused when Oman says that 'To redeem man into a sinless freedom [the Divine love] must suffer with him sympathetically and vicariously. This suffering ... is not an exceptional incident in the Divine method, but is a manifestation in time of what is eternal.'[244] But (a) does not this mode of speech minimize the Bible's witness to the once-for-all-ness of the victory of the Cross?[245] (b) While I think that there is much to be said for the view that God is not impassible, there is a case, not simply a pronouncement, to be made in favour of it.[246]

Are the difficulties lessened in what many regard as Oman's greatest work, *Grace and Personality*? A number of assertions give us pause. First, it seems a somewhat cool attenuation on the part of one to whom the parable of the Prodigal Son spoke so strongly to say that 'reconciliation to God is primarily reconciliation to our lives by seeking in them only his ends. Its immediate significance is *reconciliation to the discipline He appoints and the duty He demands.*'[247] Shortly he speaks more traditionally of God as in Christ reconciling the world to himself, and says that 'The final triumph of this

---

this being failure to know a reality which so witnesses in its own right that no other witness has any right before it.' See Oman, *Natural and Supernatural*, p. 311.

[243] Oman, *Vision and* Authority, p. 337.

[244] Oman, *Vision and Authority*, p. 343.

[245] Cf. Thomas A. Langford, 'The theological methodology of John Oman and H.H. Farmer', *Religious Studies*, I no. 2, April 1966, p. 235: '[I]t must be said that Oman is singularly free from interest in particular historical situations or mediating *kairoi*. His theory of religious awareness does not emphasise the specific historical context ...' This despite the fact that Oman can say, 'Revelation, being ... concerned with the reconciliation of God's gracious relation to us by which alone we can discover that it is gracious, must be a work of history. What is more, it must be the work of history, the work which gives it meaning and treasures up its gains.' *Grace and Personality*, p. 141.

[246] Oman's contemporary, Robert Franks, for example, denied that God could suffer. See further Sell, *Hinterland Theology*, pp. 606-10. On a number of occasions in his writings Oman dismisses views alternative to his own, and makes pronouncements, without argument (cf. n. 108 above). He brands Calvin a determinist in a quite uncritical way (which he must have known would be provocative); and, no doubt because he wishes to exclude satisfaction theories of the atonement, he brusquely disposes of the idea that God, whose honour has been abused by sin, needs to be reconciled to us. See, respectively, *Natural and Supernatural*, p. 286; *Honest Religion*, p. 99.

[247] Oman, *Grace and Personality*, p. 110. Emphasis in original.

manifestation is the Cross, the obedience unto death of the Prince of Peace in the service of God's kingdom of righteousness.'[248] But after this brief hint of what Aulén called the classical theory of the atonement, Oman reverts to something much more like a moral influence view of it: 'In the Cross ... above all else, we discern the gracious relation of our Father towards us, because there, as nowhere else, is the utter service of our brethren, unconditioned by our merit, shown to be the essential spirit of His family. The true meaning and power of the Cross we discover only as we have that spirit ...'[249] After a further eight pages and a further oscillation we learn of 'the gracious dealing of the Father with His children for victory over all the consequences of sin, without and within'.[250] In the judgment of F.R. Tennant, Oman's understanding of grace was too restrictive. For Oman, he writes, 'grace, or any divine action upon men, can only be regarded worthily when restricted to personal dealings with persons and, consequently to appeals to human reason and conscience. This restriction will be judged heretical by the larger part of Christendom ...'[251] Tennant does not explain further, but perhaps the reference is to the cosmic dimension of God's saving work in Christ (however that is most appropriately to be understood).

Oman, as we have seen, valued the modern historical method for the way in which it had helped to topple older *a priori* dogmatisms. 'The historical method,' he declared, 'is to inquire, without presupposition, what God has actually done.'[252] It is precisely because they felt that Oman's answer to his own question was vague, or an attenuation, that he came in for criticism. For a representative and balanced view we may heed Charles Duthie:

There have been Christian thinkers ... who have felt uncomfortable with the thought that God comes to dwell within. F.R. Tennant and John Oman were among them. Oman was afraid that we might construe God's grace as mechanical and irresistible. Grace, he kept saying, is just God being gracious and this gracious God always acts in a fatherly way, respecting the freedom He has given us. ... Oman's thought is a welcome correction of all Christian systems which talk of God acting upon us as a physical force acts upon another physical force; but he missed something very big in the New Testament. God does indeed respect man's freedom and never treats us as less than personal; but He knows that our freedom is not complete and has been marred by our wrongdoing. Man may be God's child but he is God's erring and sinful child; and his condition is such that

---

[248] Oman, *Grace and Personality*, p. 136.

[249] Oman, *Grace and Personality*, pp. 179-180.

[250] Oman, *Grace and Personality*, p. 189.

[251] F.R. Tennant, 'John Wood Oman', *Proceedings of the British Academy*, XXV, 1939, p. 337.

[252] Oman, *Grace and Personality*, p. 20.

he needs to be forgiven, delivered, enlightened and empowered. ... We can agree with Oman that the gracious God acts in relation to us both in accordance with His own nature and the nature he has given to us, and then go on to see how broad and deep this renewing action is.[253]

Duthie correctly adverts to Oman's horror of coercion, and of the forcing of allegedly infallible authorities upon free human beings. Least of all may the God of gracious personal relations be represented as bludgeoning people with grace against their free wills. This, I suspect prompted him to bypass almost completely traditional Christologies and, especially, soteriologies. From normally passing references we are made aware of his abomination of the notion of retributive justice, of transactional, *quasi*-commercial theories of the atonement and, above all, of penal theories – 'legal juggling of the most repellant kind,' said he.[254] He neither cared for such theories nor offered his own by way of replacement.

For his part, H.R. Mackintosh regretted that in *The Natural and the Supernatural* there was not to be found a detailed discussion of revelation. Mackintosh was persuaded that God does not wait to be discovered, he comes to us. He therefore concluded, 'If this be so, the final distribution of emphasis will be different from that of this great book.'[255] We recall Oman's view that 'Prof. Mackintosh very easily thinks of God as just doing things,' whereas he himself thinks of God as 'the ultimate real.'[256] For his part, Carnegie Simpson, in his address at Oman's funeral service in St. Columba's Church, Cambridge, on 22 May 1939, said that Oman 'was concerned, in religion, more with the foundation than with the edifice; and as regards the former, more, perhaps, with what God is than with what, in Christ, He has done for us men and our salvation'.[257]

We are at last, I think, in a position to perceive the point at which Oman's theological approach is distinct from that of his contemporaries, some of whom felt that his work needed to be balanced by what one might call more Christological-*cum*-soteriological ballast. Oman's quest is of the Supernatural, of that reality which is the environment of the natural. This Supernatural, he concludes, is personal, and he then names it God – or, 'at least' God's vehicle. We find ourselves in touch with the eternal as we deal 'wholeheartedly with the evanescent', and with 'God as the environment in which we live and move and have our being.'[258] The gracious personal God leaves manifold signs of his

---

[253] C.S. Duthie, 'A God of action', *The British Weekly*, 8 October 1964, p. 9.

[254] Oman, *Honest Religion*, p. 117.

[255] H.R. Mackintosh, review of *The Natural and the Supernatural*, in *The British Weekly*, 29 September 1931.

[256] Oman, review of Mackintosh, p. 297.

[257] P.C. Simpson, *The Presbyterian Messenger*, 1939, p. 197.

[258] Oman, *Natural and Supernatural*, p. 471.

presence, but awaits our free, un-coerced, approach. This, it may be suggested, explains the emphasis in his rather atomistic ecclesiology, according to which the Church is rather a collocation of independent, free, seekers, than an organism comprising saints who have been called by grace into union with Christ and with one another.

But let us be cautioned by the slogan, 'By their sermons ye shall know them.' To a quite striking degree the homiletic Oman is much more inclined to strike soteriological notes which are normally muted in the major works so far considered in this section of my paper. A few almost random examples must suffice:

The Cross ... is a great affirmation that God's purpose is the salvation of His children into His Kingdom, the peace and glory and possessions of which only love can win, and for which only by love can anyone be won.[259]

This power to reconcile us to God in all His way with us is summed up in the Cross, wherein every form of evil is made to work for good. Even death ... is turned into the doing of God's will and the revelation of His pardoning love and the manifestation and victory of His righteousness and peace.[260]

Christ suffered to bring us unto God. His sufferings stand between us and our sin. By his sufferings He triumphs over the world, the flesh and the evil one. All spiritual victories are contained in His death. When we suffer, we suffer with Christ who was made perfect through suffering ...[261]

The Cross of Christ is a symbol of triumph, of strength, of glory.[262]

By the resurrection ... a new light is shed upon the death of Christ and so upon the death of all who receive His grace. By death Christ has abolished death, but that is the smallest part of His work. By death He has also abolished sin.[263]

Elsewhere we have much speculation regarding God. Only here have we perfect revelation. In Christ you have the glory which a full understanding of God's purpose with His world can bestow.[264]

---

[259] Oman, *Paradox of the World*, p. 84.
[260] Oman, *Paradox of the World*, p. 115; cf. pp. 134, 166.
[261] Oman, *Dialogue with God*, p. 32.
[262] Oman, *Dialogue with God*, p. 49.
[263] Oman, *Dialogue with God*, p. 119.
[264] Oman, *Dialogue with God*, p. 136.

To borrow H.R. Mackintosh's phrase, it is pointless to speculate upon what the 'final distribution of emphasis' in his major works might have been had Oman brought to bear upon his method the more rounded Christian understanding hinted at in the above quotations. Might he, for example, come to the view that the Cross is *the* supernatural act of sovereign grace in the sense that nature could neither have imagined nor engineered it, and that its purpose is to redeem and restore nature?[265] As it is one cannot resist the feeling that, like a number of other theologians, he believed more than could readily be accommodated within the boundaries of his chosen method. Oman was, nevertheless, a profound, sincere, honest ruminator upon theological themes who, like the fishermen among whom he was raised, pushed out into the deep waters. Two or three pages of Oman can be considerably more mentally bracing than whole volumes by some of the fashionable theological gurus of our time who, in a dogmatic and unscholarly way, parrot unanalyzed theological slogans for the delectation of their groupies. We might say that his whole life was a response to the challenge posed by his loved and revered College Principal, John Cairns: 'The best apology for Christianity is a life which makes the supernatural visible to ourselves and others.'[266]

VII

Oman's works have been highly regarded by more discerning authors. Among Anglicans, Tennant surmized that those who agreed with it would regard *Grace and Personality* as 'one of the greater treasures of theological literature', and thought that Oman was 'one of the most original, independent, and impressive theologians of his generation and of his country';[267] J.S. Bezzant judged *The Natural and the Supernatural* 'one of the two ablest and most thorough works on Philosophical Theology published a generation ago, the other being F.R. Tennant's two volumes so entitled';[268] J.K. Mozley said that *Grace and Personality* 'is sufficient to place its writer among the most penetrating

---

[265] See further Sell, *Confessing and Commending the Faith*, ch. 5. When Oman thinks of sovereignty he too frequently thinks in terms of omnipotent force – something he rightly abominates. From my use of the term 'sovereign grace' it will be clear that I think it frequently advisable to use one attribute of God adjectivally in relation to another. Sovereignty without grace might, as Oman feared, become sheer untoward force; but grace without power could hardly vanquish sin and the grave. The hymn, 'Sovereign grace o'er sin abounding! Ransomed souls the tidings swell' remains a powerful blast from the Devonian shipwright, John Kent (1766-1843). Sadly, it is nowadays excluded from most mainline hymnals.

[266] Quoted by A.R. MacEwen, *Life and Letters of John Cairns*, p. 562.

[267] Tennant, 'John Wood Oman', p. 335.

[268] J.S. Bezzant, 'The theology of John Oman', *The Modern Churchman*, IX, 1965-66, p. 135.

religious thinker of his generation',[269] while C.F.D. Moule described the book 'as one of the most exquisite books on religion ever written'.[270] It is said that as he lay on his deathbed the Congregationalist, P.T. Forsyth, declared of *Grace and Personality*, 'This is a book which I should like to put into the hands of every theological student.'[271] From the ranks of the Reformed came numerous accolades. In the opinion of John Dickie, 'No one in our day has written more penetratingly on the ultimate problems of religion and theology than Dr. Oman.'[272] To the philosopher, T.M. Knox, *The Natural and the Supernatural* 'is one of the three of four most distinguished contributions to philosophy which have appeared in English-speaking countries in the last forty years, and it is a scandal that hardly any of those now teaching philosophy in these islands have read it'.[273] Finally John Hick, an *alumnus* of Westminster College after Oman's time there, deemed Oman 'one of the most original British theologians of the first half of the twentieth century'.[274]

But it is to Oman's students that we must turn for more personal reminiscences of Oman. Those who knew him said that he could be blunt, as when he remarked, on leaving the room following the presentation of a paper on *Grace and Personality*, 'I do not recognise my own portrait.'[275] His patience was tried by careless work, and he scorned what he called 'the unlit lamp and the ungirt loin'.[276] He was sometimes absent-minded, as when he fell asleep during a pastoral visit to a church member in Alnwick.[277] He could appear formidable – an impression which 'though no doubt it drew something from his fine physical stature and even more from his superlative equipment of intellectual power and vast knowledge was fundamentally that of character'.[278]

---

[269] J.K. Mozley, *Some Tendencies in British Theology from the Publication of Lux Mundi to the Present Day* (London: SPCK, 1952), p. 161.

[270] So R. Buick Knox, *Westminster College Cambridge, Its Background and History* (Cambridge: The University Library, 1979).

[271] F.G. Healey, 'The theology of John Oman', *Theology*, LXVII, December 1964, p. 543.

[272] J. Dickie, *Fifty Years of British Theology. A Personal Retrospect* (Edinburgh: T & T Clark, 1937), p. 106.

[273] T.M. Knox, review of F. G. Healey, *Religion and Reality* in *The Journal of Theological Studies*, XVII, 1966, p. 547.

[274] J. Hick, *Faith and Knowledge, A Modern Introduction to the Problem of Religious Knowledge* (Ithaca, NY: Cornell University Press, 1957), p. xix. I endorse Hick's adjective, provided that I may say that Forsyth was the most stimulating, and Franks the most scholarly theologian of the period.

[275] Healey, *Religion and Reality*, p. vii.

[276] H.H. Farmer, 'Theologians of our time', p. 132; cf.Farmer, 'Death of Dr. John Oman. An appreciation', *The Christian World*, 25 Ma, 1939, p. 9.

[277] Farmer, 'Death of Dr. John Oman', p. 158.

[278] Farmer, 'Theologians of our time. III. John Wood Oman,' *The Expository Times*, LXXIV no. 5, February 1963, p. 132.

W.A.L. Elmslie, the first Westminster *alumnus* to be called to a Chair in the College, recalled that

> Oman possessed what one can but call an encyclopaedic range of learning: complete master of his own field of theology and philosophy, he could speak with the authority of real knowledge concerning a host of other subjects. He has a penetratingly just judge of character, but had absolute respect for the rights of personality. Therefore his students not only admired and revered him, they knew that they could also trust his guidance and rely upon his kindness.[279]

Another student spoke of the honesty and authority of Oman's teaching, and also of his 'humorous stories, or taking part in party games in that homely and friendly atmosphere which Mrs. Oman and he have the secret of imparting'.[280] Some students found Oman's class lectures difficult to grasp: to Lesslie Newbigin they were 'obscure to the point of opacity', but he valued Oman's chapel utterances;[281] and many found his well-illustrated and down-to-earth conversations held at the end of the lecturing week and later gathered in *Concerning the Ministry* of great benefit. T.W. Manson wrote of the influence upon students of Oman's 'single-minded devotion to the truth,' and testified that

> There are many men in the ranks of the ministry to-day who are able to face the difficulties and perplexities of our time with some sort of inner serenity and courage because they once sat at the feet of a real hero of faith, one who never shirks a difficulty, is never content merely to defeat the opposition in argument, one who all through has striven for a unified vision of God, man, and the world, and wrought for nothing less than that whole truth that makes us free.[282]

H.H. Farmer recalled that during the painting of Oman's portrait by Hugh Rivière three visitors called at the studio on three separate occasions. The first said, 'That is the face of a fisherman;' the second, 'That is the face of a philosopher;' the third, 'That is the face of a saint.' Farmer found these responses suggestive of Oman's wrestling with the facts, his reflective mind, and his humility.[283] Following Oman's death on 17 May 1939, R.D. Whitehorn wrote,

---

[279] Elmslie, *Westminster College Cambridge*, p. 23.

[280] E.W.P., 'The new Principal. An appreciation of Dr. Oman', *The Presbyterian Messenger*, 1922, p. 155.

[281] L. Newbigin, *The Unfinished Agenda*, London: SPCK, 1985, p. 31.

[282] T.W. Manson, 'Dr. John Oman', *The Presbyterian Messenger*, 1935, p. 199.

[283] Farmer, 'Death of Dr. John Oman', p. 19.

In all his intellectual work he was concerned not with abstractions, but with the world as the home of free personalities capable of knowing God in 'a gracious personal relationship', and therefore with the Christian evaluation of men and means, souls and things. ... There has passed from among us a great teacher, a great thinker, a great Christian, and a great friend.[284]

I am sure that Oman, the Christian content to live in the half lights, saw a good deal of himself in both Pascal and Butler, of whom he wrote that they had 'precisely the same overwhelming sense of the dimness of the light with which we are compelled to act and of the need of our whole nature, and not merely our faculty of argument, in searching for that faith which the conduct of life imposes on us'.[285] But if there is one of his sentences which, more than any other, may stand as his own epitaph it is this:

To have thought God's thoughts, fathomed in some measure His creation, predicted His ways, penetrated in some measure into His working, sets man, even in this fleeting life, amid God's creatures with a radiance upon his brow which we may believe even death will not destroy.[286]

In those words are encompassed Oman's objective and his reward. The contemplative task they enshrine began for Oman when, as a solitary youth he experienced the call of the supernatural in the natural order of Orkney. Perhaps I may in conclusion resort to the kind of homely expression which this deepest of thinkers never shunned to use, and say that while you can take the man out of Orkney, you cannot take Orkney out of the man.

---

[284] R.D. Whitehorn, 'Obituary. The Rev John Oman', *Cambridge Review*, 26 May 1939. Roy Drummond Whitehorn was appointed to the Chair of Church History at Westminster College in 1933, and was Principal there from 1955 to 1963. He died on 14 November 1976, aged 85. See *Year Book of the United Reformed Church*, 1978, p. 271.

[285] Oman, *Faith and Freedom*, p. 425.

[286] Oman, *Dialogue with God*, p. 136; though in the text the last 'His' is given a capital H. It must, however refer to 'man', not God.

CHAPTER 2

John Oman: 'Thralled to Truth.'[1]

Fleur Houston

In this paper, I shall show how John Oman was impelled by the William Robertson Smith case to pursue truth through the ministry of the Church. I shall demonstrate how the case stimulated his theological thinking. And finally I shall show how the need to engage ordinary people in the pursuit of truth, combined with his war-time experience, led him to a fresh affirmation of the Gospel of Redemption.

When John Oman, a 'raw lad from the ends of the earth'[2] went to Edinburgh University, with his 'vast responsiveness to the intellectual environment,'[3] the Smith controversy was at its height.

> I had no notion, Oman writes, in those days, of ever being interested in theology, and my ignorance of the matters in dispute was profound. But I read his speeches, and, on one occasion, heard him. I seemed to find the same kind of knowledge as was making the world a place for me of incessant discovery and the same passion for reality as seemed at the moment life's supreme concern.[4]

The facts of the case are well known and there is no need to rehearse them here. Suffice it to note that in 1881, after five years of controversy in Church courts over his views on Biblical criticism and inspiration, Smith was dismissed from his chair at the Free Church College, Aberdeen, on the grounds that his teaching was a danger to theological students.[5]

---

[1] The reference is from the address given at John Oman's funeral service by P. Carnegie Simpson in St. Columba's Church, Cambridge, on 22nd May, 1939.

[2] John Oman 'Method in Theology, an Inaugural Lecture', *The Expositor*, Vol.26, (August 1923), p. 82.

[3] Oman 'Method in Theology', p. 82.

[4] Oman 'Method in Theology', p. 82.

[5] For a full account of proceedings, see J. S. Black and G. Chrystal, *The Life of William Robertson Smith* (London: Adam and Charles Black 1912); see also P. Carnegie Simpson, *The Life of Principal Rainy* (London: Hodder and Stoughton 1909), pp. 306-403.

Some of the most devout people in the Church felt sorrow and shame at this turn of events.[6] They held that Christ's promise of the Holy Spirit for the education of his Church was being fulfilled in the critical use of the Bible: they defended criticism on the grounds of faith in God and loyalty to Christ. This was certainly the view taken by Smith himself. Carnegie Simpson notes:

> William Robertson Smith had the passion of the lover for truth…and he assumed that his Church shared that love.....He believed that the Free Church of Scotland was a true depository of God's evangel and he honoured her for the courage with which she had followed God's leading into new ways of duty at the Disruption. He never doubted she would be equally ready to learn new ways of truth as these seemed to be discovered.[7]

Henry Drummond wrote at the time of the 'lynching' of Smith.[8] Some years later, in an editorial in the British Weekly,[9] William Robertson Nicholl suggested that the Free Church had 'erred most deplorably and most tragically' in its treatment of Smith. As for John Oman, he was profoundly shocked – the term is his. He thought intellectual truth the one worthy pursuit in life. He heard people condemning Smith because of this very loyalty to the results of investigation. 'Again and again, I heard people declare that, even if all he said were true, regard for useful tradition and the ecclesiastical amenities should have kept him from saying it.'[10] He cites a lawyer whom he knew to be a good man, an elder of the Church, as saying: 'granted that Robertson Smith is right, if it is truth, it is dangerous truth, and he has no right, as a professor of the Church, to upset the Church by declaring it.'[11] This suggested to Oman that the Church was not interested in truth.

> As I then understood the business, he remarked in his inaugural address as Principal of Westminster College, (the judges) were so far from being seekers after truth that…they would not have recognised it if they had met it in their porridge.[12]

The integrity of the Church was on the line.

My impression, he continues, may very likely have been hasty, crude, ill-

---

[6] Black and Chrystal, *Life of Smith,* p. 439.

[7] Carnegie Simpson, *Life of Rainy,* p. 314.

[8] Glasgow, 21st May, 1881, cited in G. A. Smith, *The Life of Henry Drummond* (London: Hodder and Stoughton 1899), p. 130.

[9] 23rd May 1912

[10] Oman, 'Method in Theology' p 83.

[11] Oman, *Vision and Authority*, p. 9.

[12] Oman, 'Method in Theology' p 83.

informed, but that does not make it less typical because the need is just to take heed not to offend one of the little ones whose chief knowledge about theology consists in thinking that no obligation is so sacred as to seek truth with all our hearts and to manifest it with all our powers.[13]

It was a crux. He made reference to it throughout his life. In 1928 he wrote:

Had I been intending the ministry, probably I should have been put off it, but this affected me somewhat as a call to my life's work...I was left with no option but to search for a truth which would shine in its own light in face of all enquiry, and complete scepticism.[14]

He opted to train for the ministry. As he suggests in *Concerning the Ministry*, he 'somehow could not escape.'[15] Many years later, he commented, 'If with open mind and courage [a man] seek truth and stand for righteousness, he will not in this service need other motive.'[16] So with a first class degree in Philosophy from Edinburgh University, he entered the United Presbyterian Church Hall. His training served him well.

In the Hall, there was, to quote A.R. MacEwan, Professor of Church History at the time,

an unusually large proportion of young men of a philosophic bent, and...this bent was emphasised by residence at German universities...The Church abounded with young ministers who...were seeking to grasp central principles and to correlate their religious principles with modern metaphysics.[17]

Oman, typically, spent successive summers in the Universities of Erlangen and Heidelberg, where he made life-long friendships and where he was exposed to German Philosophy. In particular his thought was stimulated by Schleiermacher. Although not uncritical, Oman found in the *Speeches* and *The Christian Faith* evidence of a devoutly religious philosopher who was similarly exercised by the failings of the institutional Church and was aware of the extent

---

[13] Oman, 'Method in Theology' p 83.

[14] John Oman, *Vision and Authority, or The Throne of St. Peter* (London: Hodder and Stoughton 2nd ed. 1928), p. 10.

[15] John Oman, *Concerning the Ministry* (London: SCM 1936), p. 33.

[16] John Oman, 'The Ministry of the Non-Conformist Churches' in J. A. R. Cairns, ed. *The Problem of a Career Solved by 36 Men of Distinction* (London: Arrowsmith 1926), p. 130.

[17] A. R. MacEwan, *Life and Letters of John Cairns D.D., LL.D* (London: Hodder and Stoughton 3rd ed. 1898), pp. 664-5.

to which these alienated educated people from religion.[18]

There was another influence at work at the time in the UPC. For over fifty years, the Church had been conspicuously active in foreign missions. In 1880, around 34 out of 94 students went to the mission field.[19] This contributed to the questioning of the doctrine of Limited Atonement which was particularly troubling to students at the time.[20] Debates as to the relative merits of an ethical or judicial interpretation had been current since the publication by Erskine of Linlathen's book *The Unconditional Freeness of the Gospel* in 1828 which was seen by F.D. Maurice as 'a continual witness for a God of righteousness....against that notion of a mere sovereign Baal',[21] and went into six editions. But three years later, J. McLeod Campbell, minister of Row, Dumbartonshire was deposed by an overwhelming majority in the General Assembly of the Church of Scotland for his preaching of the 'universal atonement and pardon through the death of Christ.' His book, *The Nature of the Atonement* (1856), described by James Torrance as 'one of the classics of all time on this doctrine,'[22] was to appear in many editions and reprints and contributed to a climate of opinion which is reflected in Oman's own work.[23]

It is against this background of what Oman styles 'the old controversy concerning grace'[24] that, in *Grace and Personality*, he was to present to a readership far beyond the 'study of the thinker', his belief in God's offer of love in Christ to all people.

To instance this, I point to the account by D. Ben Rees[25] of Ellis Henry Morris who in 1923 went out to serve the mission field of the Presbyterian Church of Wales in India. Morris clashed vigorously with a fellow missionary over the doctrine of the Atonement and 'immersed himself' in *Vision and Authority* and in *Grace and Personality.* These works, in Morris' eyes, combined 'a passion for truth and pastoral awareness.' So much so that five years later, he decided to further his theological training at Westminster College under John Oman.

Then there was the unmistakable personal influence of Principal John Cairns. On Cairns's death, Oman wrote: 'A great man has departed, for myself

---

[18] See Oman's Introduction to the *Speeches*; *Faith and Freedom*, chapter V; cf. his article 'Schleiermacher,' in JTS, 30, 1929 pp. 401-405.

[19] Letter from Cairns to Dr MacLagan, 1880, in MacEwan, *Cairns*, p. 681.

[20] See Carnegie Simpson, *Rainey*, p. 210; MacEwan, *Cairns*, p. 665.

[21] F.D Maurice's dedication to Erskine of *The Prophets and Kings of the Old Testament* 1852.

[22] Campbell, J.McLeod, *The Nature of the Atonement*, new edition (Edinburgh; The Handsel Press, 1996) p. 2.

[23] cf his book review of Hastings Rashdall, *The Idea of Atonement in Christian Theology, 1919, The Journal of Theological Studies*, 21, 1920, pp. 275-6.

[24] Oman, *Grace and Personality*, p. 28.

[25] D.B. Rees, *Vehicles of Grace and Hope: Welsh Missionaries in India, 1800-1970* (Welsh Books Council 2003) p. 144.

I would say the greatest man I have ever met ... whose mere presence in the world was a benediction.'[26] Cairns had an 'eagerness to master truth apart from any use to which truth may be put.'[27] His biographer suggests that: 'every fresh line of study had been attacked with a determination to go to the very roots of it and to give the result of his own research and his own thinking.'[28] His linguistic skills were legendary. Proficient in Hebrew and Greek, every now and then he would take it into his head to learn a new language – Dutch, Danish, Assyrian. He 'took a fancy' to learn Arabic,[29] as his diary shows, in the middle of an exciting meeting of the Synod in 1881, and when relaxing of an evening under doctor's orders, he took to reading the Qur'an in Arabic. In the class-room, his sense that it was a shameful thing to speak on any subject without exhaustive knowledge could sometimes be carried to extremes. 'There was some truth,' writes Oman, 'in the saying that if Cairns had to write an article on "How to blow the nose" he would have to read all the fathers through in the original to see what they had to say on the subject.'[30]

But Cairns also believed that theological students had to remain rooted in the reality of everyday life and with John Ker, Professor of pastoral theology, he instigated a system of practical placements. He himself helped with Moody and Sankey meetings, spoke from the evangelists' platforms, helped in the enquiry rooms and instructed the young converts.[31] Above all, he showed his chief strength, 'with an enthusiasm bordering upon passion, when the verities of the Christian religion had been assailed; and in an age of uncertainty, contention and pessimism, he had left in every circle the conviction that he himself had an intense and joyful belief in the growing work of a personal and living God.'[32]

Much of what Oman had learned in the UP Hall he was to put into practice in Westminster College as Professor of Theology and subsequently as Principal: the radical thinking about the nature of the Church, the importance of scholarship in order to get to the roots of things, the apologetic zeal that was grounded in the reality of people's lives. Above all, teaching theology was bound up with the search for truth. Oman made the point in his inaugural address: 'The most important matter in any seminary of learning is teaching, not organising. The real business of a theological college is being done, if men come out of it knowing how to seek truth for themselves; whereas, without it, the most efficient organisation may only be an elaborate device for wasting

---

[26] Unpublished manuscript: *Dr Cairns by one of his old students.*

[27] MacEwan, *Cairns,* p. 71.

[28] MacEwan, *Cairns ,*p. 758.

[29] MacEwan, *Cairns,* p. 716.

[30] Unpublished manuscript, *Dr Cairns by one of his old students.*

[31] see Smith, G.A., *The Life of Henry Drummond* (London: Hodder and Stoughton 1899) p. 56.

[32] MacEwan, *Cairns,* p. 786.

youth's precious years.' Students were constantly reminded to keep 'their loins girt and their lamps lit'. Oman's dislike of all that was sham or pretentious could make him a severe critic on occasion – I could instance the review he wrote of Helen Zimmern's work on Schopenhauer [33] – but he was generous in his encouragement of those students who tried their best.[34] For him, 'the true idea of a settled ministry is…to be teachers. The reason why they are expected to be able to meet regularly a regular demand is that they are dealing with abiding truth. Truth is seen not merely at his own angle but on many sides, not merely as it touches his life but as it has illumined the large experience of the saints.'

Oman's search for truth took two main trajectories. First, the Smith affair had raised in Oman's mind radical questions about the authority and nature of the Church. Many years later, he addressed these questions in *Vision and Authority*. And characteristically his intended readership was not scholars, but

> ordinary people, who read little but what our parish minister at home said he had come to in his old age – God's book and the Devil's, the Bible and a certain newspaper…Religious thinking,' he continued, 'ought to face the ordinary religious life; and it ought, as far as possible, to be expressed in ordinary language [35]

Oman takes his point of departure from the thesis that the Church has, and should have, authority. This authority is to be distinguished from external constraint. Where the Church requires unthinking submission to external authority, this is nothing more than 'exaltation of necessity over freedom.'[36] How may the authority of the Church be married appropriately with the 'authority within'? For a Christian, the eternal order is revealed, not in dogma or creed, but in Jesus Christ, who speaks with the authority of perfect truth. 'To accept Christ as teacher is not to be subjugated to the dominion of absolute truth which is not to be investigated or recognised. It is to receive intellectual emancipation.'[37] This authority appeals to each individual's insight. It does not 'dominate and silence the inward voices, but awakes them and makes them its chief witness'.[38] It makes possible a community which combines the largest freedom with the closest fellowship. 'Christ trusted to it exclusively. His whole work He committed to this Church, and He neither sought any support for his truth outside the Church, nor any other support for the Church beyond the

---

[33] Oman, Journal of Theological Studies, 1932
[34] Oman, *Honest Religion*, Memoir p. xxvii.
[35] Oman, *Vision and Authority*, preface to 2nd ed., 1928, p. 10.
[36] Oman, *Vision and Authority*, p. 94.
[37] Oman, *Vision and Authority*, p. 113.
[38] Oman, *Vision and Authority*, p. 112.

insight and faithfulness of the souls that love Him'.[39] In the Church, individual insight is corrected and supplemented through association with others who are assumed to perceive the same truth.

Disagreements arise where there are differences of insight. Scriptural interpretation is a neuralgic example, and Oman elaborates on that.[40] He starts with the premise that 'all scripture is of personal experience. Its supreme value consists in its closeness to man's highest and intensest life.'[41] Hence the inconsistency of Scripture. This is not necessarily a problem. On the contrary, its value, Oman maintains, is merely enhanced by an absence of consistency, 'for only truth could be so indifferent to consistency and so sure of it....the difference of experiences only shows more clearly the similarity of men's deepest needs'.[42] It would be wrong to infer, however, that Scripture is a matter of private opinion or of private interpretation. Oman writes,

> the final interpretation cannot be a mere matter of scholarship. The largest equipment of linguistic research, literary insight, and dialectical subtlety, however valuable as a means for helping to unfold the deep things of God, can never be the final spiritual verdict. This demands a wider and a more practical experience.[43]

The only alternative, however, is not 'an official verdict'.[44] 'Even from the wise and prudent in council truth has sometimes been hidden'[45] and their votes more often than not, 'a mere echo of party cries.' Judgments, whether of a prince of the Church or of councils may be 'warped by personal bias, tradition, formalism, prejudice, self-interest'[46] and reveal themselves to be individual opinion every bit as much as that of the commentator.

> On the other side, indifferent to party, one solitary thinker may stand, and his interpretation not be private, because it rests on the universal grounds of truth and holiness...The true representative of the Church is not the recipient of her votes, but the possessor of her highest knowledge and noblest aspirations.[47]

Possession of the highest knowledge is not confined to individual opinion; nor is it to be equated with blind obedience to creeds, it is the result of being

---

[39] Oman, *Vision and Authority*, p. 125.
[40] Oman, *Vision and Authority*, pp. 209-214.
[41] Oman, *Vision and Authority*, p. 210.
[42] Oman, *Vision and Authority*, p. 210.
[43] Oman, *Vision and Authority*, p. 210.
[44] Oman, *Vision and Authority*, p. 211.
[45] Oman, *Vision and Authority*, p. 211.
[46] Oman, *Vision and Authority*, p. 211.
[47] Oman, *Vision and Authority*, p. 211.

'faithful to our spiritual ancestry' through the Church.[48]

Oman maintained throughout his life that for a 'robust religious life' a Christian must belong to a Christian community.[49] There should always be 'a Christlike discontent with every bond of fellowship which comes short of His'.[50] And supreme effort should be made to recall the Churches to their true task as a vehicle of grace. I shall not linger over *The Church and The Divine Order* which Oman considered to be a very poor effort [51]except to indicate the continuing importance of the theme for his thinking.

We come now to the second trajectory taken by Oman's search for truth.

The relationship of infinite to the finite had, from his earliest childhood, been a key feature of Oman's thinking. 'An earnest pressing to the heart of things'[52] lay behind his observations of fishermen, shepherds and gypsies,[53] and his recollections of his own experiences whether, as a child, standing alone on the beach at full tide[54] or 'riding through the Standing Stones of Stenness on a winter afternoon when dusk was settling into darkness'.[55] In a time of war, this was translated into an urgent theological need to relate faith to reality. He writes in a sermon of meeting a young soldier who, a few weeks before had been full of the joys of life. Now he 'had the haggard, dazed look of a child that had lost all its bearings in the dark'.[56] The war sent Oman 'into camps and hospitals where fundamental religious questions were constantly being discussed'.[57] He gave David Smith Cairns 'invaluable help' in the Rouen camp when Cairns delivered addresses on the *Reasonableness of the Christian Faith* to soldiers in Rouen and Le Havre in 1916.[58] One of the most distressing experiences for Oman was to see lads 'whose religion and morality were in the army like tow in the flame'.[59] But he also saw that the war was laying bare what was true in religion, stripping away all that was not 'real religion and true sincerity.'[60] In a vivid sermon entitled *Turfing the Grave*,[61] he describes the

---

[48] Oman, *Vision and Authority*, p. 90.

[49] Oman, *Honest Religion*, p. 170; see also Oman, *Vision and Authority,* pp 140ff.

[50] Oman, *Vision and Authority*, p. 144.

[51] Cf. Oman, *Concerning the Ministry,* p. 33: 'I never wrote a book by conscious purpose but one, and it was bad, even for me.'

[52] Oman, *Concerning the Ministry*, p. 46.

[53] See Oman, *The Paradox of the World*, 1921, pp. 7, 162; Oman, *Honest Religion,* 1941, p. 165; Oman, *The Natural and The Supernatural*, 1931, p. 134.

[54] Oman, *Natural and Supernatural*, 1931, pp. 136-7.

[55] John Oman, Review of R. Otto, *The Idea of the Holy*, JTS, Vol 25, Apr 1924.

[56] John Oman, *A Dialogue with God* (London: James Clarke and Co. Ltd 1950), pp. 45-46.

[57] Oman, *Grace and Personality*, preface to the 1st ed, 1917, p. v.

[58] See Preface by David Smith Cairns to *The Reasonableness of the Christian Faith* (London, Hodder and Stoughton, 1918).

[59] Oman, *Honest Religion,* p. 16.

[60] Oman, *Honest Religion,* p. 16.

ceremony of dedication of a war memorial in Cambridge. 'Everything was right, and fitting for the occasion.' But it was all 'painting on the surface'. His mind flew back to France where after the Somme, the 'young and the strong were being gathered to the dust' and he observed how religion itself may be used 'as a pageant painted on the surface of life's mirror to distract us from looking into its depths.'

In the preface to the first edition of *Grace and Personality*, he writes: 'The War...forced upon me the reconsideration of my whole religious position. Moreover, the fact that such sorrow and wickedness could happen in the world, became the crucible in which my whole view of the world had to be tested.' He had many years before identified 'the ultimate problem' as 'the relation of Faith and Freedom, the problem of how Faith is to be absolute and Freedom absolute, yet both one'. [62] The question, which had hitherto been largely theoretical, assumed crucial importance: what is the relationship between a person's moral independence and absolute dependence on God?

A loving father does not relate to his children 'by way of irresistible might'. The way forward is surely not to 'argue from the bare idea of omnipotence, but instead to consider God's actual ways of dealing with His children....for if in all things God deals with us as a Father, His grace cannot be thus divorced from His working in nature and ordinary history.'[63] A good God, adequate to experience, can only be a God whose power is manifested in love. On the assumption that grace is not a matter of display of divine sovereignty, God can only help us 'through our own purpose, guided by our own insight, dealing with our own world'.[64] And Oman concludes: 'If the relation of God to us is one gracious dealing because it includes all things, life is made blessed in the assurance that all things work for good.'[65] This is not to deny the reality of suffering or sin, but to be

> reconciled to God in spite of sin, that we can face all evil with confident assurance of final victory over it, and by God's succour transform all its consequences, whether the evil be natural or moral, the outcome of our own sin, or from our necessary fellowship with others in His family.[66]

Grace and Personality went into several editions. Oman was encouraged 'that the book has been read by many who have no technical knowledge – some of them working men, and that they seem to have understood what I was

---

[61] Oman, *Dialogue with God*, pp. 45-46.
[62] John Oman, *The Problem of Faith and Freedom in the Last Two Centuries* (London, Hodder and Stoughton, 1906), p. 4.
[63] Oman, *Grace and Personality*, p.14.
[64] Oman, *Grace and Personality*, p. 57.
[65] Oman, *Grace and Personality*, p. 93.
[66] Oman, *Grace and Personality*, p. 231.

driving at'.[67] This was the readership he particularly wanted to reach. He had discovered through conversation with skilled mechanics during the war, that they thought

> we were all a kind of trade-union to impose upon mankind merely traditional beliefs, and that the ordinary Christian was largely a Pharisee, concerned mainly with respectabilities and negative moralities. They were mostly outside the Christian Church, but they were honest and sincere, and, in their own way, religious, and ought to be inside, which they never will be as long as the Church appeals mainly to minds responsive to assertion.'[68]

In *The Natural and the Supernatural* Oman returns to the theme. Any ultimate explanation of the world must try to make sense of the historical and contingent. If the eternal order is real and just, what are we to make of the transient and evil? In *Grace and Personality*, he had established the fact that God deals with human beings as persons whom he respects and loves. Oman now elaborates on this. A human person is called in freedom to know the truth over the whole breadth of experience. And so Oman restates his understanding of the relationship of knowing and knowledge, freedom and necessity, the transient and the eternal. He establishes that, for theological integrity, these have in each case to be held together. And he demonstrates that this can only be done as the Gospel of redemption is affirmed, incarnate in 'a life in this world which manifested God's meaning in common things and God's value in common people...a turning of earthly defeat and agony and death into victory and joy and the power of an endless life.'[69]

There is a massive unity and consistency in Oman's thought and there is also a powerful sense of forward movement and development. Divine truth, revealed in personal experience, grows and deepens as he seeks to discover further truth. In *Honest Religion*, his final work, he writes: 'Man's restless mind will ever try to think things together. But religion has ever been the creative force in history, and man's central interest must ever be in reaching forward and upward towards a world not yet realised.'[70] And so 'we pursue truth till we know that our knowledge ends with what is most worth knowing.'[71]

The William Robertson Smith case stimulated Oman's quest for truth in ways which still challenge us today: his repudiation of dishonesty in the Church's conduct of its affairs, his belief that faith is cultivated by free intellectual enquiry, his insistence that theology ought to resonate with the

---

[67] Oman, *Grace and Personality*, preface to 3rd edition, 1925, p. x.

[68] Oman, *Method in Theology*, p. 85.

[69] Oman, *Natural and Supernatural*, p. 464.

[70] Oman, *Honest Religion*, 1941, p. 51.

[71] Oman, *Honest Religion*, 1941, p. 193.

experience of ordinary people, above all, his affirmation of a gracious God in whom all opposites are reconciled.

CHAPTER 3

Oman and the University of Cambridge

David M. Thompson

I had always been intrigued by the fact that *Grace and Personality*, and indeed all Oman's later books, apart from *Concerning the Ministry* (SCM Press, 1936), were published by Cambridge University Press, rather than the traditional publishers for nonconformist theology, such as Hodder and Stoughton. Why was this? I wondered, and what did it tell us about the relationship between Oman and the University. As soon as I began to investigate this, I discovered two things: first, that *Grace and Personality* was not the first of Oman's books to be published by the Press – that was *The War and Its Problems* (1915); the other was that Oman's involvement with the Faculty of Divinity was much deeper and longer than I had supposed. Oman was actually the first Westminster Professor to hold a University Post, that of University Lecturer in the Philosophy of Religion (what is now the Stanton Lectureship), which he held twice, as it had been established under the pre-1926 Statutes. So this paper will have three main sections. The first is a general discussion of the relationship between Westminster College and the University from its move to Cambridge in 1899, and particularly the relationship of Oman and the University after the opening up of the Faculty to nonconformists, following the removal of religious tests for degrees in Divinity in 1913. (I do not propose to address the discussions which led to the move to Cambridge in 1899, as that story is well-known.) The second will be a reflection on Oman and his books, particularly those published by the Press from 1915; and the final part will be a discussion of the visions of Oman, and also John Skinner, on the requirements of a theological syllabus, in the Cambridge context.

The relationship of Westminster College and the University from 1899

There is no indication in the Minutes of the meetings of either the Professors of Divinity or the Special Board for Theology of any comment on the forthcoming arrival of the Presbyterian College in Cambridge in the years from the Synod's decision in 1895 to the opening of the College in 1899. The only decision that might possibly have any relevance is one taken by the Special Board for Divinity on 10 May 1897 on the motion of the Norrisian Professor (H.C.G.

Moule, later Bishop of Durham, and a friend to Westminster in its opening
years) 'that Defoe's *Shortest Way with Dissenters* should not be set among the
subjects for the Special Examination in 1899'.[1]

This is more interesting because of a significant Discussion in the Senate on
3 March 1898 concerning the proposed recognition of St Edmund's House as a
Public Hostel of the University. The original buildings of what is now St
Edmund's College had been purchased from Mr Ayerst, who had attempted to
run them as a public hostel for university students but without ever gaining
official recognition, partly because it had been run as a speculative enterprise
based on the profits gained from renting rooms. When bought by the Council of
St Edmund's College, Ware, as a place where intending candidates for the
Catholic priesthood could read for University degrees before engaging in their
seminary studies, the property was owned freehold, with an additional
benefaction of £5,000 from the Duke of Norfolk. The Council of the Senate had
recommended that St Edmund's House be recognised as a public hostel, and it
is not without interest that Donald MacAlister of St Columba's was a member
of the Council at that time.

Nevertheless the Liberals (often so self-described) in the University queued
up to speak against the proposal, led by Charles McTaggart, who even
suggested that after fifteen years' experience, it was possible to see that the
recognition of Selwyn College as a Public Hostel might have been a mistake.
All of them denied any No Popery sentiment of course; their concern was 'an
institution whose whole essence was its exclusiveness' (McTaggart) or 'the
multiplication of Colleges which were not free and unrestricted' (J.R. Tanner).
In other words, the enemy was sectarian education.[2] The Council nevertheless
persisted with its proposal, and on 12 May 1898 it was defeated by 471 votes to
218.[3] Why am I telling you all this? Because I do not know whether it was ever
hoped by the Twins and their other Cambridge supporters that Westminster
might actually be recognised as a Public Hostel like Selwyn College. I have
never come across any reference to the idea. But if it might have been a hope in
the minds of some of the dons at St Columba's, the University's decision on St
Edmund's House killed that possibility before the College even opened.

There was one possible echo of that debate at the beginning of the College's
second year in Cambridge in October 1900. The Senatus received a letter from
Mr Huddlestone, the Censor of Non-Collegiate Students (who had supported
the St Edmund's proposal), concerning an application from a student who
wished to be a non-collegiate student and reside in Westminster. The Lodging
Houses Syndicate gave permission for him to keep terms at Westminster, and
by December 1900 Huddlestone had written to the Senatus to suggest that

[1] *Minutes of the Special Board for Divinity*, p. 247: University Archives, Min
V.101A.
[2] *Reporter*, 4 March 1898, pp. 584-91 (quotations from pp. 584-5, 587).
[3] *Reporter*, 17 May 1898, p. 825.

Westminster men preparing for the Theological Tripos should be directed and advised in their studies by the teachers at Westminster.[4]

Let us therefore turn to the internal discussions in the Church and the College about the implications of the move to Cambridge. At the very first meeting of the Senatus of the College held in Cambridge after the move (13 October 1899) 'Dr Gibb informed the Senatus that he had obtained the consent of Professor Moule for Students in the first term to attend lectures in the Divinity School on the First Epistle to the Corinthians'; and Dr Skinner said that he had reached a similar arrangement with Professor Kirkpatrick for students in their fourth term to attend his lectures on Isaiah. 'The Senatus resolved to require attendance on these Lectures as part of the regular curriculum.'[5] The Minutes contain various other references in the first decade to different sets of Tripos Lectures being required for Westminster students.

Also from an early date there were requests first from ministers and then students from the other Free Churches, most obviously Baptists and Congregationalists, to study at Westminster as private students – requests which the Senatus usually readily agreed to. In October 1905 the Senatus received a request from the Rev'd E.W. Johnson of Cheshunt College about the possibility of their students attending Westminster lectures; and the Senatus 'expressed a hearty welcome to Cheshunt on their removal to Cambridge and hoped they would find the University of Cambridge of assistance to them'. It is interesting, I think, that the reference is to the University of Cambridge; from its part the Senatus agreed to give every facility to Cheshunt students.[6] Within ten years of its arrival in Cambridge, therefore, Westminster had put down firm roots with the University. Its existence was further recognised by the award of honorary MAs to Oswald Dykes, the Principal, on 25 October 1900, John Skinner on 14 May 1903, and John Gibb on 24 May 1906.[7] So, although Aberdeen, St Andrews and Glasgow Universities had been in touch about counting work done at Westminster towards eligibility for their DD degrees under their new regulations, Westminster itself was already making provision for students, who did the Cambridge Theological Tripos to continue their ministerial studies in Cambridge. This meant that the Church's existing regulations for scholarships to support pre-ministerial undergraduate studies could actually be used, with certain amendments, to support Cambridge

---

[4] *Senatus Minutes*, 8 and 30 October 1900, 4 December 1900; cf *Senatus Letter Book*, Dykes to Huddleston, 5 December 1900; Westminster College Archives, WCR1/4.

[5] *Senatus Minutes*, 13 October 1899.

[6] *Senatus Minutes*, 27 September 1905.

[7] Grace 3 of 25 October 1900, *Reporter*, 1900-1901, p. 170 (this was the same day as Elgar's honorary MusD); Grace 1 of 14 May 1903, *Reporter*, 1902-3, p. 808; Grace 2 of 24 May 1906, *Reporter*, 1905-6, pp. 986, 988.

undergraduates in the Theological Tripos as well as other Humanities subjects.[8]
By 1907 the Synod heard with satisfaction that the proportion of vacancies
filled by Probationers of the Presbyterian Church of England remained high.[9]

Oman's link with Westminster was established before he was formally
appointed to the staff in 1907. In 1902 the Westminster College Association
agreed to suggest to the Senatus that the Revd John Oman, BD, should be the
Westminster Lecturer for 1904, and the Senatus accepted this proposal on 9
October 1902.[10] The Lectures which he gave were an early version of what
became his Kerr Lectures at New College, Edinburgh in 1906, subsequently
published as *The Problem of Faith and Freedom in the last Two Centuries*.[11]
This was in part a survey of theology since Pascal, but it also contained a
statement of Oman's own position, essentially a critical version of Ritschl's
theology. In this respect it followed up the line of thought developed in his
book, *Vision and Authority* (1902), which originally had the title, 'The Throne
of St Peter'. It established a position from which he scarcely deviated in later
years. Oman's resolute defence of freedom in theological enquiry was to
become less fashionable after the First World War; but it is not surprising that
someone, whose boyhood ambitions were to ride a horse bare-backed and to
steer a boat in a gale, set a high value on freedom and was unimpressed by
constraints of necessity.[12] When the Barbour Chair of Systematic Theology at
Westminster fell vacant by the resignation of Dr Oswald Dykes in 1907, the
Synod elected Oman to it. 402 voted for Oman and 101 voted for the Rev'd
Carnegie Simpson, whereupon Oman was elected unanimously. At the same
time Charles Anderson Scott was elected to the newly established Dunn Chair
in New Testament.[13]

Anderson Scott was already a Cambridge MA, having taken the Classical
Tripos in 1882, gaining an Upper Second at St John's College. Oman obviously
had no Cambridge connections but was made a member of Queens' College in
1908, and was given an honorary MA in March 1909.[14] With the arrival of
these two new members of the Senatus, who had no links with the former
college in Queen Square, a new era was more clearly beginning. In 1909
Anderson Scott was appointed to be a member of the Special Board for

[8] *Reporter*, 13 March, 8 and 22 May 1900.
[9] *Minutes of the Synod of the Presbyterian Church of England*, 8 May 1907, p. 38.
[10] *Minutes of the Synod,* 9 October 1902.
[11] John Oman, *The Problem of Faith and Freedom in the last Two Centuries*
(London: Hodder and Stoughton, 1906).
[12] John Oman, *Honest Religion* (Cambridge: Cambridge University Press, 1939), p.
36. Having been struck by that sentence, I was disappointed to find that it is also cited
by John MacLeod in his article 'John Oman, as Theologian', *The Hibbert Journal* xlviii,
4 (July 1950).
[13] *Minutes of the Synod of the Presbyterian Church of England*, 9 May 1907, pp.
46-7.
[14] Grace 2 of 6 March 1909, *Reporter*, 11 March 1909, p. 698.

Theology, and in 1910-11 he gave lectures in the Faculty on 'Paulinism'.[15] In 1912 the change came which was to transform the relationship between Westminster College and the University. At a meeting of the Professors of Divinity on 8 February 1912 a letter was received from Professor Scott Holland, 'explaining the steps which were about to be taken in Oxford with a view to throwing open the degrees of BD and DD to others than persons in Anglican Orders'. The Professors therefore agreed to consider what they should suggest to be done in relation to Cambridge degrees at their next meeting. Accordingly on 17 February 1912, 'a memorial to the Vice-Chancellor on Divinity degrees was considered and signed by the Professors'.[16] This memorial, which proposed the same steps as at Oxford, was published in the *Reporter*, and was followed by a Report of the Council of the Senate, proposing Graces to give effect to the change. Unsurprisingly this went to a vote, but was approved by 433 votes to 323. The Statute on Degrees on Divinity was amended by the omission of the declarations to be subscribed and the requirement to preach in the University Church.[17] Thus the final act of a saga, which had begun in 1833, when it was first suggested that Dissenters be admitted to degrees, was completed, with an almost striking lack of controversy – though the size of the vote and the relative closeness of the result should not be overlooked. Perhaps even more significant is the fact that Anderson Scott was appointed to be a member of the Divinity Degree Syndicate on the Regulations for admission to Degrees in Divinity.[18]

In 1912-13 Anderson Scott was once again a member of the Special Board for Divinity and also an Examiner for the Ordinary BA Degree; and his lectures on 'The Christology of the Apostolic Age' in Westminster College were advertised in the University Lecture List. In 1913 Oman was appointed to the University Lectureship in the Philosophy of Religion endowed by Professor Stanton in 1904 for three years; and reappointed from 1919 to 1922; he gave his first University lectures on the 'Introduction to the Philosophy of Religion' in the Michaelmas and Lent Terms.[19] W.A.L. Elmslie, who was not on the staff of Westminster at this point, but was a graduate of Christ's, was also down to lecture on 2 Samuel in Hebrew, and to this in 1913-14 he added lectures on Isaiah xl-lxvi in Hebrew. John Skinner and Anderson Scott were members of the Special Board for Divinity in 1913-14; and both Elmslie and Anderson

---

[15] *Minutes of the Special Board for Divinity*, University Archives, Min V.101A, p. 18 November 1907, p. 309; *Reporter*, 1910-11, p. 52.

[16] *Minutes of the Divinity Professors, 1907-16*, University Archives, Min V.292, pp. 17-18.

[17] *Reporter*, 1911-12, p. 638; 1912-13, pp. 42, 1007.

[18] *Reporter*, 25 May 1914.

[19] *The Historical Register of the University of Cambridge, Supplement, 1911-20*, (Cambridge, 1922), 14; *Reporter*, 1912-13, pp. 13, 17, 64, 70.

Scott were Examiners in the Tripos.[20] Oman lectured on the Philosophy of
Religion – the Psychological Nature of Religion in 1914-15, and on the
Philosophy of Religion in 1915-16. In 1917 Anderson Scott and Oman were co-
opted to the Degree Committee of the Faculty of Divinity and from this point
on the involvement of the Westminster Senatus in the life of the Divinity
Faculty became so much part of its routine that it would be tedious to list all the
ways in which this happened.[21]

There is, however, an important coda to this whole story, which relates to
the discussion of the New Statutes of 1926 (as they became) in 1924-25. In
1925 T.R. Glover wrote an obituary of John Skinner in *The Eagle*, the
magazine of St John's College, in the course of which he noted that Skinner
had only been given an '*honorary* MA' by the University of Cambridge (in
contrast to Oxford's DD).[22] Notwithstanding Glover's eventual appointments as
University Lecturer in Ancient History and University Orator, as a Baptist he
had felt a sense of exclusion in an Anglican-dominated University in the 1890s,
but still had always hoped for a post in the Faculty of Divinity, rather than
Classics. Without making any judgement on whether Skinner's name should
have been among the first nonconformists to be considered in the early 1920s
after DDs were open to non-Anglicans, I need to note that at the time Glover
was writing in 1925, an honorary MA was still the only way to recognise those
not educated at Cambridge as members of the University. This was in fact
changing as Glover wrote. In October 1924 a Report of the Council of the
Senate on Statute A II 18 proposed a distinction between degrees given to those
holding office in the University, a College or Public Hostel from degrees
honoris causa. One of the speakers at the first Discussion wanted what he
called 'proper DDs' by making learning the main criterion. At the second
Discussion a month later Mr McTaggart once again led the attack on the
privileges of the Church. Professor Burkitt suggested that the category of *ex
officio* DDs be extended from Bishops and Deans in the Church of England to
include the Moderator of the Presbyterian Church, any official approved by the
Congregational body, any Roman Catholic Bishop and the Chief Rabbi.
Another speaker interestingly pointed out that these proposals were one
consequence of the 1918 Franchise Act disenfranchising honorary MAs from
voting in the election of the MP for the University.[23] A Revised Report was
published in January 1925 to meet the criticisms of the original proposals; and

---

[20] *Reporter*, 1913-14, pp. 13, 1234-5.

[21] *Reporter*, 1914-15, p. 74; 1915-16, p. 66; 1917-18, p. 13.

[22] T.R.G., 'John Skinner', *The Eagle*, July 1925, p. 151. This point is picked up a
little more slightly by Roger Tomes in his entry for Skinner in Clyde Binfield & John
Taylor, *Who They Were in the Reformed Churches of England and Wales, 1901-2000*
(Donington, 2007), p. 205.

[23] *Reporter*, 1924-25, 21 October 1924, pp. 155-6; 4 November 1924, p. 217; 2
December 1924, pp. 314-8. (University MPs were abolished in 1948.)

in the vote on 7 February the recommendation that DDs should continue to be given to Bishops, Deans and Heads of House *ex officio* was defeated by 77 votes to 58.[24] Once this had been embodied in the 1926 Statutes, DDs were only awarded on the basis of published work. (Oxford, unlike Cambridge, retained the possibility of a dissertation until after the Second World War.) The Scottish Universities were also in the process of tightening the basis upon which they awarded DDs in the 1920s; essentially until this time, provided one had a basic theological qualification, DDs were given to those who were 'good chaps'.

The changes I have described in the first quarter of the twentieth century were obviously not just the result of the arrival of Westminster College in Cambridge, and in some respects substantial change only took place in the last quarter of the century. But there is no doubt that Westminster acted as a catalyst, not least because of the outstanding intellectual calibre of its Professors.

Oman and the Cambridge University Press

As I indicated at the beginning, before starting the research for this paper I had always supposed that the first book of Oman published by the Press was *Grace and Personality* in 1917. I was wrong. The first book published by the Press was one that is now almost forgotten, *The War and its Issues*, published in 1915. 130 pages long, its origin was a speech at Queens' College, but Oman expanded it 'through the impulse to think out my own relations to the present crisis'.[25] Although the precise way in which the Press came to publish it is obscure, it seems probable that a key link was the Rev'd C.T. Wood, Dean of Queens', who is noted in a manuscript list of periodicals to which the book was being sent for review.[26] It is also likely that it was Wood who invited Oman to speak at Queens' in the first place. The book was published by the Press on a profit-sharing basis, and the Syndics bought the rights to it from Oman on 1 January 1932.[27]

Even at that stage Oman was emphasising that 'we are face to face not merely with a new event but with a new age'.[28] Indeed, he had seen this within a month of war breaking out in August 1914, because in the last week of August 'Watchman' of the *British Weekly* remembered meeting Oman on the sand at Warkworth in Northumberland, when he said 'Chaos has come again!' and continued, 'I feel that never will you and I look upon a world recognisably

---

[24] *Reporter* 1924-25, 20 January 1925, p. 522; 10 February 1925, pp. 578-82.

[25] John Oman, *The War and its Issues* (Cambridge: Cambridge University Press, 1915), Preface.

[26] Letter of 3 March 1915, Cambridge University Press Archives, Pr A O.96.

[27] CUP to Few & Kester, 27 May 1939, CUP Archives Pr C/O.39-40, p. 2.

[28] Oman, *The War*, p. 5.

like anything we have known!'[29] In January 1915 Oman had been one of seventeen ministers – W.F Halliday, William Paton and John Skinner were three others – who signed a Statement in *The Presbyterian Messenger* setting out the reasons why they believed that the Church should 'refrain from official declarations which may be regarded as sanctioning war'.[30] The Church was called, in war as in peace, to bear witness to the truths of the Eternal Order – the binding claims of peace and goodwill between nations, the sacredness of human life and the horror of its wholesale destruction, love of enemies, forgiveness of injuries and national penitence for sinful ambitions and false standards, and particularly the Church's failure to impress Christian ideals on civilisation. But the last point drew attention to the need for what might today be called an 'exit strategy': in view of the task of healing and reconciliation which would be necessary at the end of the war, it was vital that the Churches 'should not be justly chargeable with having taken a merely national view of the situation'.

This point was echoed in Oman's book, when he remarked that the conspicuous failure in 'this death struggle of the nations' was 'the absence of true catholicism', which transcended national boundaries.

> The Salvation Army and the Student Movement, and, in some wider but less intense because less personal way, the Church of Rome, alone suffer. For the rest to maintain their catholicity in any sense, individual or corporate, is a pretence which can hardly to-day delude even ourselves. All our churches in consequence have become mere national churches…in the sense of having no interest or charity beyond the national call.[31]

In later chapters he developed his argument that once again (because he had outlined this argument before in *Vision and Authority* and the Kerr Lectures) the Church had succumbed to the temptation of becoming a state, using the methods of a state, and failing to distinguish itself from the state. Indeed he took particular pains to criticise the view of Richard Rothe that the goal of the church was to create 'a Christian state prepared to do the Church's work'. But, Oman argued, 'the state, even as perfectly moralised force, would still be neither wide enough, nor deep enough, nor high enough to embody the kingdom of God'. Whereas Rothe assumed that the progress of civilisation and the realisation of the kingdom of God were identical, the mutual succour of religion and civilisation was largely derived from their antagonism. The religious man had to be in the world yet not of it; 'to live as a stranger and a pilgrim and yet with the assurance that all things, the world as well as Cephas,

---

[29] *British Weekly*, 25 May 1939.
[30] *Presbyterian Messenger*, January 1915, p. 9.
[31] Oman, *The War*, p. 56.

things secular as well as sacred are his; ...to have...a joyous use of the present with a self-denying outlook upon the future'.[32]

These sentiments so offended the reviewer in *The Presbyterian Messenger* that he remarked that it was 'a statement which is so far from truth and charity that on all grounds of internal evidence it must be regarded as non-Omanic, having been inserted in the manuscript by a malicious brownie while the good professor slept'![33] It has indeed taken many Protestants a very long time to appreciate the fundamental ecclesiological deficiency of Protestantism, which much grand talk about the invisible Church can never completely dispel. Whilst the reviewer looked forward to another book about the War, which would 'in the strict sense be a theological book', this exchange illustrates that Oman's book on the War was not so untheological after all, and that it was in keeping with his earlier writing. In any case Oman was not outlining a pacifist position in the strict sense, but rather exploring some of the dilemmas posed by the War. Incidentally, it is not clear whether the original letter in the January 1915 issue of the *Messenger* was in any self-conscious sense a response to the so-called Declaration of the Intellectuals in Germany in support of the War that so offended Karl Barth. There is certainly no reference to it, and it is constructed very much as an internal Presbyterian document.[34]

Oman's second publications by the Press came a year later, with two lectures on 'Human Freedom' and 'War' in a collection of essays, edited by Professor Stanton. These were originally given as part of the Theological Lectures under the University Local Lectures' system. The theme for 1916 was the difficulties for Christian Theism raised by the spectacle of conflict and suffering in the world.[35] These two snappy lectures encapsulate much of the essential character of Oman. Both of them, but particularly that on 'Human Freedom', fasten on the mechanical nature of much scientific thinking – a criticism which has subsequently become commonplace in the critique of Enlightenment rationalism in recent years. So he could write that, 'A world built up of hard, elastic atoms, which evolve order out of chaos by impinging upon one another according to Newton's laws, satisfied minds much occupied with neat mechanical methods'. But he immediately went on to note that our

---

[32] Oman, *The War,* pp. 110-11, 114-5.

[33] *Presbyterian Messenger*, July 1915, p. 255.

[34] There is an interesting discussion of the different responses of Oman and Forsyth to the War, though with some over-simplification of Oman's view, in S.P. Mews, 'Neo-Orthodoxy, Liberalism and War: Karl Barth, P.T. Forsyth and John Oman 1914-18', in D. Baker (ed), *Renaissance and Renewal in Christian History* (Studies in Church History, 14), Oxford 1977, 361-75. More recently some have questioned whether the Declaration of the Intellectuals really had so much influence on Barth as he subsequently claimed.

[35] V.H. Stanton (ed), *The Elements of Pain and Conflict in Human Life, considered from a Christian Point of View* (Cambridge: Cambridge University Press, 1916), pp. 56-73, 157-72.

conception of the atom itself had changed very much in recent years (presumably an oblique reference to Einstein), suggesting that 'the new idea of the atom leaves measureless room for the possibilities of the universe'.[36] The lecture on 'Human Freedom' also reveals Oman's characteristic use of sailing metaphors. The question of freedom, he notes, only arises in relation to those issues which we have power to determine. Though they are a small section of life, they may have vast consequences, and he adds, 'we can accomplish nothing by trying to push round the ship, but we can bring her round by applying ourselves to the helm'.[37] The idea that people may be led but not forced was fundamental to Oman's thought. Oman was the only non-Anglican invited to contribute to this series, probably because of his University Lectureship, but it indicates the high regard in which he was held by the senior members of the Faculty of Divinity.

Grace and Personality, which was published in 1917, was more closely connected to the War than might at first sight be supposed. The origins go back to a series of articles in *The Expositor* in 1911-12, which was reworked in the light of the War. As Oman wrote in the Introduction, 'the work, as it now stands, is the effect of the War'. This had scattered his students, interrupted his historical and philosophical studies, and sent him 'into camps and hospitals, where fundamental religious questions were constantly being discussed, and forced upon me the reconsideration of my whole religious position'.[38] Perhaps in a sense it was the 'strictly theological book' that the *Presbyterian Messenger* reviewer had wanted. Before commenting on Oman's argument and its relationship to the rest of his work, it is interesting to reflect on some of the evidence from the Press archives about the book. Most striking is the fact that this book was published at Oman's expense, and although in the end it went through three editions, proved substantially profitable to him and was still selling a hundred a year in 1941, it caused him considerable anxiety early on.[39] There was a long discussion initially about the price and the number of copies, eventually fixed at 1,000 at 6/- each. Oman wrote in November 1917 that 'the ladies (*sc* Dr Lewis and Dr Gibson) seem to think that people are as likely to give the price of a pound and a half of butter for it as a pound and a quarter'. But he reflected wryly that this assumed an equal relish for theological literature, and 'there is no sign yet, of what is here seen every day for the humble substitute margarine, of the formation of a queue from the Senate

---

[36] Stanton, *Elements of Pain*, pp. 58, 63-5 (quotations on 64), also p. 165; Chapter 1 of Part III of *Grace and Personality* is entitled 'Mechanical Opposites'.

[37] Stanton, *Elements of Pain*, p. 61.

[38] John Oman, *Grace and Personality*, 3rd edn., (Cambridge: Cambridge University Press, 1925), p. v.

[39] CUP to Few & Kester, 27 May 1939, CUP to Ballard, 8 September 1941: Cambridge University Press archives, Pr C/O.39-40, pp. 2 & 11.

House to the Press to wait for it'.[40] In 1917 Oman had been in the Midlands –
as he described it, 'exercising somewhat episcopal functions', which he found
'a monstrous business of dull letters and troublesome people'. 'How anyone
who knows anything about it should imagine it the foundation of religion is
more a mystery to me than ever.'[41] By 2 February 1918, he had had a bill for
£80 for the production of the book, which he wondered whether he should pay
at once, or wait for the sales to come in. In May he wrote that he had a learned
friend who said every time he met him, 'I've read that book of yours again.
Biggest thing in theology since Ritschl's *Reconciliation*. But it won't sell.'
However, by the time a second edition of 1,000 was printed in 1919, he had a
credit balance of £51.6s.1d. A third edition was published in 1925, which was
distributed in the USA by Macmillan, New York; and a reprint of 2,000 copies
was made in 1930.[42] By this time Oman's publishing reputation was secure.

As with *Faith and Freedom*, Oman began *Grace and Personality* by
affirming the centrality of the Enlightenment rather than the Reformation. The
significance of this was that 'the dogmatic form itself began to crumble', to be
replaced by the historical method. All this suggested that God did not govern
his world 'by infallible direction and irresistible power'.[43] Oman therefore
suggested an understanding of God's grace, which accepted the autonomy of
each moral person, because doctrines of grace are doctrines of love rather than
power. For this reason I am rather hesitant about Stephen Bevans's use of the
term 'a God of omnipotent love' to describe Oman's position in his own book
on Oman's Doctrine of God, because it is very difficult to use 'omnipotent' as
an adjective in a sufficiently nuanced way to catch what Oman is trying to say.
The argument is not helped by a series of crucial quotations from Oman used
by Bevans, which work backwards chronologically from Oman's essay on
'Human Freedom' of 1916 via *Faith and Freedom* to *Vision and Authority*,
thereby ignoring, in my view, the significance which Oman attached to the War
in leading him to reconsider his whole religious position.[44] If Bevans's phrase is
understood in terms of Oman's definition of God in *Honest Religion* as 'the
final and absolute power', with the love of God which Jesus commends to us as
'nothing less that the absolute might', we are closer to the mark.[45] The
difficulty always is to conceive of power or omnipotence as anything other than
the ability to ensure that things turn out the way the omnipotent agent wills,
when we are not that agent and therefore do not know what is willed. But

---

[40] Oman to Waller, 4 November 1917, CUP Archives, Pr A O.96, 15i & ii.

[41] Oman to Waller, 1 October 1917, CUP Archives, Pr A O.96, 12ii.

[42] Oman to Waller, 2 February 1918, 21 May 1918, 8 February 1919, 8 July 1925,
25 October 1930, CUP Archives, Pr A O.96, pp. 17, 18, 19, 35b & 43.

[43] Oman, *Grace and Personality*, pp. 6, 8.

[44] Stephen Bevans, *John Oman and his Doctrine of God* (Cambridge: Cambridge
University Press, 1992), p. 91, nn. 56-74.

[45] Oman, *Honest Religion*, p. 95.

Oman was not rejecting the idea of the Kingdom of God, only what he took to be false understandings of it. The final two chapters of *Grace and Personality* are on 'The Rule of God' and 'Eternal Life'. The link between them may be illustrated by the following quotation:

> God's Rule cannot be the order of the world, without limit or suspension, like the law of gravitation, because it is of the nature of love to endure restriction and even rejection, seeing it has respect for persons with their responsibilities in the world they create for themselves, and cannot be content with any lower success than the acceptance of its order as blessedness and freedom. Yet it alone has might and dominion.[46]

Such an understanding of omnipotence, or ultimate power, is very different from the way most understand it; and the fact of eternal life is necessary to bring all things to their ultimate climax. Tim Healey wrote that 'P.T. Forsyth, while confined to bed with his last illness, was discovered reading *G[race and] Personality]*. To his astonished visitor Forsyth remarked: "This is a book which I should like to put into the hands of every theological student".'[47]

In 1921 the Press published a collection of Oman's sermons under the title, *The Paradox of the World*. This was also published at his own expense, but the sales were relatively small and Oman was out of pocket on the exercise. The same was true of his *Book of Revelation* in 1921 and *The Text of Revelation* in 1928.[48] What many have regarded as Oman's most significant book was *The Natural and the Supernatural*, which the Press published in 1931. Oman wrote to Sydney Roberts in May 1929, saying that he had a large book coming to completion. Two publishers had approached him, 'but I would like the Press to see it first'.[49] Obviously the readers' reports were favourable. Although there is no clear evidence, it seems probable that it was published by the Press at its own cost. By 1939 there were 111 copies in stock.[50]

The Natural and the Supernatural was certainly Oman's most ambitious book, offering in effect a theory of religion as such. His friend, F.R. Tennant, who wrote Oman's obituary for the British Academy, saw this book as a development of Schleiermacher's view in the *Speeches on Religion* that 'religion is an "original" element in human nature'. This line of thought was pursued 'with originality and adventurousness' in *The Natural and the Supernatural*, in which he argued that 'knowledge of a supernatural environment is not inferentially acquired but is of the nature of direct,

---

[46] Oman, *Grace and Personality*, pp. 296-7.
[47] F.G. Healey, *Religion and Reality: The Theology of John Oman* (Edinburgh: Oliver and Boyd, 1965), p. 156.
[48] CUP to Few & Kester, 27 May 1939, CUP Archives, Pr C/O.39-40, p. 2.
[49] Oman to Roberts, 4 May 1929, CUP Archives Pr A O.96, p. 38.
[50] CUP to Few & Kester, 27 May 1939, CUP Archives Pr C/O.39-40, p. 2.

unmediated, intuition'. Tennant goes on to remark that Oman's argument in support of this conviction 'is different in several respects from Schleiermacher's more cloudy advocacy of it; and it ventures farther in maintaining that religion is presupposed in all natural knowledge and is determinative of the progress of human culture'. The signs of first-hand observation, reflection and synthesis, which the book displayed, proved Oman (in Tennant's view) 'to be one of the most original, independent, and impressive theologians of his generation and of his country'.[51]

By concentrating on the books that Oman published with the University Press, I do not imply any adverse judgement on his earliest works – the translation and introduction to Schleiermacher's *Speeches on Religion* (Kegan Paul, Trench, Trübner & Co, London 1893), *Vision and Authority* (Hodder & Stoughton, London 1902), *The Problem of Faith and Freedom in the Last Two Centuries* (Hodder & Stoughton, London 1906), and *The Church and the Divine Order* (Hodder & Stoughton, London 1911). *Vision and Authority*, for example, is often regarded as a crucial work, though in some ways the Introduction to Schleiermacher's *Speeches*, more often skipped over than read, is the signpost for Oman's ambiguous relationship with the great Pietist theologian. What, however, that list makes clear is the significance of Oman's shift to Cambridge University Press. Quite apart from the argument that *Grace and Personality* and *The Natural and the Supernatiural* are Oman's greatest books, it demonstrates the extent to which Oman had become a part of the University. One of the things which surprised me in the research for this paper, was the discovery that several of those books were published at his own expense. True, it was wartime, but Oman could have published elsewhere, had he chosen to do so. He obviously wanted to be published by the Press; and that to me shows a significant consequence of Westminster's move to Cambridge.

The requirements of a theological course

I turn finally to my third heading, What is needed in the study of Theology? I have demonstrated how Westminster became part of the University of Cambridge in effect, if not constitutionally; I have discussed how its teachers became involved in the work of the Faculty – Oman's book on *Revelation*, for example, was a result of his attendance at Professor Burkitt's seminar, when the Apocalypse was discussed, to his mind unsatisfactorily.[52] But there was never any question of adapting Westminster's theological syllabus because of the move to Cambridge, apart from taking advantage of the possibility of attending certain lectures in the Faculty. The Theological Tripos had never been designed as a theological training for the ministry. Instituted in 1870, it was still regarded

---

[51] F.R. Tennant, 'John Wood Oman', *Proceedings of the British Academy* 1939 (London: Humphrey Milford, 1939), pp. 334-5.
[52] *Proceedings of the British Academy*, 1939, pp. 337-8.

thirty years' later as an inferior route to ordination than that provided by the Classical Tripos, though useful for weaker men. More particularly, its weakness was perceived to be that it provided no obvious teaching in the principles of the Church of England.[53] Yet for a Presbyterian its weakness was that it provided no teaching in Systematic Theology – the Tripos papers, which most closely corresponded to those for a century after its introduction were those in 'Christian Life and Thought' in various periods, from the early Church to the more recent past, which was until the Second World War the eighteenth century. The basic pattern of the Westminster syllabus did not change in any way with the move from Queen Square, and was based on the traditional division of Theology into Biblical, Systematic and Pastoral: Apologetics tended to float around from time to time, and from 1907 there were distinct chairs in Old and New Testament.

But even this pattern was not regarded as sacrosanct. The First World War disrupted the operation of Westminster, and training was moved to Birmingham in 1916 after the introduction of conscription, with the Professors also helping congregations whose ministers were serving at the Front. The Synod of 1918 appointed a Special Committee, without executive power, 'to consider the whole situation in, and of, the Church', inviting it to examine with courage, and 'such insight and foresight as God will give it in answer to prayer' to examine measures which will better equip the Church to play its part in winning England for Christ at the conclusion of the War.[54] This Committee was to include representatives from all the main Committees of the Church. As a result of this the Convener of the College Committee, the Rev'd R.C. Gillie, made his own suggestions about a revision of the Westminster curriculum, to which the Professors were invited to respond. No copy of those original suggestions seems to survive, but their contents can be inferred from the comments of both John Skinner (Old Testament) and John Oman (Systematic and Philosophical Theology); Anderson Scott's response does not survive.

The Organisation Sub-Committee was primarily concerned with the structures and operation of the Church nationally, but it did also urge that ministers pay special attention to the instruction of young people, both by teaching them the fundamental truths of Christianity and by preparing them for service in various aspects of church work – teaching, social service, public prayer and the conduct of religious meetings. This last point was regarded as so important that ministers should concentrate on such duties alongside preaching and pastoral visitation. They were especially to take the lead in teaching Training Classes and in the organisation and conduct of graded lesson schemes in Sunday Schools. The Sub-Committee recognised that such an emphasis would require congregations to excuse the minister 'from attending to many of

---

[53] 'Religion in Cambridge', *Church Quarterly Review*, lix, 117 (October 1904), pp. 1-28.

[54] *Minutes of the Synod of the Presbyterian Church of England*, 1918, p. 853.

those minor functions which at present absorb so much of his time'.[55] It is clear from what eventually happened that there were particular concerns about education in teaching methods, specific training in preaching, and a knowledge of the social context of the Church's work.

Skinner was, of course, Principal of Westminster at the time and he published his observations in a pamphlet for private circulation. Oman's comments survive in a cyclostyled version. Although expressed in characteristically different ways, the comments of the two men were very similar. Skinner identified the key issue as being two distinct conceptions of education: one, which he called the liberal ideal aiming at the development of personality; the other aiming at practical efficiency. He indicated his scepticism about the latter ideal immediately, and also dismissed the view of theological education 'as a dry-as-dust imparting and assimilating mere information for its own sake' as mistaken. The aim rather was 'to stimulate thought, to inspire imagination, to quicken susceptibility, and to enlarge experience, through contemplation of the Christian religion as it has manifested itself in the life and thought of the world'.[56] If it were argued that this view represented an unrealised ideal, the remedy was to reconsider the methods of effecting it, not to substitute a lower and easier aim. Oman summed up the same issue by saying that in his time of teaching he had become aware of the enormous difference between knowing a subject and knowing about it. More dramatically he said that the central question was, 'Do we propose to put shots in men's lockers for every occasion that may arise or to teach them how to make their own munitions?' He admitted that he had not heard of the returns from church members, but remarked that 'to go round to your people and say, What kind of a minister would you have us produce for you, is sheer spiritual insolvency'.[57]

Skinner identified two faults in the proposed alternative. It was suggested that the College should provide only the 'theory' directly related to ministerial work by omitting 'the theoretical portions which will be less serviceable'. But it was a mistake 'to speak of theology as the theory of ministerial activity'; and it was 'wrong to suppose that administrative ability, homiletical proficiency, the arts of clear exposition and address' were the be-all and end-all of ministerial education; and he doubted whether preachers with an urgency of message could be produced by training at all, especially if that were made a direct aim.[58] Skinner then turned to what he regarded as the nub of the problem: the view of many that the study of Hebrew and Greek occupied a disproportionate amount

---

[55] 'Moderator's Committee: Report of Organisation Sub-Committee', n.d., especially 5; Westminster College Archives, WT1/16.
[56] J. Skinner, *Some Observations on Theological Education*, Westminster College, 1918, pp. 4-5.
[57] Sub-Committee on Ministry; Memorandum by Rev Professor John Oman, Westminster College Archives, WT1/16, p. 2.
[58] Skinner, *Observations*, pp. 7-9.

of time in the present curriculum. The real question, however, was whether it was worth teaching them at all. The proposal before the Board of Studies to reduce the time allotted by half was, in effect, an attack on Hebrew. Unsurprisingly for an Old Testament scholar he defended Hebrew vigorously not only on the ground of the ability to understand the original, but also because he felt the difficulty was exaggerated and there was no guarantee that more would be accomplished in other subjects – 'even in matters like Church History and dogmatic Theology, it is no good preparation to accustom students to think they can dispense with the study of original documents'.[59] Oman also touched on the relevance of Hebrew, Greek and Church History. On Hebrew particularly, he noted that the usual question was, what time was spent on it, whereas the important question is, how is it studied? 'Is it as a linguistic exercise or as the sole key to the mind which lies behind not only the Old Testament but the New?'[60]

Skinner argued that the ministry was an arduous profession, and its test was not the first appearance in a pulpit but staying power over many years. If a low standard were set, a low average would result, which was hardly likely to appeal to those 'accustomed to the keen stimulus of a University atmosphere'. One course would maintain the respectable level of ministerial education, which had been 'the chief contribution of Presbyterianism to the religious life of England'; the other would forfeit a position of influence and 'fall into the rear where once we led in the van'.[61] Oman also noted the value of the University context of Westminster's work. He noted the danger of 'becoming a mere Seminary'. 'Sometimes the whole College lives very keenly in the great current of this very cosmopolitan place.' Then those who are the source of that leave and an isolation sets in; but there was nothing the Committee could do about that.[62]

Oman's memorandum, which was on the whole pithier and more trenchant, also explained his approach to Apologetics. He spent two terms out of six on this, both to meet difficulties in the students' own minds and to equip them to meet current difficulties about belief. The books he set were Bishop Butler, Rudolf Otto and James Ward. He added his experience in France (with the YMCA) which had shown him the enormous gain given 'by our type of training in dealing with ordinary people and their religious difficulties', and this was likely to be even more important with the growth of education and greater social equality in England. His experience in the previous two years had made him even more familiar with the difficulty of Presbyterian work in England, and he asked several pertinent questions: why did ministers who left us usually have rapid and even marked success in the other Churches to which they go,

[59] Skinner, *Observations,* pp. 9-12.
[60] Memorandum by Oman, Westminster College Archives, WT1/16, pp. 1-2.
[61] Skinner, *Observations*, pp. 12-14.
[62] Memorandum by Oman, pp. 3-4.

whereas those who come to us, without Presbyterian training, only rarely escape disaster? 'Why is it that in Birmingham, away from Presbyterian Churches, I could always get an audience, while I doubt if five people ever came to hear me in ours, and, if they did, they would likely be ministers?' 'Why are there so many large Churches where a call to the ministry has never been heard of?'[63]

Oman also tackled the questions of choice in the syllabus and practical training. He had been told several years before of the large number of options and practical subjects in the American theological colleges, and at the time had a completely open mind; but the almost unanimous opinion now coming back, even from those who had introduced it was that it had had disastrous results. On practical training he made several suggestions: a year's training of the kind they had in Birmingham during the war – 'the experience of trying to revive struggling causes, on their own, with someone to beard the lions occasionally, enabled men far better to cut their wisdom teeth than assistantships in large and prosperous churches'; regular contact with work such as that formerly undertaken at Kentish Town, which he thought more instructive to the students 'than pottering away on their own at a mission'; and a regular relay of visiting ministers from all over the Church. 'I often dream,' he said, 'that we might make the college a Mecca to overcome the isolation mere space imposes on us; for the real failure is not what the college fails to do for men, but that there are few helps to keep it going afterwards.'[64]

Oman left his depth charge until last. He admitted that he did not know much about training in methods of education, except how difficult it was; but he feared the development of rules which made the system mechanical; and he concluded, 'none of these things will reform the Sunday School for which we need a new ideal from start to finish'.[65]

Skinner and Oman did not prevent the College Committee from going ahead with their proposed changes. The Moderator's Committee Report for 1920 contained proposals, which acknowledged the valuable memoranda submitted by the Professors, resisted the request to offer a general statement reviewing the whole system of theological education, and confined itself to practical suggestions, which the Committee felt would result in increased efficiency. The only concession that was made on language teaching was the suggestion that if the Senatus judged a student not to profit by linguistic study, they should make alternative arrangements for adequate instruction in the religion of the Old and New Testaments.[66] The Synod of 1920 instructed the College Committee, in consultation with the Senatus, 'to arrange for the instruction of the students in the Principles and Practice of Teaching and in Social Science, also carefully to

---

[63] Memorandum by Oman, pp. 2-3.

[64] Memorandum by Oman, p. 3.

[65] Memorandum by Oman, p. 4.

[66] *Reports to the Synod of the Presbyterian Church of England*, 1920, pp. 565-8.

consider the important subject of training in the Art of Preaching, and to report to next Synod what has been done in those respects'.[67] Accordingly the College Committee Report of 1921 indicated that the Senatus had proposed the engagement of Dr John Adams to give a course of lectures on the Principles and Practice of Teaching; arrangements should be made for students to attend lectures in Sociological Study at the University. Vacation Courses were to be arranged at the College in June; and the custom was revived of having Westminster Preachers visit the College for long week-ends to be in close contact with the students.[68] And there the matter rested, though I find it interesting how little the questions have changed in the last ninety years. It may or may not be a coincidence that the same College Committee Report indicated that Dr John Skinner wished to resign as Principal 'on the ground of advancing age'. The Synod delayed making a new appointment to the Principalship until 1922, when Oman was elected.

These events give an added interest to Oman's Inaugural Lecture, when he was appointed Principal of Westminster in 1922, entitled 'Method in Theology'. Some of the same themes emerge as in his Memorandum of 1918. The study of theology is a duty of honesty, because the only ground for speaking about religion is that one knows what one says to be true. Furthermore the real business of a theological college is done, if those leaving it know how to seek truth for themselves. Finally, open-minded enquiry is essential. 'Theology is bankrupt the moment there is any suspicion that it seeks something else than truth.' Oman suggested that the greatest hindrance to religious appeal at the present time was 'the idea that religious people are more concerned about what is correct than about what is true, and that the ecclesiastical leaders, in particular, are more concerned about unanimity than veracity'.[69] He went on to refer to the impression that the Robertson Smith case[70] had made upon him as a student (which he later discussed at greater length in the Preface to the second edition of *Vision and Authority* in 1928). Oman had read Robertson Smith's speeches and heard him on one occasion; he found in him 'the same kind of knowledge as was making the world a place for me of incessant discovery and the same passion for reality as seemed at the moment life's supreme concern'. But his trouble was 'not in the least that the judges were not critics and philosophers, even though all my interest at the time was in history and thought, but that, as I then understood the business, they were so far from being seekers after truth, that, as we said, they would not have recognised it if they had met it in their porridge'.[71] He referred again to his

---

[67] *Minutes of the Synod of the Presbyterian Church of England*, 1920, p. 402.

[68] *Reports to the Synod of the Presbyterian Church of England*, 1921, p. 833.

[69] John Oman, 'Method in Theology', *The Expositor*, eighth series, xxvi (1923), p. 82.

[70] See chapter 2 for a full discussion of this case.

[71] Oman, 'Method in Theology', p. 83.

wartime experience:

> Everyone who spoke to working men, especially the skilled mechanics, during the war, discovered that they were very little troubled by our divisions, but that they constantly thought that, in spite of our divisions, we were all a kind of trade-union to impose upon mankind merely traditional beliefs, and that the ordinary Christian was largely a Pharisee, concerned mainly with respectabilities and negative moralities.[72]

How could this problem be overcome? Oman looked for personal faith – a God 'credible only on clerical guarantees' was distressing as well as worthless. History was of supreme importance for interpreting any purpose there may be in the word, but it was history as prophecy and not merely as facts. Philosophy was, as it were, the grammar of experience. 'Religion alone reaches out to what eye hath not seen and ear not heard, as it were to life's poetry and prophecy.'[73] Religion was concerned with history, not to live in the past, but because the past was the chief means for reaching out to the future. 'Yet, unlike science, it is not the uniformities of the past that interest it, but the new, the exceptional, the experience above our own.'[74] Physical science 'leaves out everything except the uniformities which we may hope to meet again, whereas a true theology leaves out nothing of the concrete varied world that is within the grasp of our finite minds, in the hope of seeing the things unseen manifested in the things which do appear.'[75]

In that lecture – and I have no idea what impression it made on the minds of his audience – one sees Oman in transition from some of the themes which had preoccupied him in his earlier writings, to the concerns of *The Natural and the Supernatural*. As a historian I find that it chimes very much with my own experience, which is why I have always been attracted by his writing. It shows, as his 1918 Memorandum did, the significance of the effect which the War had had upon him, both in France and in the West Midlands. What it also shows, I think, is the significance of the wider sea in Cambridge, which he was now navigating. As well as the traditional themes of philosophy and theology, in the ancient world as well as the modern, the rapid development of modern physics in the Cambridge of the 1920s created a context in which large ideas could be envisaged. In understanding any writer it is important to grasp the context: this is one reason why I am suspicious of post-modernism. Notwithstanding Oman's Orkney origins and his Scottish training, the context for all his writings was England, and for his mature works it was the University of Cambridge. He was a respected figure in the Faculty; this was why he was eventually elected as

---

[72] Oman, 'Method in Theology', pp. 84-5.
[73] Oman, 'Method in Theology', p. 91.
[74] Oman, 'Method in Theology', p. 92.
[75] Oman, 'Method in Theology', p. 93.

a Fellow of the British Academy. To see Oman in context, particularly the context of the 1920s, which was the time of his greatest influence on students and contemporaries, brings out most clearly the significance of Oman and the University of Cambridge.

CHAPTER 4

Oman and Scottish Philosophical Traditions

Eric McKimmon

Introduction

A characteristic of John Oman's work is that it is free-standing. He gives a
vision rather than a map with co-ordinates. In *The Natural and the
Supernatural*, he explains the reasons for this approach. It is not that he 'wants
undue credit for originality by ignoring his intellectual ancestors'.[1] It is, rather,
that he thinks the proper place for names and sources is a text-book. He even
recommends one, George Galloway's *The Philosophy of Religion*[2], where 'a
long list of authorities is given with learning and discrimination'.[3] The reader of
Oman, in consequence, has to do homework to establish the text beneath the
text, to see what sources contributed to his thinking. This essay will examine
the contributions to Oman's thinking of two prominent streams in Scottish
philosophy: Realism and Personal Idealism.

Realism shaped the philosophical environment in which Oman began his
studies in Edinburgh in 1877. Scottish Realism, or the Common Sense school,
originated with the work of Thomas Reid.[4] It was both a reply to the skepticism
of David Hume and a critical questioning of the ideal theory of reality.
Thinkers in the tradition of Locke and Berkeley posited that the immediate
objects of knowledge are ideas in the mind. Indeed, the existence of anything
outside the mind, or indeed the mind itself, is not subject to proof. Reid called
this assumption into question and argued for the real existence of mind and
matter, as well as a real relation between the powers of the mind and an
objective order. This philosophy, sometimes called natural realism, or simply
dualism, was predominant in Scottish universities into the late nineteenth

---

[1] John Oman, *The Natural and the Supernatural* (Cambridge: Cambridge
University Press, 1931), Preface.

[2] George Galloway, *The Philosophy of Religion* (Edinburgh: T&T Clark, 1914).

[3] Galloway, *Religion.*

[4] There is an extensive commentary available on Reid's philosophy. Ronald E.
Beanblossom provides text and discussion in *Thomas Reid's Inquiry and Essays*
(Indianapolis: Hacket Publishing Co., 1983).

century.[5] Oman's teachers, Henry Calderwood in Moral Philosophy and Alexander Campbell Fraser in Metaphysics, were amongst the last representatives of the realist tradition. Another philosopher in the Scottish School was John Veitch, in Glasgow. They were all pupils of Sir William Hamilton, who taught in Edinburgh from 1836 until 1856. As we shall see, realism was not a static tradition, indeed Hamilton sought to find an accommodation with Kantian idealism.[6] However, for a young undergraduate from Orkney, Realism was the first port of call on a great academic adventure. Oman arrived aged seventeen, a mere 'raw lad from the ends of the earth, with little equipment except a vast responsiveness to the intellectual environment'[7]. What were the lasting influences of this intellectual awakening?

Whereas Scottish Realism may be characterized as an antecedent influence: it was the old, established, philosophical tradition in Edinburgh: waiting, as it were, to be discovered. Personal Idealism was relatively a more recent phenomenon: taking shape late in the nineteenth century and coming to maturity in the early twentieth. Personal Idealism emerged as a critique of Absolute Idealism. Finding its orientation in the philosophy of Hegel, Absolute Idealists regarded Mind, or Spirit, to be constitutive of reality. History is an unfolding of Eternal Consciousness and human reason is a mirror of Universal Reason.[8] Personal Idealists didn't quarrel with the finality of Mind. However, they feared that the significance of the individual would be lost in a monist philosophy of the Absolute; and, consequently, they were insistent on a substantive place for personality in their philosophy of being and existence. As we shall see, another of Oman's teachers, Andrew Seth Pringle Pattison, more than any other in Scotland, gave Personal Idealism its shape, writing some of its seminal texts.[9] Our interest will be to compare and contrast the Personalism of Oman with that of Personal Idealism that was current at the end of the 1st World War.

---

[5] A succinct summary of main tenets of Scottish realism is found in W.R Sorley, *A History of English Philosophy* (Cambridge: Cambridge University Press, 1920), pp. 204-210.

[6] John Veitch, *Sir William Hamilton: the man and his philosophy* (Edinburgh and London: William Blackwood & Sons, 1883).

[7] F.G. Healey, *Religion and Reality* (Edinburgh and London: Oliver & Boyd, 1965), p. 9.

[8] F.H. Bradley, T.H. Green and Bernhard Bosanquet represented the high point of Absolute Idealism in Britain in the nineteenth century. A sympathetic and comprehensive study of these thinkers, and others, is found in T.L.S. Sprigge, *The God of Metaphysics* (Oxford: Oxford University Press, 2006).

[9] For example: Andrew Seth, *Hegelianism and Personality* (Edinburgh and London: William Blackwood & sons, 1887); Andrew Seth Pringle Pattison, *The Idea of God in Recent Philosophy* (Aberdeen: Aberdeen University Press, 1920 [1917]).

Scottish Realists: Calderwood, Fraser and Veitch

Henry Calderwood

We begin our investigation with Henry Calderwood,[10] born in Peebles in 1830 and Professor of Moral Philosophy from 1866 until his death in 1896. Oman's friendship with Calderwood extended beyond his student days; and he paid tribute to Calderwood in the latter's biography.[11] Both were ministers in the United Presbyterian Church. However, it is with respect to Oman's thinking on personality, and what it means to be a person, that we are able to observe the proximity of their thought. In *Grace and Personality*, Oman defines personality in fundamentally moral terms: a moral person is 'self-determined, according to his own self-direction, in the world of his own self-consciousness'.[12] There is a mantra like quality about this definition: self-determined, according to our own self-direction, in our own world of self-consciousness. Where does it come from? It is when we turn to Calderwood's *Hand-book of Moral Philosophy* that we find Oman's source. Calderwood's *Hand-book* was first published in 1872; it had run to its sixteenth edition and 14,000 copies by 1888. It was a text-book for students of philosophy and widely used as such. Calderwood's definition of personality reads: 'Man is self-conscious, intelligent, self-determining power – a Person, not merely living Organism, not a mere Thing, Personality involves self-conscious being, self-regulated intelligence and self-determined activity.'[13]

Here is a definition of personhood essentially the same as Oman's concept of personality. It is grounded in self-consciousness, shaped by self-directed intelligence and expressed in self-determined activity. In Calderwood's subsequent digressions there is a rejection of deterministic theories of personality, whether naturalistic or Hegelian. Positively, there is a Kantian affirmation of the centrality of will and of the unity of personality. In a person, will, intellect and consciousness cannot be compartmentalized. He writes: "Intellect is knowing power. Will is controlling power. These two are so related that the one presupposes the other. The phenomenon of intelligence and the direction of intelligent activity are in constant relation."[14]

Likewise with Oman, when he moves from self-determination to self-direction, he cautions that 'this is only another aspect of the same activity, and not a new attribute'.[15]

In Oman's writing, however, the concept of personality does not remain

---

[10] For Henry Calderwood, see also chapter 1.

[11] W.L.C. Calderwood and Rev. David Woodside, *The Life of Henry Calderwood* (London: Hodder & Stoughton, 1900), pp. 390-394.

[12] John Oman, *Grace and Personality* (Cambridge: Cambridge University Press, 1925 [1917]), p. 44.

[13] Henry Calderwood, *Hand-Book of Moral Philosophy,* (London: Macmillan, 1891 [1874]), p. 26.

[14] Calderwood, *Hand-Book*, p. 177.

[15] Oman, *Grace and Personality*, p. 51.

static. In that respect, we have a contrast with Calderwood. For Calderwood, principles of morality are intuitive and self-evident; conscience can only err in application, but not in principle; and, Kant's categorical imperative has the force of universal law. With Oman, however, by the time he writes *The Natural and the Supernatural*, his concept of person is set in an evolutionary paradigm. Accordingly, he argues for a morality that is inspirational, ever reaching out to new insight, ever climbing new heights. Human beings develop in moral awareness and, therefore, the person can transcend the moral maxims characteristic of older intuitionalism. Oman writes: 'By what a man is he perceives what he should be…we thus, as it were, rise up on the stepping stones of our dead selves to higher things.'[16]

Accordingly, conscience though sacred, may err, and needs continual education; furthermore, the categorical imperative is inadequate to meet 'the clamour of appetite and desire'. The categorical imperative 'could only rule them if they are well chilled already'.[17] Thus, the moral person is not free, but is being made free, through living in a higher environment. 'We cannot be strong to do anything without a wide atmosphere to breathe in….'[18] This is the atmosphere of the supernatural, or, in terms of Oman's earlier work, the atmosphere of grace.

In *Grace and Personality*, Oman's great imaginative contribution was to hold together the autonomy necessary for the moral aspect of personality and the dependence on Divine aid that is characteristic of religious personality. The language of self – self-determination, self-direction, self-consciousness – finds redemption in a dialogue of grace. Grace, for Oman, is essentially a relational, nurturing experience. It is an I-Thou relationship that aids personality to make a journey of self-realization, under God or, more particularly, with God.

Interestingly, Calderwood, in a short chapter on 'Morality and its relation to Religion,' affirms that the moral life is also the blessed life.

> The religious life and the moral life are thus essentially one, for we yield true homage to the author of our being when we use our whole nature aright, realising moral law in action, as having been vitalised in personal character.[19]

So, whilst writing from the older intuitive perspective, Calderwood, too, believed that moral maxims and religion combine in personality. As we have seen, the view that the religious life and a moral life are essentially one – and vitalized in personal character – is a good description of how Oman understood the outcome of grace in the human sphere.

---

[16] *Morals*, an unpublished essay in Oman Papers, WT1/12-14, Westminster College, Cambridge.

[17] Oman, *Natural and Supernatural*, p. 303.

[18] Oman, *Natural and Supernatural*, p. 304.

[19] Calderwood, *Hand-Book*, p. 317.

Alexander Campbell Fraser

We turn to the second of Oman's teachers, Alexander Campbell Fraser. He was the father of Scottish philosophy in Edinburgh at the turn of the nineteenth century. Born in 1818, Fraser's life spanned that of four monarchs. He saw Queen Victoria come and go; he knew an old woman in his native Argyll who had been an eye witness to events at Culloden. He died in 1914, in the reign of George V. Fraser was born a son of the manse and his father came out at the Disruption. There was predictability in his going to New College; as, he hoped to fulfil a call to the Free Church ministry. However, his destiny was to be in the field of philosophy. His life was not without stress. So troubled was his mind as a student that he was 'environed in deepest darkness, and utterly deprived of the use of every faculty'.[20] He found solace in Descartes and rested in the principle of moderation. Of opinions, he wrote, 'the most moderate are probably the best, since extremes are commonly erroneous'.[21]

Fraser describes the most significant encounter of his life as being with Sir William Hamilton. He writes: 'I owe more to Hamilton than to any other influence.'[22] The Edinburgh Town Council, who were the benefactors of the Chair of Philosophy, did not permit Hamilton to teach a 'useless' subject like Metaphysics. And so, Fraser was part of a select group that attended a metaphysics class at Hamilton's home in the evening. It must have been a stimulating time. Fraser, however, was not a blind follower of Hamilton and went on to edit Locke's *Essay,* as well Berkeley's works. These studies moved his thinking in the direction of a type of Personal Idealism, or what he preferred to call 'Spiritual Realism'. However, it was in his Gifford Lectures of 1894-96, published as *Philosophy of Theism,* that he gave an apologia for theistic faith.

In the themes Fraser lays out in his Gifford lectures, we find a perspective that carries through to Oman. Take, for example, the terms 'Natural' and 'Supernatural': Fraser uses these to describe reality in its two-fold aspect of material and spiritual.

> The complex order of nature is God speaking to us. The elaborate web, weaved according to laws of natural connection, is a means to an end of its being a revelation to us of each other and of God. Living in and through his order, we are living in and through his active providence; in a process that may be without beginning, and may persist without end – at once natural and supernatural – outward nature significant of super-nature with which it is animated.[23]

---

[20] Alexander Campbell Fraser, *Biographia Philosophica* (Edinburgh and London: William Blackwood & Sons, 1905), p. 52.

[21] Fraser, *Biographia*, p. 58.

[22] Fraser, *Biographia.*

[23] Alexander Campbell Fraser, *Philosophy of Theism,* second edition (Edinburgh and London: William Blackwood and Sons, 1899), p. 131.

Like Oman, Fraser held that the natural world and the supernatural could not be understood apart from each other. Both appealed to Berkeley, who posited that the physical world is a system of signs that mediate the transcendent. Much later, Oman would write:

> Berkeley has not been wrong in thinking, as one of his critics expressed it, that sense experience has the intelligibility of language whose conventions are one and all determined by a spirit akin to our own; and his argument against matter without meaning is valid to this day.[24]

It is in this last point – namely, that reality is fundamentally personal and meaningful – that Fraser's perspective was anticipatory of Oman's. Fraser uses a striking phrase: the Creator is 'on speaking terms with humanity'. Speaking is the operative word. Consciousness is not, as with neo-Hegelianism, a mere unfolding of cosmic reason. God can speak through the created order because, argues Fraser, that order is both natural and supernatural and virtually personal. It is because our human experience is personal that we can ascribe the attributes of personality to God. Our deepest relationship to one another is ethical trust; and, our relationship to the universe is one where we trust its laws and rationality. So, asks Fraser:

> does this not mean that the universe is virtually personal, for us a revelation of a person rather than a Thing?....this practically means that our deepest relation to reality is ethical not physical: that *personality* rather than *thingness* is the highest form under which *man* can perceive God. This is the final moral personification, or religious conception, of the universe of experience.[25]

As well as reality being personal, the universe was also for both writers essentially spiritual. In *The Natural and the Supernatural* Oman could write of atoms: 'for aught that it [physics] can show, they may think'.[26] And mind, Oman argued, may reasonably be taken as the presupposition of evolutionary processes, rather than the end result. 'The mind by which we know everything, science included,' is 'first in principle'.[27] This view of reality resonates with Fraser's phrase: 'conscious life is the light of the world'.[28] For Fraser, matter, apart from perception, is an unrealizable abstraction. 'The sciences themselves – physical, chemical and biological – exist only in and through the conscious activity of a person; so that it is through spiritual life and agency that existence

---

[24] Oman, *Natural and Supernatural,* p. 170.
[25] Fraser, *Theism,* p. 251.
[26] Oman, *Natural and Supernatural,* p. 245.
[27] Oman, *Natural and Supernatural,* p. 264.
[28] Fraser, *Theism,* p. 141.

is realised in sensation or in science.'[29]

In this Subjective Idealism, or 'Spiritual Realism',[30] we have a shared perspective. In their distinction between the natural and the supernatural, in their emphasis on the personal nature of reality and in the centrality of mind in their metaphysics, Fraser and Oman may be termed kindred spirits.

John Veitch

For our third Scottish realist, we make the journey west to the University of Glasgow where John Veitch was Professor of Logic and Rhetoric from 1864 until his death in 1894. John Veitch was a school friend of Henry Calderwood in Peebles. They came to Edinburgh as undergraduates. Veitch was the son of a Free Church mother and a Church of Scotland father. His father had been in the Napoleonic wars. He wore a medal on Sundays to Church, but only to the Established Church. When he had occasion to go to the Free Kirk with his wife, discretion was the greater part of valor: he left the medal at home!

John Veitch was also intending to fulfil a calling to the ministry. But he too opted for a career as a philosopher. Unlike Fraser, he was a realist of what we may call the 'unreconstructed' kind – a stout defender of Hamilton and an unyielding opponent of Hegelian influences in Scotland.

Our interest in Veitch, however, arises from his reflections on poetry and on transcendence. He was a poet himself.[31] Veitch was especially inspired by border landscapes and collected the ballads of the Borders' poets. He considered poetic awareness as a bridge from the natural world to the transcendent. In his own words: 'the poetry of Wordsworth is the natural compliment to the realism of Hamilton.'[32]

Oman, too, had an interest in the epistemological significance of poetry. Readers of Oman find digressions on poetry in the section 'Knowledge and Knowing' in *The Natural and the Supernatural.*[33] There Oman asks the question: to whom shall we turn to find widest knowledge and the deepest meaning: to the scientist, or the philosopher, or to the poet and to the child?

> We shall, therefore, not betake ourselves to the scientist and the philosopher as authorities on what is known by awareness and apprehension, because they are precisely those persons whose eyes are in the back of their heads, looking for understandings and explanations, and

[29] Fraser, *Theism*, p. 141.

[30] Alexander Campbell Fraser, *Berkeley and Spiritual Realism* (London: Thomas Constable & Co., 1908).

[31] John Veitch, *Merlin and other poems* (Edinburgh and London: William Blackwood and Sons, 1889).

[32] John Veitch, *Sir William Hamilton: The Man and his Philosophy* (Edinburgh and London: William Blackwood and Sons, 1883), p. 49.

[33] Oman, *Natural and Supernatural*, pp. 120-143.

who, even when they do look at their environment are most in danger of only seeing it with the their judgements and theories, but to the poet and the child whose gifts are for perceiving not for explaining.[34]

Oman was writing some thirty years after Veitch; nevertheless, there is shared appreciation of the place of poetry in the field of knowledge. Both believed that the natural world yields levels of meaning that are not accessible to discursive thinking. The quotation above is indicative of how Oman was the more polemical, setting the cognitive value of poetry above the conceptualities of science. Veitch, more accommodatingly, stressed the complementary nature of the rational and the intuitive. 'Science,' he writes, 'observes and interprets in its own way, so does poetry'. [35]

The 'holy' is another area that makes for interesting comparison between Oman and Veitch. Oman ascribes his understanding of the holy to his reading of an essay by Wilhelm Windelband, *Das Heilige*, published in 1902.[36] For Windelband, experience of the holy is not a specialized aspect of awareness, nor the sphere of the irrational, but the ground of '*Normalbewusstsein*:'[37] normal consciousness of truth, goodness and beauty. Oman is particularly strong on this emphasis on the normality of the holy; it was the basis of his criticism of Rudolf Otto.[38]

Veitch does not speak of experience of 'the holy' *per se*. However, in his descriptions of how human beings experience transcendence, he touches on similar issues. Veitch believed that experience of transcendence is realized 'by most reflective minds,'[39] though the poet experiences it at its 'highest reach'.[40] In a collection of essays, published in 1895, under the title *Dualism and Monism*,[41] he reflects on how the mind can 'be equally open to the world of sense – the finite, and to the sphere of the infinite that borders and surrounds

---

[34] Oman, *Natural and Supernatural*, p. 125.

[35] Veitch, *Hamilton*, p. 49.

[36] Wilhelm Windelband, *Präludien* Vol, 2, (Tübingen: J.C.B. Mohr [Paul Siebeck]1919 [1902]).

[37] Windelband, *Präludien*, p. 304. (*Das heilige ist also das Normalbewusstsein des Wahren, Guten und Schönen, erlebt als transzendente Wirklichkeit*.) The original is in Gothic script.

[38] John Oman, Review of 'The Idea of the Holy', *The Journal of Theological Studies*, 25 (April 1924). Oman, *Natural and Supernatural*, Appendix A. For a critical perspective on the debate between Oman and Otto, see John Macquarrie, *Twentieth Century Religious Thought* (London: SCM, 1998), p. 72. A more recent discussion of Oman's understanding of the holy is found in Adam Hood's comparative study of John Baillie, John Oman and John Macmurray: Adam Hood, *Baillie, Oman and Macmurray: Experience and Religious Belief* (Hants, England; Ashgate Publishing Ltd.).

[39] John Veitch, *Dualism and Monism* (Edinburgh and London: William Blackwood and Sons, 1895), p. 175.

[40] Veitch, *Dualism*.

[41] Veitch, *Dualism*, pp. 175-221. 'The Theism of Wordsworth'

this world of ours'.[42] The resulting experience is one of awe and reverence.

> There is revealed to us that far wider and higher sphere of being which
> holds for us awe, reverence, and rebuke, incentives to action here that can
> never allow us to rest in the sphere of mere contentment of earthly
> enjoyment or bounded prospect.[43]

The reference to 'incentives to action' is significant. The experience is not
merely a matter of awe, but carries with it moral imperatives. As Veitch
continues, he reiterates that such experience is 'a catholic element' in
humanity: to 'feel and know a Transcendent Power' is 'not a peculiarity of the
individual, but open to every man who has singleness of vision and purity of
heart'.[44] Experience of transcendence is not alien to ordinary experience.
Nevertheless, Veitch gives a privileged role to nature. It is landscape and
environment that for Veitch are most likely to raise consciousness to an
awareness of a Presence 'above' and 'beyond' the natural. He describes the
impact of his native Borders.

> Its hills and glens, widespread moorlands had nourished it, for nowhere
> does a man feel his littleness more, nowhere does he feel the awing, and
> purifying of solitude and mystery greater than on the far reaching, often
> mist darkened, moorlands of 'the north cuntré'.[45]

Oman, too, gives a key role to nature in stirring a primary experience of
awe. But, it is possible that he would have looked upon Veitch's feeling for the
mystery as an instance of primitive religion,[46] an example of the 'awesome'
holy. Or, to use another Oman concept, Veitch's description of the revelatory
power of nature is an instance of the 'particular' holy, inspired by places and
objects, like the standing stones in Stenness, the altar in the tabernacle, or the
binding of the Koran.[47] However, while Veitch shows a particular relish for awe
and mystery, his views on how awareness develops, are strikingly similar to
Oman's wider categorization. Oman believed that the primitive holy has the
potential to evolve into ethical awareness, moral sensitivity and binding
conviction, apart from any material context.[48] A comparable continuum is
observable in Veitch. Awe can be 'sublimated' into a 'revelation of moral and
spiritual truth'.[49] Thus, when Veitch digresses on his own experience of awe, he

---

[42] Veitch, *Dualism*, p. 177.

[43] Veitch, *Dualism*, p. 181.

[44] Veitch, *Dualism*, p. 214.

[45] Veitch, *Dualism*, p. 185.

[46] Oman, *Natural and Supernatural*, pp. 372-389.

[47] Oman, *Natural and Supernatural*, p. 65.

[48] Oman, *Natural and Supernatural*, p. 308.

[49] Oman, *Natural and Supernatural*, p. 187.

explains it in aesthetic, moral and cognitive terms. 'This power independent of me, outside of me, yet uniform, passing on before me in endless process-vision, yet linked to me in bounds of reason, feeling and imagination, makes me patient, observant, teaches me waiting and reverence.'[50]

This link, in terms of 'reason, feeling and imagination', indicates that, for Veitch, experience of the Infinite is never simply context bound, nor purely irrational, and always has the potential for refinement. Nature may have a privileged role to play as epiphany; poetry may be well suited to cognitive expression; but these do not negate a sense of transcendence – of the holy – in ordinary experience. Thus, though Oman came to his understanding of the holy via Windelband, Veitch illustrates that an interest in poetry and knowledge, in reverence and transcendence, was not unknown in the Scottish philosophical tradition.

Conclusion

Oman wanted to avoid a text-book genre, and so there is no paper trail to sources and influences. But, perhaps we can make a modest claim to have found text beneath text: not a text shinning vividly beneath the surface, but more like an archaeological artifact, suggestive of earlier inhabitants on the site. Setting Oman's work in an historical perspective has enabled us to see how some of his main themes were anticipated. With respect to Henry Calderwood, we find a quite direct link to Oman's definition of personality. In the work of Alexander Campbell Fraser, we have a complementary metaphysics, built around the relation between the natural and the supernatural, and a vision of reality that is spiritual and personal. Fraser's use of the terms 'natural' and 'supernatural', in his Gifford lectures of 1889, were, I think, worthy of acknowledgement by Oman. John Veitch, in 1895, wrote concerning poetry, knowledge and experience of transcendence. It would have been interesting had Oman brought Veitch's insights into his discussion.

Finally, because of Oman's extensive knowledge of Schleiermacher and Ritschl, he is rightly credited with keeping alive liberal Protestant thought in the English speaking world. Perhaps his failing was not to acknowledge his Scottish philosophical antecedents. In late nineteenth century Scotland there was lively debate around the very issues that Oman deemed important. Had his old teachers, and the figures that were part of his intellectual awakening, been engaged more in his writing, they would, I think, have had a worthwhile contribution to make.

---

[50] Veitch, *Hamilton*, p. 49.

Personal Idealists: Sorley and Pringle Pattison

William Ritchie Sorley

William Ritchie Sorley was also from the Borders. He was born in Selkirk in 1855, where his father was a Free Church minister. He studied for the ministry at New College, Edinburgh, before, like Fraser and Veitch, moving to a career as a philosopher. However, his interest in theology never waned and he remained a practicing Christian. Sorley read philosophy at Trinity College, Cambridge, and later took up university appointments in London, Cardiff and Aberdeen. He returned to Cambridge as Professor of Moral Philosophy in 1900, a post he held until his retirement in 1933.

If we compare Sorley's work to that of Oman, we have a good example of the shared horizons. An emphasis on human autonomy, the dignity of personality and the personal nature of grace are central *foci* for both thinkers. Most notably, Sorley abandons the traditional concept of irresistible grace. In Divine-human relations there is an absence of all coercion and an invitation to free response. As we have noted, this was the cardinal idea in Oman's *Grace and Personality*. One could say that *Grace and Personality* was an extended theological commentary on this fundamental insight.

For both writers, the sphere in which the relationship of grace is realised is the natural world. What Sorley describes as the 'whole region of common life' is, for Oman, the 'whole breadth of experience'. There is for each something of a disenchantment with organized religion, and a belief in the universality of God's presence, awaiting to be realized in secular vocation. Grace for Oman is, 'not merely in some special sacred sphere of ecstasy or rite or even duty. Nothing less is at stake than the whole nature of the world when rightly used as God's world.'[51]

In these insights and emphasis there is, one could argue, an anticipation of the secular Christianity of theologians such as Bonhoeffer and Ronald Gregor Smith.[52] Experience of war in any era inevitably exposes institutional marginality.

It is illuminating, also, to compare Sorley's *Moral Values and the Idea of God* with *The Natural and the Supernatural*. Though written over twenty years later, in 1931, *The Natural and the Supernatural* exhibits a broad continuity with Sorley in both theme and method. For example, methodologically, Oman adopts a similar empirical approach and is scathing of abstraction. He writes: 'Unless theology is, like true science, about experience and not in place of it, it is worthless.'[53]

---

[51] Oman, *Grace and Personality*, p. 81.

[52] Jeffrey C. Pugh, *Religionless Christianity: Bonhoeffer in troubled times* (London and New York: T&T Clark, 2008); Ronald Gregor Smith, *Secular Christianity*, (London: Collins, 1966).

[53] Oman, *Natural and Supernatural*, p. 97.

However, Oman focuses on experience on a wider front than moral awareness. The reality of the transcendent for Oman is apprehended through the ideal values of truth and beauty, as well as through moral sensibility. Sorley, of course, recognized the intellectual and aesthetic aspects of experience; but he believed that moral values are primary. 'Man is not a cognitive being in the first instance, and only thereafter an active being. Knowledge is sought by him in virtue of some interest; and the interest in knowledge for its own sake is a late interest.'[54]

In contrast, for Oman, beauty takes the lead. The human quest for beauty is 'the true search for unity and harmony and perfection in all things'.[55] For instance, in morals, a search for beauty inspires 'striving for harmony in thought and action'.[56] Equally, in a highly intellectual field such as science, 'beauty is a conspicuous element in the abstract completeness aimed at in the higher mathematics'.[57] Beauty, Oman concludes, 'ought at least to be the inspiration of the study of all life'.[58] In a secondary sense, beauty belongs to religion. However, this latter belonging has been often a negative experience. Beauty suffers at the hands of religion because of traditional piety. Oman writes: '...by few things has it been limited and stereotyped and formalised more than by having imposed upon it narrow or external or sentimental or traditional forms of piety'.[59]

Yet, beauty is an essential part of 'true religion' in that 'a sense of beauty and a sense of the holy are not far apart'.[60] Neither beauty nor the holy are apprehended 'by the clear hard light of understanding', but rather by 'intuitions and anticipations which go far beyond what can be justified by understanding'.[61] In this focus on aesthetics, Oman reveals the abiding legacy of Schleiermacher; whereas Sorley, in his moral emphasis, is a disciple of Kant.

Beyond these differences, however, there is a shared conviction that the natural world and the world of values belong together in One Divine reality. Of the intimate connection between the material and the spiritual, the Natural and the Supernatural, Oman writes: 'The two are not in opposition, but are so constantly interwoven that nothing may be wholly natural or supernatural.'[62]

For both writers this duality in unity is the proper context in which to understand evolution. There is, Sorley argues, 'a design greater than Paley ever dreamed off'.[63] In other words, the mind finds the purpose and meaning that is

---

[54] Sorley, *Moral Values*, p. 25.
[55] Oman, *Natural and Supernatural*, p. 209.
[56] Oman, *Natural and Supernatural*, p. 210.
[57] Oman, *Natural and Supernatural*, p. 211.
[58] Oman, *Natural and Supernatural*, p. 211.
[59] Oman, *Natural and Supernatural*, p. 210.
[60] Oman, *Natural and Supernatural*, pp. 209-210.
[61] Oman, *Natural and* Supernatural, p. 210.
[62] Oman, *Natural and Supernatural*, p. 72.
[63] Sorley, *Moral Values*, p. 326.

not reducible to, or circumscribed by the material world.

It is not owing to natural selection, but rather in spite of it, that the mind of man affirms an affinity with truth and beauty and goodness, and, undismayed by opposition, seeks its home among ideals. To them as well as to nature the mind has adapted; and this adaption can neither be explained nor explained away by biological laws.[64]

Oman, similarly, believed that human beings 'adapt' to their spiritual environment. He draws an analogy between the challenge of natural environment and that of the spiritual reality. 'The creature that has learned to live in the air, if it returns to the water, does not become a fish but a corpse.' Likewise, at the human level, wrong choices have consequences that are no less grave. It is perilous to be indifferent to the absolute values. In reality, 'the Supernatural is only a higher bar of judgment being a sacred call and a decisive opportunity'.[65] Oman concludes: 'Man is the only creature we know who has consciously entered into this heritage.'[66] Or, as Sorley expresses it, 'conscious purpose is known to us directly only as it exists in the mind of man'.[67] In these ways, for both thinkers, all of reality – natural and spiritual – is construed in an evolutionary framework of purpose that has to be freely chosen in order to be realized. Divine purpose may seem at odds with nature, and the thought of it may be dismissed by science, but it is, nevertheless, a valid moral and spiritual hypothesis. Of this, adds Oman: 'we do not need the biologist's kind permission to believe'.[68]

Conclusion

We see that Oman and Sorley have a great deal in common, even though with contrasting emphases. We may also note a philosophical antecedent in the thought of Alexander Campbell Fraser, for whom Sorley worked as an assistant. Fraser also sought to understand the natural world within a spiritual perspective, and all three acknowledge a debt to Berkeley.[69] But apart from shared roots, Sorley and Oman have a family resemblance in their articulation of a Theism that is grounded in experience, affirmative of freedom and

---

[64] Sorley, *Moral Values*, p. 327.
[65] Oman, *Natural and Supernatural,* p. 294.
[66] Oman, *Natural and Supernatural*, p. 280.
[67] Sorley, *Moral Values,* p. 417.
[68] Oman, *Natural and Supernatural*, p. 277. A comprehensive contemporary discussion of the issues surrounding evolution and belief is found in David Fergusson, *Faith and its Critics* (Oxford: Oxford University Press, 2009).
[69] Sorley makes a distinction between Idealism of the Platonic type and that of Berkeley. He adds: 'the view at which this book has arrived if of this latter type'. Sorley, *Moral Values*, p. 468.

protective of personal autonomy. Both sought to integrate the personal and the natural world in a larger spiritual whole. With regard to theology, Sorley and Oman set aside 'irresistible grace' in favour of grace as love, gift and invitation.

Andrew Seth Pringle Pattison[70]

Pringle Pattison was a transitional figure between the Scottish Realism of the late nineteenth century and the Personalism of the early twentieth.[71] He was born in Edinburgh in 1856, and baptised Andrew Seth. Later, he changed his name to Pringle Pattison as a condition of receiving a bequest: the Haining Estate, near Selkirk, in the Scottish Borders. In 1878 he graduated from Edinburgh and, afterwards, went to study in Germany. On return to Edinburgh in 1880, he became an assistant to Alexander Campbell Fraser, in succession to W.R. Sorley. He held various appointments in the Universities of Wales and St Andrews before succeeding Fraser, in 1891, as Professor of Logic and Metaphysics. It was a post he held until his retirement in 1919.

Recent, renewed interest in Scottish philosophy in the early twentieth century regards Pringle Pattison not merely as transitional, but pivotal to the emergence of Personal Idealism. David Boucher writes:

> Andrew Seth is of immense importance in the history of British Idealism because for years after he edited what was the manifesto of Scottish Hegelianism he more fully developed his doubts he had hinted at earlier. He now questioned the metaphysical conclusions that Absolute Idealism projected and was at the forefront in Britain of leading the revolt against them and championing the cause of personal idealism.[72]

Even more recently, Cairns Craig, in his panoramic review of Scottish philosophical culture since the Enlightenment, argues that Pringle Pattison's criticism of the Kantian-Hegelian tradition and his return to the Scottish tradition was, in effect, a quest for a post-modern philosophy. It was Pringle Pattison, argues Cairns, who cleared the way for the constructive thinking of John Macmurry, later in the twentieth century.

> In Seth's effort to create a post-modern philosophy by a return to Scottish traditions and by a critique of the whole Kantian-Hegelian tradition we

---

[70] For Pringle Pattison, see also chapter 1.

[71] Gordon Graham, 'The Nineteenth Century Aftermath', *The Cambridge Companion to the Scottish Enlightenment* Edited by Alexander Broadie (Cambridge: Cambridge University Press, 2003), pp. 338-350.

[72] David Boucher, (Edited and Introduced) *The Scottish Idealists* (Exeter: Imprint Academic, 2004), pp. 8-9.

can see a pre-figuration of the most important philosophy of the twentieth century, that of John Macmurry...[73]

From this contemporary evaluation of Pringle Pattison's significance, we turn to his personal journey from neo-Hegelianism to Personal Idealism. If we consider three of his seminal works – *Essays in Philosophical Criticism*,[74] *Hegelianism and Personality* [75] and *The Idea of God in Recent Philosophy*[76] – it is clear that his Personal Idealism was born of considerable heart searching, and of rigor in sifting competing intellectual opinions.

Essays in Philosophical Criticism was the 'manifesto of Scottish Hegeliansim'.[77] It was dedicated to the memory of T.H. Green and the *Preface* was written by Scottish neo-Hegelian, Edward Caird. The volume aimed to carry forward the work of Green, for whom philosophy was not 'a study of the words of men that are gone' but 'a life expressing itself with that power and authority which belongs to one who speaks from his own experience, and never to the "scribes" who speak from tradition'.[78] Seth, as he was then known, as well as being joint editor, contributed an essay entitled: 'Philosophy as Criticism of Categories'. The essay was devoted to a critical examination of Kant's polar categories of the phenomenal and the noumenal. It was on Kant's part, he felt, 'a mischievous step' to isolate 'the conditions, principles or categories from the experience in which they are disclosed to us'.[79] On the contrary, argues Seth: 'The individual is individualised only by his relations to the totality of the intelligible world.'[80]

Clearly, at this early point in his thinking, he was committed to an Hegelian perspective. However, within four years of the publication of *Philosophical Criticism* things became very different. In 1887, in Seth's second series of Balfour Lectures, published as *Hegelianism and Personality*, he gave a cogent criticism of Absolute Idealism coupled with an affirmation of the importance of personality in metaphysics. 'The radical error both of Hegelianism and of the allied English doctrine I take to be the identification of the human and the divine self-consciousness, or, to put it more broadly, the unification of

---

[73] Cairns Craig, *Intending Scotland: explorations of Scottish Culture since the Enlightenment* (Edinburgh: Edinburgh University Press, 2009), p. 169.

[74] Andrew Seth and R.B. Haldane, (eds.) *Essays in Philosophical Criticism* (London: Longmans, Green and Co., 1883).

[75] Andrew Seth, *Hegelianism and Personality* (Edinburgh and London: William Blackwood & Sons, 1887).

[76] Andrew Seth Pringle Pattison, *The Idea of God in the Light of Recent Philosophy* (New York: Oxford University Press, 1920[1917]).

[77] Boucher, *Idealists,* p. 8.

[78] Seth, *Essays,* p. 3.

[79] Seth, *Essays,* p. 16.

[80] Seth, *Essays,* p. 34.

consciousness in a single Self.'[81]

Idealism, he believed, is a valid philosophy but only if it finds a place for the threefold reality of nature, personality and God. The merit of Idealism is its affirmation of unity; but, within that unity, the individual must be given a role, not as a means to an end, but as an end. 'Self', he writes, 'is the very apex of separation and differentiation'.[82] This is in contrast to the Absolute Idealism of, for example, John S Haldane, who saw personality in terms of its contribution to social unity. '… personality is no mere personality of one individual amongst others. We find in social life that it unites and does not separate us'.[83]

For Haldane, the only personality one can truly speak of is the personality of God, in which the whole of experience finds unity.[84] It is important to note, however, that though disagreeing with neo-Hegelians and Absolute Idealists Seth maintained a great respect for Hegel. 'In all this, Hegel is the protagonist of Idealism in the historical sense of that word, and champions the best interests of humanity. It is Hegelianism as a system, and not Hegel, that I have attacked.'[85]

When we come to Pringle Pattison's mature reflections in the *Idea of God*, published in 1917, we find a continuing twofold emphasis: an Idealist insistence on Mind and unity, together with an insistence on diversity and personality. It was a narrow road to travel and the alternative seemed broad on either side. If self is not, as the Absolute idealists thought, 'adjectival', then could it be that reality is in fact fundamentally pluralistic? This was the course taken by radical pluralists like Pringle Pattison's contemporary, J.M.E. McTaggart. The latter posited that finite selves 'exist in their own right' in a 'systematic whole', and in 'reciprocal dependence'.[86] But, reciprocal dependence was too 'weak' a concept for Pringle Pattison. Just as humanity stands in an organic relationship to nature, so the humanity is also organic to God. Ideals are the presence of God, immanent in the human spirit. He writes: 'But as soon as we begin to treat God and man as two independent facts, we lose hold on the experienced fact, which is the existence of *one in the other and through the other*.'[87]

Thus, we can see why critics accused Pringle Pattison of never resolving the essential conflict between Idealism and Personalism.[88] However, I feel the

---

[81] Seth, *Hegelianism*, p. 215

[82] Seth, *Hegelianism*, p. 217.

[83] John S Haldane, *Materialism* (London: Hodder & Stoughton, 1932), p. 131.

[84] Haldane, *Materialism*.

[85] Seth, *Hegelianism*, p. 230.

[86] Pattison, *Idea of God*, pp. 391-392. For McTaggart's metaphysics, see John M.E. McTaggart, *The Nature of Existence* (ed.) C.D. Broad (Cambridge; Cambridge University Press, 1927[1921]).

[87] Pattison, *Idea of God*, p. 254.

[88] 'Pringle Pattison's position is a half-way one with no firm ground beneath it, and failing at the very point which he has made the speculative climax of his metaphysics,

criticism is harsh, and fails to acknowledge his attempts to find a solution. In two articles in *The Philosophical Revue* of 1892,[89] he makes a distinction between metaphysics and epistemology, a distinction which he consistently maintains. His argument is that knowledge is always 'trans-subjective' and presupposes a relation between knower and known. But, this doesn't, he argues, obviate metaphysical identity. This point, he believed, was often obscured by neo-Hegelians.

> Hegelianism, in fact, offers an eminent example of the confusion between Epistemology and Metaphysics on which I am dwelling. With Hegel the essence of the universe is thought, here in the subject, and thought there in the object; and there is some temptation, therefore, to think that metaphysical identity absolves use from epistemological enquiry. But, this is not the case. However much the objective world and the individual knower may be identified in essence, the objective thought which he recognises is still trans-subjective…[90]

Pringle Pattison adds that 'Hegelians are not the only sinners in this respect'.[91] If it were the case that Hegelians 'swamped epistemology in metaphysics'; it is also the case that realists of the Scottish school were guilty of projecting the dualism inherent in knowledge unto reality. Often, the so called 'Natural Realist' was left defending metaphysical dualism of mind and matter as two generically different substances. Thus, realism 'falls at once into the most un-philosophical crudities'.[92]

With this distinction between epistemology and ontology, Pringle Pattison was able on the one hand to identify with the metaphysical Idealists and yet maintain that knowledge is by its very nature personal. The following two quotations sum up his distinction between the epistemological individuality and ontological identity in Divine Being. 'Knowledge means nothing if it does not mean the relation of two factors, knowledge *of* an object *by* a subject.'[93]

> The universe is once for all a whole and the external world as the Hegelians put it, is essentially related to intelligence, in other words it is

---

namely the definition of God.' Rudolf Metz, *A Hundred Years of British Philosophy* (London: George Allen and Unwin, 1938), p. 389.

[89] A. Seth, 'Psychology, Epistemology and Metaphysics', *The Philosophical Revue*, 1892, Vol. 1, No. 2, pp. 129-145; and A. Seth, 'The Problem of Epistemology', *The Philosophical Revue*, 1892, Vol. 1, No. 5, pp. 504-517.

[90] Seth, 'Psychology', pp. 129-145.

[91] Seth, 'Psychology', p. 145.

[92] Seth, 'Psychology', p. 145.

[93] Seth, 'Problem of Epistemology', pp. 504-517.

not a brute fact existing outside the sweep of divine life and its intelligent ends. In all this I most heartily agree with the neo-Hegelians.[94]

When, therefore, in the concluding chapter of the *Idea of God*, Pringle Pattison reflects on what personal idealism means for divine-human relationships, we find a theology of both intimacy and freedom. He compares the creation of the soul 'not to the manufacture of an article, which remains throughout something separate from its maker'; but, rather, to 'the addition of a child to a family'. It is a strong image of identity and belonging. 'But there is something more intimate still; for its filaments which unite the finite spirit to its creative source are never severed.'[95]

And, in this identity and belonging the relational aspect is not lost. There is continual opportunity for growth in knowledge and self-discovery. 'The Productive Reason remains at once the sustaining element of the dependent life, and the living content, continually offering itself to the soul which it has awakened to knowledge and the quest of itself.'[96]

Having committed himself to the personal nature of the divine-human relationship, Pringle Pattison makes several critical adjustments to theology. He abandons the traditional concept of Omnipotence. He argues that the 'real omnipotence' is 'atoning love'; and God is 'no far off theological mystery', but is found 'in the very texture of our human experience'.[97] He concludes, the theological interpretation of the Spirit as the third person within 'the inner constitution of a transcendent Godhead' is fundamentally misplaced. For him, the 'doctrine of the Spirit' is the 'profoundest, and therefore, the most intelligible attempt to express the indwelling of God in man'.[98] In his theology of the Spirit, Pringle Pattison is far removed from Trinitarian orthodoxy; yet, in his theology of the Spirit's working, his views are perfectly at home in the mystery of grace.

Pringle Pattison and Oman

In Pringle Pattison's Personal Idealism and Oman's Personalist theology, there is obviously a mutual emphasis on personality. However, there are differences. Generally, Oman considered that Pringle Pattison leaned too much towards the nineteenth century understanding of 'individuality' at the expense of Kant's more robust concept of the 'individual'. It was Pringle Pattison's contention that what German idealists had done was 'to enlarge and complete Kant's conception of intrinsic value by making it include all the higher reaches of

---

[94] Seth, 'Problem of Epistemology'.
[95] Pattison, *Idea of God*, p. 255.
[96] Pattison, *Idea of God*, p. 255.
[97] Pattison, *Idea of God*, p. 417.
[98] Pattison, *Idea of God*, p. 410.

human experience'.[99] He regarded this as a good thing. For Oman, however, this broadening of personality compromised its autonomy and self-determining character. He expressed his disagreement in *The Natural and the Supernatural.*

> But what Prof. Pringle Pattison thinks success was rightly achieved by discarding the eighteenth century framework of the Kantian scheme, which is what I call the question of the individual: my contention, on the contrary, is that the essential weakness and failure of all Romanticist philosophies was in taking the easy road and over-looking it.[100]

Perhaps Oman may be characterized as a 'hard' personalist in comparison to Pringle Pattison's 'softer' variety. In this emphasis on autonomy and self-determination, Oman is much closer to Henry Calderwood than to Pringle Pattison. It was Oman's view that Pringle Pattison, though a critic of neo-Hegelianism, continued to think within essentially Hegelian horizons. Reviewing the *Idea of God*, he comments: 'Pringle Pattison has not adequately settled his account with Hegelianism and relies more on mere 'organic unity' for solving problems like perception and the moral ideal, than his own view of the individual justifies.'[101]

In reality, Pringle Pattison probably considered that his account with Hegelianism had been settled, at least to his own satisfaction. Besides, in terms of theology, there were gains in neo-Hegelianism. It could accommodate an appreciation of spiritual presence and sacramental realism. Because Pringle Pattison allowed for an ontological identity between the 'finite spirit and its creative source',[102] he was much more creative than Oman with his doctrine of the Holy Spirit. His philosophy was compatible with the New Testament focus on 'indwelling'[103] and he did not regard this as a violation of personality. If the Divine relationship is – as he characterizes it – '*the existence of one in the other and through the other*',[104] then grace can be experienced *in* us. Consequently, the Spirit and Sacraments can be appropriated in more than a relational way. Divine presence does not stop at the boundary of self-directing, self-legislating, self-conscious personality. The mystery of the Spirit transcends Kantian categories.[105]

---

[99] Pattison, *Idea of God*, p. 38.

[100] Oman, *Natural and Supernatural*, Appendix B, Kant and Hegel, p. 475.

[101] John Oman, Review of Andrew Seth Pringle Pattison, *The Idea of God in the light of Recent Philosophy*, *The Journal of Theological Studies*, 19 (January and April 1917), pp. 246-7.

[102] Pattison, *Idea of God*, p. 255.

[103] For example, John 15:1-11; Eph.3:16-17; or Rom.8:11-12.

[104] Pattison, *Idea of God*, p. 254. (Italics in text)

[105] Helen Oppenheimer criticizes Oman for his exclusive relational understanding of grace. 'We want to be able to say that people are full of grace, not only that God is

In contrast, Oman's theology both of the Spirit and the Sacraments is entirely relational and symbolic. Nevertheless, one could argue that Oman, in making human autonomy sacrosanct, is a prophet of a more radical theology. For Oman, the experience of freedom is the experience of God; in this respect, he anticipated a more secular spirituality.

Final Comments

This essay began as an inquiry into Oman's relation to Scottish philosophy; in particular, to the Realist and the Personal Idealist traditions. Root and branch is probably an appropriate metaphor for the relationships we have discovered. Oman's roots were in the tradition of Scottish Realism that was still a live tradition in Edinburgh University when he arrived as a student from Orkney in 1877. We noted that some of Oman's main themes bear the hallmarks of his antecedents. For example, Calderwood's definition of personality and Fraser's understanding of the universe – as natural and supernatural and personal – are illustrative of a common horizon. Veitch shared the same philosophical culture: with particular interest in poetry and epistemology, mystical awareness and the significance of the sacred. This shows that the themes we find in Oman were not novel, nor alien to Scottish philosophy. They had a native complexion and were not merely imports, via Windelband or Otto.

The other half of the metaphor, branches, is suggestive of Oman's relation to his philosophical contemporaries. The period immediately after the First World War gave birth to a broad interest in Personalism. Pringle Pattison was the pioneer of Personal Idealism; a branch of philosophy that had in it something of the soil of the older Realism as well as the sap of Hegelianism. Sorley's interest in personality was developed into a philosophy of Ethical Idealism, with a focus on moral values. Oman's was the more explicitly theological work, relating the category of the personal to the Christian tradition. The tools he used, however, were almost exclusively philosophical. He is not easy to categorize, not least because of the eclectic nature of his thought. Nevertheless, I think it fair to say that Oman's work reflects antecedent influences from Scottish Realism; and bears a family resemblance to the various branches of Personal Idealism that flourished in the early twentieth century. This does not negate influences born of his direct interaction with wider European traditions. He was both a Scottish and European thinker.[106]

---

looking favourably upon them.' Helen Oppenheimer, *Incarnation and Immanence* (London: Hodder & Stoughton, 1973), pp. 44-7.

[106] I would like to thank David Fergusson for his helpful comments on this essay.

PART TWO

THEOLOGICAL FRAMEWORKS

CHAPTER 5

Seeing with a Prophet's Eye: John Oman's Experiential Method[1]

Stephen Bevans

Introduction

In 1922, on the occasion of his inauguration as principal of Westminster College, Cambridge, John Oman delivered a lecture entitled 'Method in Theology.'[2] This lecture is a summary statement of what after many years he had found to be 'the best method of trying'[3] to do theology and it represents his most direct statement on the subject. It is, indeed, 'in parts difficult and even obscure,' as his student and successor F. G. Healey wrote,[4] and what it says will need some fleshing out from other methodological passages in Oman's writings. The main ideas, however, of Oman's theological method are present in his 1922 lecture, and a closer study of it amply repays the effort needed to understand it. What emerges in the lecture and in Oman's other methodological writings is an understanding of theological method that takes human experience as the principal theological source. One does theology as one reads human experience with a 'prophetic eye.'

We shall begin with a summary of Oman's inaugural lecture and then move on to a wider discussion of method in his other writings.

'Method in Theology'

The first part of the inaugural lecture is basically a negative statement: the method of theology is *not* concerned with the repetition or maintenance of

---

[1] This essay is adapted from Stephen Bevans, *John Oman and His Doctrine of God* (Cambridge: Cambridge University Press, 1992 / 2007), pp. 41-62.

[2] John Oman, 'Method in Theology, An Inaugural Lecture,' *The Expositor*, 26 (August, 1923): pp. 81-93.

[3] John Oman, 'Method in Theology', p. 81.

[4] F.G. Healey, *Religion and Reality: The Theology of John Oman* (Edinburgh: Oliver and Boyd, 1965), p. 69.

traditional ecclesiastical authority or of doctrinal statements. Oman's time was one in which the truth of religion was being questions from all sides by science, history, psychology and philosophy. Oman argues that theology must show that its own investigations are inquiries into something real, and that its method of investigation, while different from that of these other fields, is nevertheless one that is complementary and not in contradiction to their methods. Theology, in other words, 'ought to be common to all inquiry that is seeking the truth simply as truth.'[5]

Such openness to the truth, however, is not always the impression that theology gives. 'The greatest of all hindrances to religious appeal, at the present time, is the idea that religious people are more concerned about what is correct than about what is true, and that the ecclesiastical leaders, in particular, are more exercised about unanimity than veracity.'[6] As an example of this dishonest and ultimately self-defeating attitude, Oman shares his own experience as an undergraduate at Edinburgh of the 'Robertson Smith' case that has been related in other articles in this volume. Oman recalls specifically the dishonest attitude of people who were saying that 'even if all [Robertson Smith] said were true, regard for useful tradition and the ecclesiastical amenities should have kept him from saying it.'[7] That this same spirit was still alive in the Church is evidenced, Oman says, by a letter he had recently received which accused ministers of not being 'honest and sincere' because 'they did not accept every word in Genesis as an exact account of the origin of the world and that they did not take the whole traditional creed as the soldier the army regulations.'[8]

It was an attitude such as this that fuelled psychologists in America – perhaps Oman refers here to disciples of Freud – who contend that religion's power comes not from the power of its own arguments, but from 'the vehement ecclesiastical temper, sustained by the mere confidence of obscurantism.'[9]

The reason, insists Oman, why religion is losing its appeal to students is because an unquestioned submission to ecclesiastical authority and theological tradition 'is so opposed to the methods of science, philosophy and historical inquiry, in which they are being trained,'[10] and even common working people look on religion as 'a kind of trade-union to impose upon mankind merely traditional beliefs.'[11]

Since 'theology is bankrupt the moment there is any suspicion that it seeks

---

[5] Oman, 'Method in Theology', p. 82.
[6] Oman, 'Method in Theology', p. 82.
[7] Oman, 'Method in Theology', p. 83.
[8] Oman, 'Method in Theology', p. 84.
[9] Oman, 'Method in Theology', p. 84.
[10] Oman, 'Method in Theology', p. 84.
[11] Oman, 'Method in Theology', p. 85.

something else than the truth,'[12] the first demand of theological method is that it must be open to all honest inquiry. This does not mean, as will be insisted upon later in the lecture, that theology must adopt the same method as that of science and philosophy, but it does mean that theology must admit the insight of modernity that we must 'be responsible for our deepest beliefs and … decide for ourselves our highest duties,'[13] independent of any external authority. Rather than repetition or defense of traditional authorities and formulations, in other words, theology must be concerned with the expression of one's own understanding, one's own insight, one's own experience of faith. Theology's method, to put it in terms that might have resonance today, must be 'public.'[14] Theology's task is not to explain what the Bible says or make credible what a Magisterium says, but to inquire openly and honestly into life's meaning by means of the light that life gives it.

Having said this, however, Oman moves a step further by means of a qualification. Such open inquiry has certain limits. Theology, as does all modern thought, owes a great debt to the Enlightenment's insight that all knowledge must be personally appropriated. However, when this insight into independent inquiry and judgment was reduced by the rationalistic tendency of the time to a quest for clear and distinct certainty in religion, theology lost sight of the fact that it does not produce but is itself produced by experience: that experience of ultimate meaning and value that is called religion.

What rationalism did was to reduce theology to intellectual propositions, but such 'intellectual argument, which Rationalism regarded as the only method of intellectual honesty, is not the method of theology.'[15] The problem is with the word 'only.' Rationalism so narrowed the idea of genuine knowledge that it deprived theology of its experiential foundations. It lost sight of the fact that theology only *served* experience and does not set experience's agenda. Rationalism made religion depend on theology in that it set out a few 'evident' doctrines as the only true basis of faith, and did not allow theology to spring from religious experience. Theology's purpose, according to the rationalistic mentality, was to give religion a certain, rational (understand: mathematical) basis, but the result was to make religion into a barren list of doctrines and not a way of being open to the highest calling in life.

Rationalism, to put it another way, replaced the ecclesiastical authorities with a new authority, that of speculative reason. In this way it distorted what theology was as much as the authoritarian method that it opposed. Rationalism, in short, put the cart before the horse and made experience of God depend on intellectual certainty of divine existence and action. But 'to make religion

---

[12] Oman, 'Method in Theology', p. 82.

[13] Oman, 'Method in Theology', p. 85.

[14] See David Tracy, *The Analogical Imagination: Christian Theology and the Culture of Pluralism* (New York: Crossroad, 1981).

[15] Oman, 'Method in Theology', p. 87.

depend on theology is like making art depend on intellectually demonstrated rules of criticism or morals on inferences from utility.'[16]

Rationalism was right in saying that theology has to be the result of personal conviction and not mere assent to authority. But it limited the scope within which personal conviction could be ascertained. It reduced truth to mathematical certainty and neglected the fact that knowledge comes not only from the intellect but from the whole range of our experience. Like the knowledge of the world that poets and artists have, that prophets are able to discern, knowledge is intuitive and experiential but nonetheless real. The religious person comes to knowledge of God by being attentive to the richness and depth of all that she or he can experience.[17] Religion, therefore, is not something that one can prove in the same way that one can prove a mathematical equation, but it is nonetheless real because it reveals itself in the power of experience.

So far in the lecture Oman has said pretty clearly what the method of theology is not, only hinting at what he thinks it is. Now he begins to move toward a positive statement: theology method is the interpretation first and foremost of the religious dimension of human experience.

Although we have to look elsewhere in his writings to understand more precisely what Oman means by experience, he develops this positive statement here by comparing and contrasting the method of theology with the method of the physical and natural sciences. Theology, as much as science, is concerned with comprehending reality, but each discipline approaches reality from a different angle. Science is concerned with the world as it appears to the senses, and its method is to understand by focusing its attention more and more narrowly on its object. Theology, in contrast, is concerned with the meaning *beneath* the world, and its method is to understand by opening up to the unity of the whole. Theology and science interpret the same world, but do it in different ways. This is why their methods differ even though their concerns are the same. Science, says Oman, looks *backward* at experience; theology, in its search for the meaning of the whole, looks *forward*,[18] as it were *through* experience.

> Theology reaches out beyond the world's meaning, while science concerns itself with origins and uniformities. As science aims at manipulating experience and not passing beyond it, it seeks these uniformities, not in the meaning of our experience, but in what we may call the fixed symbolism which lies beneath it.[19]

---

[16] Oman, 'Method in Theology', p. 87.

[17] Oman, 'Method in Theology'. p. 88.

[18] Oman, 'Method in Theology', p. 90.

[19] Oman, 'Method in Theology', p. 90.

This basic contrast is developed by means of two illustrations, one from language, the other—as the title of this essay indicates—from the biblical understanding of the prophet.

One can reduce the words of a paragraph to syllables or individual letters. One can say, for instance, that there are so many vowels and so many consonants, or that there are so many syllables in each line, etc. Or one could also approach the sentences of a paragraph from the point of their grammatical structure. One could speak of so many sentences, so many dependent and independent clauses, nouns and adjectives, verbs and adverbs. From a certain point of view, this is valid and in certain cases may be very helpful (for instance in learning about an African language which so far has never been written down or studied by Western methods). Such phonetic and grammatical analyses, however, do not come near to understanding what the paragraph *means*. One can only do this by the mysterious yet real process of grasping the letters and syllables and words and sentence structure *as a whole*.

> As thought is the reality of writing, all the possibilities of experience are the real world. The notion that science gives the true picture of complete reality was the mere illusion of a dominant interest, which is no longer entertained by serious scientific thinkers. Scientists are, as it were, merely the writing masters of experience, fulfilling a very important task for the managing of the world, but with no right to set for us the limits of its possibilities.[20]

The second analogy from the Hebrew prophets is one that is only hinted at in the lecture. Given the interpretative task of theology, it should be 'of the nature of prophecy.'[21] As the prophets of Israel saw meaning, purpose, and pattern behind the elements of the physical world and the events, however catastrophic, of history, the theologian should, with the same insight, attempt to discern and articulate what God is doing in her or his own personal, communal, and historical experience. It is this striving for insight in order to be able to see through experience – with a prophetic eye – to its deepest meaning which is what Oman understands as the correct method of theology.

> [Theology] necessarily works on the frontiers of intuition and anticipation; and it asks what relation to the present reality best manifests what is beyond it. Its prime conviction is that a higher reality is seeking to reveal itself to us through our whole experience in this present world, and is calling us to participate in its life, and that, with all fuller life, we enter it as we reach out after our farthest vision and are loyal to its highest even vaguely concerned requirements.

---

[20] Oman, 'Method in Theology', p. 90.
[21] Oman, 'Method in Theology', p. 91.

Wherefore, the business of theology is to deal with life and actual experience, but with them as they speak of things beyond demonstration, things or moments of deeper insight and higher consecration.[22]

At the end of the lecture Oman returns again to the idea with which he began: the question of authority, and in particular here the authority of the past (scripture, tradition, and the creed). Since theology is concerned with the whole of experience, the theologian, while working out of his or her present, must be attentive to the experience of the past. But such attention is not in order to copy that experience or merely to repeat its insights. It is to allow that experience to illumine his or her own. The past is to be regarded 'as an enlargement of our experience, not as a substitute for it … It is not a mere question of learning what they saw … The supreme thing is to learn their bearing towards life whereby men were prophets of the highest.'[23]

Authority and tradition have their place in theology, but they are subordinate to personal insight and prophetic vision into the meaning of the present. Theological method takes account of the past. The past is definitely to be taken as a theological source. But theology is guided by it, not whole governed by it. 'A true theology leaves out nothing of the concrete varied world that is within the grasp of our finite minds, in the hope of seeing the things unseen manifested in the things which do appear.'[24] Theology needs the past. It needs the independence as well of reason and rational thought. But it does not serve its purpose if it is not trying to articulate a person's deepest yearnings and highest aspirations. These are moments when one can see, however dimly, with a prophet's eye.

Authority, Reason, and Experience: A Wider Perspective

In the preface to the second (1928) edition of *Vision and Authority*, Oman relates a parable that vividly illustrates the theological method which he had sketched out a few years earlier in his inaugural lecture, and that can serve as a starting-point for trying to understand his theological method from the wider perspective of his other writings.

Suppose yourself on a wide moorland, without anything very distinctive, at any time, in any direction, and in the dark, wholly without character or feature or visible landmarks, with the mist settling in the boggy hollows, and a somber heaven above, with too few starts for any one to be identified with certainty. If being accustomed to such a situation, you are still calmly assured that you will reach home safely, and even directly, to

---

[22] Oman, 'Method in Theology', p. 91.
[23] Oman, 'Method in Theology', p. 92.
[24] Oman, 'Method in Theology', p. 93.

what guidance are you trusting?[25]

In the first place, of course, there is the beaten trail in front of you, made by others who have gone before, and in the darkness you can make out this trail step by step. This well-trodden path is good as long as it leads you in the general direction of where you want to go, 'but you may not commit yourself to it implicitly.'[26] There are times when the path forks, and you have to decide which is the right way. And after a time, when you realize that even the well-chosen path will not take you as directly as necessary to your destination, 'you have to take the risk of leaving it and of faring forward as straight as you can, across such country as you chance to meet.'[27]

Now that you have left the well-worn path, however, another guidance takes over and not the work of others but your own resources need to be even more fully called upon. Still, it is the 'guidance of what you see on earth,'[28] and this guidance is twofold. First, you have to be attentive to every step you take, so that you do not step into the soft earth of a bog and lose your footing. This becomes easier as you get more accustomed to the darkness and are able to judge where the higher, firmer, ground is most likely to be. But ultimately even this guidance is not enough, because 'this use of sight for what is near would be worthless for guidance, without a sense of general direction from what is not near.'[29] This guidance is more of heaven than of earth, and it is the brighter sky that gives a sense of the dark horizon toward which you need to go. And despite the fact that there are not many stars visible, there is 'one solitary star, the name of which you may not know, but the direction of which you can confidently trust,'[30] because it leads you on in a way that you know, however vaguely, is right. And so 'in loyalty to the authority of this double vision of the near and changing and of the remote and abiding, you can make straight paths for your own feet and perhaps straighten out the track a little and make it a little plainer for those who may follow.'[31]

It takes little reflection to understand that three sources of guidance are functioning in the parable, each with its own role to play in getting the wayfarer home. First, there is the trail blazed by those who have gone before which provides a general but not necessarily infallible direction. Then there is the necessity of personal risk and application in leaving the trail and fending for oneself, moving step by step, wary of the possibility of floundering in the soft

---

[25] John Oman, 'Preface to the Second Edition,' *Vision and Authority* (London: Hodder and Stoughton, 1928), p. 7.

[26] Oman, 'Preface' to *Vision and Authority*, p. 7.

[27] Oman, 'Preface' to *Vision and Authority*, pp. 7-8.

[28] Oman, 'Preface' to *Vision and Authority*, p. 8.

[29] Oman, 'Preface' to *Vision and Authority*, p. 8.

[30] Oman, 'Preface' to *Vision and Authority*, p. 8.

[31] Oman, 'Preface' to *Vision and Authority*, p. 8.

bogs and losing one's way in the pockets of fog. Finally, there is the vision of the horizon outlined against the sky and the 'solitary star,' both of which have provided direction for those who have gone before, provide direction at the present moment, and will provide direction for future travellers who will use the present wayfarer's path with appropriate corrections of their own.

The point is, of course, that the living of a Christian life and the articulation of a Christian theology demand attention to three similar sources of guidance. One is greatly helped, but not infallibly guided, by the path that others have trod before (the theological sources like scripture, tradition, the creed). One needs to break out on one's own and blaze one's own path when the old path moves in a direction which one suspects will lead to a dead end or in the wrong way (personal rational appropriation). Finally, one needs the lighted sky and the light of a trusted star to make sure that, despite personal caution, one is moving the in the right direction (what Oman calls religious experience).

The wisdom of the past, human reason, and human experience – all three are necessary, but for Oman it is the third that is the primary source in which all Christian living and theologizing must be rooted. Each of these three aspects of theological method needs some further reflection.

The Traditional Theological Sources[32]

The final pages of *The Church and the Divine Order* deal with the 'task of the present' – the need to come to a knowledge of God that is neither the result of submission to authority nor to mere reason, but that is 'prophetic.' Knowledge of God, in other words, can only be genuine knowledge if it rises out of personal experience, and if there is any role of authority in religion today, it is the role of offering interpretations of experience that will foster such knowledge. 'It is true indeed,' concludes Oman, 'that the consecrated individual is the special organ of revelation, and we will depend on him, whether through Scripture or through life, *yet it is not to lend us his flame, but*

---

[32] 'Theological Sources' are what Roman Catholics call the *'loci theologici.'* In their classic form, for instance in Melchior Cano's *De Locis Theologicis*, they are of two general types: scripture and tradition, the latter of which contains various sub categories. Protestant theology tends to refer to *loci theologici* in terms of the topics of classical systematic theology: God, Christ, Church, sin, etc. See, for example, Carl Braaten and Robert Jensen, eds., *Christian Dogmatics* I and II (Philadelphia: Fortress Press, 1984). In this section I have chosen to deal with only three sources: scripture, tradition and creeds. Scripture and tradition will be relevant for both Catholics and Protestants. Creeds will be particularly relevant for Protestant Churches like the Presbyterian Church which insists on allegiance to certain 'Standards,' among which is the Westminster Confession. By analogy, Catholics might think of this third source in terms of what has come to be called 'the Magisterium.'

to kindle ours.'[33]

It is this last phrase that is significant for understanding the role of the traditional sources of theology. Their role is *inspiring* rather than being inspired, as *enabling and persuading* rather than coercing, and as *facilitating* theological insight rather than substituting for it. Nothing can claim to be a theological source if it attempts to eclipse the authority of personal experience: not an inerrant scripture, not a revered tradition, not a normative creed. And yet, if regarded in the right spirit, these sources can be of considerable service in bringing a person to a deeper and more accurate interpretation of the religious dimensions that she or he can experience in life.

Scripture

Oman understands Christianity as a religion of the present experience of God and not as a religion of a book. That this is so is indicated by the fact that Jesus spent 'His life on lake and mountain, in synagogue and temple, eating with publicans and sinners, and speaking to shortlived men.'[34] Jesus' life was one spent with men and women, not in writing an autobiography or a compendium of theology.

The fact that Jesus lived in an age in which writing was an essential means of communicating (both Roman and Hebrew cultures had great bodies of literature) and the fact that he spoke so strongly about the permanence of his message though both heaven and earth pass away (Mt 24:35) point to the fact that Jesus must have had a deliberate purpose for not writing anything himself. This purpose was to show the kind of authority he wanted the written word to have: it was to be a *memory* of him, one that would stir up his message in the hearts of all who would read it. It was not intended to be an indelible, intractable word, valid in its apparent literal meaning for all time and in all circumstances.

> If it were His first purpose to set all dubiety for ever aside, He might have made every word be continued to man as a royal proclamation, with an imperative authority behind it which none might doubt and few disobey. But this enslaving authority over man's mind and will He ever shunned; and to find a reason why He put no word in writing, we only need recall how He dealt with the men among whom he lived.[35]

Jesus himself never used scripture as an absolute authority, Oman says. His 'appeal was never to Scripture but to the hearts of living men, and the true use

---

[33] John Oman, *The Church and the Divine Order* (London: Hodder and Stoughton, 1911), p. 322. My emphasis.

[34] Oman, *Vision and Authority*, p. 194.

[35] Oman, *Vision and Authority*, p. 126.

of Scripture was only an aid in his final appeal.'[36] The appeal of Jesus was to
one's own experience; this is how he taught and this was why he taught in
parables: so that people could come to their own conclusions and see the truth
for themselves. Theology, we might conclude, is called to follow Jesus'
method, and not just to repeat his words.[37]

Jesus' method of appealing to the human heart is a powerful one, and it is
perhaps the church's abandonment of his method that is the basic problem
behind its lack of real influence in a world in which reason and scholarship
have thoroughly discredited the claim for an inerrant and infallible Bible. Oman
sees this modern skepticism, however, as a blessing. It is an opportunity to
view scripture in its proper and still powerful perspective, and to rediscover the
method of Jesus, which really is the method of a personal God.[38]

Today, despite the inroads that scholarship has made into the fortress of
inerrancy and infallibility, scripture can be a powerful source to 'kindle our
flam' by the way it appeals to heart and conscience. 'Its great power to
persuade' in its images, its teachings, and its challenges is 'never more certain;
its right, or even its desire, to demand obedience without persuasion' is 'never
more dubious.'[39]

The Bible is still the 'most wonderful book in the world;'[40] but it is 'the
literature of our goal and freedom in God,'[41] and not something to be
swallowed unthinkingly or uncritically. What must be remembered is that the
Word of God is something that even the Bible serves,[42] and a reverence for
scripture should lead us to experience that Word, or help us interpret and
articulate it. It should never be a substitute for it. A line from *Grace and
Personality* fairly well sums up scripture's use as a theological source: 'Only
what speaks to the image of God in us has a right to be called a word of God.'[43]

Tradition

But what of tradition? 'There is no breadth of judgment without help from the
past, but there is no using the past to good purpose without independent
judgment on it of our own conscience of truth and right.'[44] As strongly as Oman

[36] Oman, *Vision and Authority*, p. 103.

[37] Oman, *Vision and Authority*, p. 191.

[38] See Bevans, *Oman & Doctrine*, pp. 84-87.

[39] Bevans, *Oman & Doctrine*, p. 94.

[40] John Oman, *Concerning the Ministry* (London: SCM, 1936), p. 228.

[41] John Oman, *The Problem of Faith and Freedom in the Last Two Centuries*
(London: Hodder and Stoughton, 1906), p. 324.

[42] Oman, *Concerning the Ministry*, pp. 228 and 236.

[43] John Oman, *Grace and Personality*, Third Edition (Cambridge: Cambridge
University Press, 1925), p. 258.

[44] John Oman, *Honest Religion* (Cambridge: Cambridge University Press, 1941),
pp. 13-14.

insists on the judgment of the individual in matters of religion ('slavery to tradition, fear of inquiry, submission to institutions are not religion but the want of it, not faith but unbelief'),[45] he insists on dialogue with others and with the great proven lights of tradition ('a conscience repudiating all guidance except its own is barren').[46] Insofar as the past helps us to 'kindle the flame' of our insight into God's working in our past collective life, it is of invaluable help. After all, our knowledge of God comes 'like all other knowledge, by one man building on another's foundation' and 'we are built upon the foundation of the good and faithful in all ages and in all nations.'[47]

The Church is built on the foundation of apostles and prophets, and their wisdom is a precious possession and an abundant source for theology, but we remain faithful to our apostolic and prophetic foundation on when we realize that we ourselves are called to the same apostolic and prophetic vision.[48] Being faithful to the apostles and prophets does not mean

> that, because they knew God immediately, we may only know Him at second-hand – that, because they recognized God's rule directly, we may only do it indirectly. It means, on the contrary, that through them we also are helped to be apostles and prophets, to hear the Spirit of God's Son in our own hearts and see for our own lives the Divine rule working good through all things.[49]

To do theology faithfully one must take into account the fact that we are historical beings, and therefore 'heirs to the past.' But 'we are heirs to the past only as we can make it live in the present and we leave nothing after us, if no one can keep it alive for his own need.'[50] The past is important, but it stays important by interpretation and retrieval for the present. Tradition is more than a body of knowledge to be preserved. It is being faithful to the meaning of past achievements in the context of the present.

Creeds

Like scripture and tradition, creedal statements must serve and not dictate experience. The creeds of the church are like one's communal and personal history which can neither be unquestionably accepted nor totally rejected. In order for them to be of value, one has to 'travel through and go beyond'[51] them.

---

[45] Oman, *Honest Religion*, p. 51.

[46] Oman, *Grace and Personality*, p. 255.

[47] Oman, *Vision and Authority*, p. 98.

[48] Oman, *Honest Religion*, p. 55. This is one of Oman's main contentions in *Vision and Authority* as well. See pp. 125-38.

[49] Oman, *The Church and the Divine Order*, pp. 320-21.

[50] Oman, *Vision and Authority*, p. 173.

[51] Oman, *Honest Religion*, p. 161.

For Oman, creeds do not represent infallible statements that must be upheld over against worldviews that call the truth of their formulation into question. They represent a grasp of deep truth, but truth articulated within very particular contexts. Because of this they cannot be taken literally and are not above criticism. Creeds represent 'less an illumination than points of light in the darkness, rather lighthouses to direct the course than sun or moon to display the prospect.'[52]

In an address in 1931, Oman spoke of a creed as having four purposes. It can be (1) an instrument to refute error, or (2) to establish uniformity of opinion. It can be (3) a means of instructing men and women about the essentials of the faith or it can be (4) a way of expressing in summary form the faith that the church stands for, an expression of its insight into God's dealing with humankind. This last purpose is the most important, and points to the basic reason for creedal formulation.[53]

Despite the fact that the four main doctrines of the Westminster Confession (the authority of scripture, predestination, the covenants of works and grace, the visible and invisible church) are hardly doctrines 'by which we can patiently and joyfully live and for which, if need were, steadfastly die,'[54] the main point of the Confession is clear: that Christian faith is in God and not in human goodness or strength. Thus the substance of the creed, or what it affirms, should be distinguished from its form.

Oman believes that creeds such as the Westminster Confession should be radically reinterpreted in terms that enhance and do not obscure the essential insight of faith that it attempts to articulate. An interpretation which is faithful to both Christian and human experience, in his judgment, would be one in which God's sovereignty would be expressed in terms of the perfection of God's gracious, personal relationship to humankind. Although this would mean the 'end of old forms' of doctrine, it would be 'capable of a more spiritual presentations.'[55] Such a reinterpretation would highlight a greater trust in God's truth (scripture), in God's work (election), in God's purpose (covenant theology) and in the community that God has founded in Christ (church).

The task of reinterpretation will not be a particularly comfortable one for the theologian, who 'may well mourn the vanished past and think enviously of his predecessors, who were only required to enunciate the Church's creed to find it received everywhere and always,'[56] but the task is nevertheless necessary. After all,

---

[52] Oman, *Vision and Authority*, p. 217.
[53] John Oman, 'The Moderator's Address. The Westminster Confession of Faith,' *The Presbyterian Messenger*, 1035 (June, 1931), p. 48.
[54] Oman, 'Moderator's Address', p. 48.
[55] Oman, 'Moderator's Address', p. 50.
[56] Oman, *Vision and Authority*, p. 184.

confidence ... is not conviction, and assertion is not truth; and even articulated consistency is not demonstration; and to receive anything on the assertion of another, though it be an infallible Church, is not knowledge. We travel by this method into yet greater uncertainties and into inquiries lying further away from the track of our common practical life. But, when the demonstration is in our own hearts, when it is the truth that proves itself by making us free, when as we grow in grace we grow in knowledge, the manifestation is altogether human, and, while it is far short of omniscience, it is adequate when tested by practical endeavor.[57]

Creeds, then, are important for what they affirm, and in regard to their substance, they are beacons to guide us on our way to understand our faith more deeply. But in order for that light to shine to its capacity, creeds must be constantly interpreted, and old forms left behind. Like scripture and tradition, they exist not to lend us their flame, but to kindle our own.

And so, while the traditional theological sources are not for Oman the most important part of theological method, they are nevertheless useful and quite necessary. Theology can never be a slavish repetition of what others have said in the past, no matter how 'authoritative.' But neither can it do wholly without them.

The Use and Limits of Reason

It was the Enlightenment which decisively changed the idea that theology was merely the faithful repetition of traditional formulas and doctrines, but the rationalism which emerged as a result was an imposition of another authority which was perhaps even worse: the authority of pure intellectual reasoning. Oman speaks of the Enlightenment in terms of two movements, one the positive movement of 'Illuminism' or 'the Illumination,' and the other the more negative movement of 'Rationalism.' While 'Illuminism' contained the 'true lesson and call'[58] of the times, and expressed the basic attitude and principle from which it worked, 'Rationalism' expressed the cultural mood out of which it emerged and the method by which it proceeded.[59] Oman intended the former

---

[57] Oman, *Vision and Authority,* p. 184

[58] Oman, *Grace and Personality*, p. 9.

[59] Oman never seemed satisfied by any English designation of the movement. The French, he said, spoke of the movement as *Illuminisme*, and the Germans called it *Aufklärung*, but the British 'never realized its significance enough' to make them give it a 'native designation' (*Grace and Personality*, p. 3). In *The Problem of Faith and Freedom* Oman said that the word 'Emancipation' captured what was intended by the movement, but the words 'Illuminism' or 'Enlightenment' were closer translations (p. 147). In *Grace and Personality* he said 'Age of Reason' might be a candidate, 'had not the title acquired a cheap association' (p. 3). The distinction I am using is that used by

term to express all that was of lasting value in the Enlightenment, and the latter to express the imperfect, negative, and shallow spirit which the movement took on as it progressed.

What made Illuminism important was its insistence that

> truth is not truth for us, except as we ourselves see it; and that right is not righteous, except as we ourselves determine it; and that to determine our own beliefs by our own reason and our own duty by our own conscience, is man's highest and most personal concern, which he may not delegate with honour.[60]

What this meant for theology was that theology had to be determined not by the 'external authorities' of church office, scripture, tradition or creed, but by open investigation into the spiritual reality was its object, subjected only to the 'internal authority' of personal insight. Illuminism held that one is a religious person not when she or he affirms certain facts or propositions but when she or he 'has realized the utter loneliness of his spirit and desires to hear nothing but what speaks in this aloneness, and no deliverance from it except harmony with the reality of this sacred world which sets him in this isolation.'[61] Theology, because of the insights of Illuminism (the positive aspect of the Enlightenment), was thrown back on personal reflection and personal experience.

However, the rationalistic mood of the age began to turn what was positive and far-seeing into what was negative and short-sighted. Rationalism began equating personal insight and personal experience with intellectual certainty, and 'insight into the whole depth of reality and consecration to the whole requirement of the highest had no place accorded to it compared with the mere negative insistence on being independent.'[62] So what began as the insight into the necessity for personal appropriation of knowledge and duty ended up as an emphasis on speculative reason alone, with knowledge emptied of much of its richness. One could only know what one understood 'clearly and distinctly,' and anything else was only worthy of skepticism.

> Thus man was made a much poorer measure of the universe than he has it in him to be; and it was forgotten that, while his own knowing is the only measure man has, it is used to profit only when he realizes how very far the universe is beyond his measuring, and how with his best knowing and groping, he is, as Newton said, only a child gathering pebbles on the

---

Oman in *The Natural and the Supernatural* (Cambridge: Cambridge University Press, 1931), p. 100.

[60] Oman, *Natural and Supernatural*, p. 100.
[61] Oman, *Natural and Supernatural*, p. 102.
[62] Oman, *Natural and Supernatural*, p. 102. See also p. 321.

shore of the great ocean of truth.[63]

The consequences of this rationalistic epistemology for theology was to make it not, as Illuminism had held out in promise, 'a science of experience in putting its truth to the test,'[64] but a barren discipline of intellectual speculation, striving for a 'natural religion' based on common denominator doctrines of God's existence, divine providence, and personal immortality. And so from these clear, distinct and rationally certain ideas, all theological doctrines could be deduced.

We might take Oman's summary of Matthew Tindal's *Christianity as Old as Creation* as a case in point. Tindal starts with what he considers the perfectly rational and self-evident proposition that God is perfect. If this is the case, argues Tindal, then the perfect religion must be knowable by every person, and that of course is discoverable by reason. Since neither the scriptures nor church teaching are very reasonable sources as they are so historically unreliable ('pious fraud leaves every document doubtful'), the only way to reach true Christianity is 'not to admit anything but what our reasons tell us is worthy to have God for its author.' There then follows a safe but sterile laying out of what Chrsitianity means, guided by the general principal that 'actions that tend to promote happiness are always good.'[65]

The rationalist argument for God, Oman points out, used 'every argument for religion except religion itself.'[66] Its insistence, after Descartes, on mathematical certainty as the only model for truth led it to abandon or neglect the whole experiential dimension of life. There were voices to the contrary. Blaise Pascal spoke of encountering not the God of the philosophers but the God of Abraham, Isaac, and Jacob, not by speculation but through the reasons of the heart.[67] Similarly, Joseph Butler spoke not of mathematical certainty but of probability as the guide to life.[68] But Butler, as well as Pascal, were, with their intuitions of the experiential basis of religion and theology, 'farthest away from what the age thought was obligatory—such an apologetic as would put Christianity on the lowest possible intellectual franchise.[69]

It is precisely this rationalist neglect of the priority of experience in theology that Oman identifies as the root of its wrong theological method. This contention was expressed strongly in Oman's first book, *Vision and Authority*. Arguing against both the abuses of authority and reason in religion and

[63] Oman, *Natural and Supernatural*, pp. 102-103.
[64] Oman, *Vision and Authority*, p. 190.
[65] Oman, *The Problem of Faith and Freedom in the Last Two Centuries*, pp. 114-115, quoting Tindal.
[66] Oman, *Faith and Freedom*, pp. 96-97.
[67] Oman, *Faith and Freedom*. pp. 58-77, esp. pp. 71-72.
[68] Oman, *Faith and Freedom*, pp. 118-134.
[69] Oman, *Faith and Freedom*, p. 118.

theology, he says that in the area of secular knowledge, men and women have learned to doubt not only the validity of unquestioning submission to authority, but to doubt also the validity of arguing from abstraction to concrete reality. To put it positively, men and women 'have discovered at once the glory of inquiry and the folly of *a priori* assertion.[70] The problem is that such inductive, empirical thinking has not fully informed the method of theology. In regard to the doctrine of God, for example, people still want to reason from their idea of perfection and project that on to God, rather than to inquire into what perhaps God is really doing in their lives.

It is assumed that, God being perfect in Himself, and all His ways being perfect, His orbit can have nothing errant or oblique, so that, through it is infinite, it may be more easy to predict than man's finite but irregular course. Yet, this is a method of reasoning which has only a superficial plausibility. True reverence would lay down no rules for God. It would endeavour rather to discover what rules He has laid down from Himself. Presumption cannot go further than to argue on the postulate that God cannot transcend our highest conception of the method He ought to follow. In the spiritual, as in the material world, God's real method may turn all our presuppositions to ridicule. The highest method may be precisely what we have rejected.[71]

Theology, in other words, should not be constrained by *a priori* assertions, assumptions, postulates, and presuppositions derived from speculative reason. The task of theology is the discovery of the method that God actually uses in relation to the world, and this can only be done if theology is rooted in the richness of human experience.

In *Grace and Personality* the question of method does not occupy many pages, but 'Oman regarded what he had to say about method in theology as a particularly valuable feature'[72] of the book. As Oman says in the Preface,

My application of it may not seem greatly to approve the method, but the method is more important than any particular application: and it may be permitted me to hope that even my limitations may stimulate some one to use it to better purpose.'[73]

The actual statement of the method comes in the context of asking how to approach the issue of the relationship between divine grace and human freedom, the fundamental theme of the book. Does one proceed, asks Oman, by

[70] Oman, *Vision and Authority*, p. 49.
[71] Oman, *Vision and Authority*, pp. 49-50.
[72] Healey, *Religion and Reality*, p. 66.
[73] Oman, *Grace and Personality*, p. vi.

speculation from abstract principles, or by attending to experience?

> Is it to be in the old way of arguing down from the throne of God, of propounding what seems to us fitting in the relation of an Infinite Being to His finite creatures, or is it to be upward from the actual position we occupy here below?'[74]

In answer to these questions, the first thing to be admitted is that if we opt for the 'old way' of 'mapping out from above God's operations,' we really have no criterion for judging its truth. After all, 'we occupy no vantage ground. We are not able at all to soar, and we look up with no eagle eye.'[75] It would be both ridiculous and blasphemous to pretend that *our* reasoning can capture divine motives and purposes.

We cannot 'second guess' God, but we can have recourse to 'the actual position we occupy below.' We can have recourse to an analysis of, and reflection on our experience. And, in fact, says Oman, 'only if we can see grace as it works on earth and understand how it affects our own experience, can we possibly hope to have either clearness or certainty.'[76]

When this shift in theological starting-point takes place, and one begins from a reflection on one's experience, the presuppositions about God's actions in grace drop away, and one can begin to realize that divinity can best be characterized by the wisdom of patience, the power of love, and the strength of persuasion. 'To look up from earth will not be a disadvantageous position forced upon us by our lowliness, but the only place from which to understand a relation to us which is of love, in the sense at least of being considerate of what we are.'[77]

The next section will reflect about what exactly this 'experience' is. The point here, however, is merely to illustrate Oman's caution that to start from an *a priori* understanding of God as omnipotent, omniscient, eternal, and so forth, can only be a projection of our finite minds and 'impatient, domineering spirits.' It is to be 'misled by a vain imagination of how we ourselves should act on the throne of the universe.'[78]

Oman was committed to the fact that theology needed to be conducted in reasonable, public discourse. But reasonable and public, he insisted, did not necessarily mean coldly rational. Any kind of 'intellectualism,' as well as any kind of authoritarianism, needed to be avoided if theology was to speak relevantly and truly in the contemporary world.

---

[74] Oman, *Grace and Personality*, p. 40.

[75] Oman, *Grace and Personality*, p 40.

[76] Oman, *Grace and Personality*, p 40.

[77] Oman, *Grace and Personality*, p. 41.

[78] Oman, *Grace and Personality*, p. 15.

Experience

'Unless theology is, like true science, about experience and not in place if it, it is worthless.'[79] Passages like this are found throughout Oman's works and emphasize that his is a method that relies not merely on past formulations of scripture and doctrine, nor on speculations founded on pure rational reflections. Oman's method is rooted in experience.

But what did Oman mean by experience? 'Of all the words in the philosophic vocabulary,' wrote Michael Oakeshott in 1933, experience is the word 'most difficult to manage; and it must be the ambition of every writer reckless enough to use the word to escape the ambiguities it contains.'[80] Oman, unfortunately, did not escape all such ambiguities in his use of the word 'experience,' but I think that a close study will reveal that his understanding of it, if not always clearly expressed, is quite profound and quite contemporary.

There are times when Oman uses the word 'experience' in general, unreflective ways. For example, just paging through *Grace and Personality* one can come across an idea of experience as mere common sense – like, 'that just doesn't fit with what I know from experience.' At other times, 'experience' is used I a way that corresponds to a definition of experience that I once heard offered by American story-teller / philosopher Garrison Kiellor: experience is what you get when you don't get what you want. Experience is also used in a way that seems to reflect the common understanding as 'kind of just what happens to you,' and in this sense it is something passive, something one undergoes.[81]

More often, however, though it is never *defined* as such, Oman uses experience in quite a different, I would say even technical, way. Experience is not, for Oman, something purely passive, something that merely 'happens' or 'breaks into' human consciousness. One gets the impression, rather, that it is an activity in which a person is actively involved. But what must immediately be added is that experience is not pure activity, for that would make experience the result of personal, individual projections. The activity that one needs to be engaged in is basically a personal authenticity in the way one faces life. The way one thinks, the way one critically appropriates one's culture and history, the way one relates to people the way one does one's job and chooses one's politics – all these things equip a person for the way the world is perceived in general, and people and events are perceived in particular. To the extent that

---

[79] Oman, *Natural and Supernatural*, p. 97.
[80] Michael Oakeshott, *Experience and Its Modes* (Cambridge: Cambridge University Press, 1933), p. 9. These lines are quoted on page 10 of Nicholas Lash, *Easter in Ordinary: Reflections on Human Experience and the Knowledge of God* (London: SCM, 1988). Lash's masterful book has been of utmost help in unravelling some of Oman's meanings of 'experience.'
[81] See Oman, *Grace and Personality*, pp. 187, 289 and 290.

one lives authentically, or, as Oman would say, conscientiously or sincerely,[82] to that extent one's world or environment will be perceived as something graciously given, challenging one to and rewarding one with personal identity and personal freedom.[83] For the person who lives authentically, therefore, all of one's life, simple things like taking a walk with a friend or spouse, or awesome things like giving birth or facing death, are occasions when one experiences the *reality* of life. It is in this kind of experience that theology needs to be rooted.

Oman never really expresses himself as clearly as all this, but toward the end of *Honest Religion* he provides an account of one of his own experiences that I believe expresses as clearly as anything what he means. One day Oman had been driven around the county of Suffolk. The weather had been perfect, the spring was in full bloom, and 'the variety of greens and browns infinite, the light of unearthly perfect,' and the farms and villages he had seen were 'a panorama of varied beauty.' Then he arrived at Flatford Mill, where the artist John Constable had lived and worked as a young man. Oman entered into the mill, and looked out the window, seeing what he thought Constable might have seen 'any time he lifted his head from his work.' That which was framed by the window was, after all the glories of the day, a rather commonplace scene. And yet what the window framed was the scene of one of Constable's masterpieces, 'The Hay Wain.'

In one sense, as Constable saw the scene day after day, it was always 'there.' But it was not until he saw it with his artist's eyes that he actually *experienced* it. It was not simply a matter of the beauty of the scene 'breaking in' on the artist. It was because of his artist's sensitivity and openness to the reality of nature that he could see the ordinary as it really is: something of *extraordinary* beauty.

So it is with all our knowledge, as Oman sets out to prove in *The Natural and the Supernatural*. We come to know something not by having reality bombard us with images. Reality is not just 'out there,' and we the passive observers. The fact that our knowing comes when we begin to discern a meaning in the world around us – as when we begin to perceive a melody in a piece of music instead of so many notes, or when we begin to perceive sense in a paragraph instead of just so many letters and words[84] points to the fact that knowing is an activity to which we attend, and in which 'interest' holds an

---

[82] '... all sincerity, being patient, laborious, teachable, is in the way of the manifestation of the truth which life provides ...' (Oman, *Vision and Authority*, pp. 185-186). 'In Oman sincerity was a broad, steady, powerful, open-eyed, confident, mature – every adjective is necessary – intention to grasp and be grasped by the truth over the whole range of experience and knowledge, no matter how it presents itself' (H. H. Farmer, 'Memoir of the Author,' *Honest Religion*, p. xxvii. For Oman's idea of 'conscientiousness,' see *The Natural and the Supernatural*, p. 329.

[83] How this actually 'works' is explained in Bevans, *John Oman and His Doctrine of God*, pp. 63-81.

[84] Oman, *Natural and Supernatural*, pp. 174-175.

indispensable place.[85]

But while knowing is such an activity, it does not simply create reality.[86] Rather, its perception of meaning deals with a reality that is truly external to the mind, and takes on sharper focus as one attends to it. Various hues of colours only become visible to the eye as our interest is developed. Oman points out that a language as precise as Greek has a surprisingly limited number of terms for describing colours, but that does not mean that the various velocities of light were not present to the Greek eye.[87] To give a further example, even though a person might not have the slightest idea about writing, marks on a page will still appear within the range of that person's vision. It is only by learning and attending to what they really are that one can read a sonnet by Shakespeare or a page from a novel by Chinua Achebe.

The requirements for experience are in the same vein. Just as Constable's artist's eye revealed to him the beauty of Flatford Mill, or our twenty-first century sense of colour allows us to see a broad range of colours, or the prophet's vision allows him or her to see the meaning of events, so our openness to life (what Oman calls 'sincerity') allows us to experience the ordinary happenings of our life in a way that manifests their true meaning. As we have seen from our summary of Oman's inaugural lecture as principal of Westminster College, Cambridge, while science is concerned with the individual components of trees and water and earth and light waves / particles, theology begins and remains concerned with *experience*, or, in other words, with the unity or full reality of the whole.

Oman's comments following his experience at Flatford Mill point to a further understanding of his use of the word experience. He writes that the true blessedness of life would unveil itself to us if we could only live it more honestly and sincerely: 'the real infinity of meaning and value is in the common folks around, could we love and serve them better, and in the common tasks, were they freed from imperfection of motive and purpose.'[88] The more honestly we try to live our lives, in other words, the more life's wonder and mystery will be revealed to us. As Oman expresses so many times in his writings, a fidelity to 'discipline and duty,' to living one's life as faithfully and honestly as possible, will reveal the whole of life's meaning, and will manifest the fact that *all* life is revelation, a gracious gift that continually calls us to ourselves and beyond ourselves.[89]

In many ways, it seems to me, this kind of approach to experience anticipates what in contemporary thought is spoken of as 'praxis.' Only if one lives one's life responsibly and reflectively, trying to be faithful to the demands

[85] Oman, *Natural and Supernatural* pp. 188-192.
[86] Oman, *Natural and Supernatural* p. 154.
[87] See Oman, *Natural and Supernatural* pp. 188-189.
[88] Oman, *Honest Religion*, p. 194.
[89] See, for example, Oman, *Vision and Authority*, p. 57.

of life on the one hand and the insights of one's community, culture, and tradition on the other is one thinking correctly. And if one does this in the context of faith, one is doing theology.[90] If there have ever been true theologies, 'they were not intellectual inferences, but the outcomes of the greatest of all experiments, which is the endeavour to live rightly in our whole environment – natural and supernatural, the seen and the temporal and the unseen and the eternal.'[91]

Speaking of the content of preaching in one of the chapters of *Concerning the Ministry*, Oman says that one's preaching should be from 'experience,' but that does not mean that it should be a sharing of 'experiences,' gushy, emotional moments of 'mysticism.' Rather, if one is faithful and reflective in living one's life, one will truly experience what life is – and that is the 'matter' for preaching. That is the way of the Bible as well: 'On the whole, the Bible is concerned with all kinds of events and demands and practical commitments and with what God means in relation to them, with remarkably little about psychological experiences or personal feelings at all.'[92]

In the same way, theology is not done by reflecting primarily on abstract doctrines, but on concrete circumstances and actions. The prophets did not arrive at their doctrine of monotheism, says Oman, 'by meditating on the ideas of unity and omnipotence and their reflection in their souls.' Rather, monotheism emerged 'from learning in face of the disasters that God has a purpose no evil can defeat, and that for themselves He was greater than all that could be against them.'[93] Jesus also taught out of his own openness to life and nature, saying with his parables about 'kings and slaves, and bailiffs and debtors, and farmers and fisher-folk, and housewives and children' that 'every mortal is occupied with God, and, as he is rightly or wrongly occupied, all his life is right or wrong.'[94]

The experience, then, that Oman talks about as being necessary for theology is a knowledge of reality that comes from an attentiveness and faithfulness to life. It is open to the deepest and most risk-filled callings of one's spirit, which

---

[90] I want only to be suggestive here, but it does seem that what Oman is getting at is similar to what, for example, Brazilian theologian Leonardo Boff says in an article on Third World theologies: 'The first word is spoken by what is done, that is, by a conscious act aimed at changing social relationships. It is therefore an inductive theology. It does not start with words (those of the Bible or the Magisterium) and end in words (new theological formulations), but stems from actions and struggles and works out of a theoretical structure to throw light on and examine these actions' ('What Are Third World Theologies?' in Leonardo Boff and Virgilio Elizondo,eds., *Theologies of the Third World: Convergences and Differences. Concilium* 199 (5 / 1988) (Edinburgh: T. and T. Clark, 1988): p. 10.

[91] Oman, *Natural and Supernatural*, p. 356.

[92] Oman, *Concerning the Ministry*, pp. 146-147. The quotation is from p. 147.

[93] Oman, *Concerning the Ministry*. pp. 146-147.

[94] Oman, *Grace and Personality*, pp. 81-82.

challenges women and men to go beyond themselves, requiring them to reach out after the 'farthest visions and follow even the dimly discerned beckoning of its requirements.'[95] But it is not anything rapturous, emotional or mystical (unless by 'mystical' one means 'that sense of touching through experience the deeper things which give experience meaning' – but then that is 'just another name for religion'[96]). The experience in which theology needs to be rooted comes in an attitude that is open to see the whole in the particular, the pattern in the random, the graciousness of God in the midst of imperfection and evil.

Conclusion

We may summarize the method that Oman proposes for theology in the following way. The first requirement is that theology come out of experience in the profound sense in which Oman means it: an experience of the graciousness and challenge of one's life which is the result of authentic human and religious living. And so theology is first and foremost the attempt to articulate and reflect critically on this experience, which is, as Oman maintained, the experience of God's self in grace, God's personal self-disclosure and invitation to relationship and responsible partnership.

As one struggles to be authentic, however, one realizes that authenticity demands both fidelity and independence, and these have a crucial role to play as theologizing takes shape. One's experience comes out of the whole web of relationships that stamp a person with a particular identity, and these relations include one's culture and one's history, one's community, social location, and one's heritage. In reflecting on and articulating one's experience in theology, the experiences of Israel and the church in the scriptures, and the experience of the church in its tradition and creeds are useful and even necessary.

But these sources are always to be personally appropriated if they are truly to be sources, and here all the working of one's reason is to be employed. Nevertheless, even reason has to be subordination to the higher but dimmer, more immediate but less clear experience of oneself as being challenged to, and endowed with, personal freedom. The theologian must avoid constructing a theology that is a mere 'compendium of traditional dogmas' or a rational system which is 'founded off by abstract speculations.' He or she must rather approach theology as 'the science of such Divine truth as we are able to experience.'[97] Theology must be rooted in life, and must be a reflection on life's deepest dimensions. Experience is what poses theology's questions, and what validates its answers.[98]

Such rootedness in experience does not mean that theology cannot profit

---

[95] Oman, *Natural and Supernatural*, p. 109.

[96] Oman, *Grace and Personality*, p. 263.

[97] Oman, *Vision and Authority*, p. 215.

[98] Oman, *Honest Religion*, p. 30.

from the past, nor does it mean that theology is not a scientific, that is, rational enterprise. It only means that theology's object – God and God's action – is a reality that can only be understood and penetrated by personal appropriation, and that such appropriation is a much deeper one that mere logic can sustain. Any and all theological truth is achieved when the theologian, in dialogue with the past, opens himself or herself fully to the present.

An adequate theology, therefore, will be one that has been constructed in dialogue with tradition, but which is articulated in a way that allows tradition to shape its expression and to challenge it, but not to 'schoolmaster'[99] it. Such a theology will be expressed in a coherent system, but one constructed out of fidelity to the experience from which it emerges. Today we would say that all theology must be contextual.[100]

---

[99] Oman, *Honest Religion*, p. 154.
[100] See Stephen Bevans, *Models of Contextual Theology*, Revised and Expanded Edition (Maryknoll, NY: Orbis Books, 2002).

CHAPTER 6

God's All-Conquering Love: Oman's Preaching, its Style and Content

Adam Hood

It has been said of William Robertson Smith that his preaching, which was conventionally pious and somewhat sentimental, bore little relationship to his critical biblical scholarship.[1] In contrast, John Oman's preached message is one of a piece with his theology. In his published orations as found in *A Dialogue with God* and *The Paradox of the World*, which have been judged as representative of his preaching as a whole, one finds considered, biblical, pastorally aware, and down to earth sermons in which are articulated Oman's most deeply held theological commitments.[2] They aim to fructify the faith of his hearers by pointing to the spiritual freedom and victory that can be achieved in life through an awareness of and response to the love of God active across the whole range of human experience. They hold out a view of faith as willing obedience to the duties that God ordains. They present a vision of Christ, the one who both reveals the love of God and the true pattern of human faith, as lying at the heart of faith. Thus do Oman's sermons provide an accurate and accessible starting point in understanding his work as a whole. Indeed, it can be argued that there is little of real spiritual importance in his scholarly work that is not intimated in his sermons. His scholarly work might be construed, in the main, as an attempt to justify and underpin the insights that inform his sermons.

The present essay will begin by looking at the ecclesial context in which Oman's preaching developed. It will argue that he represents a style of preaching prevalent in the United Presbyterian tradition. Next, there will be a discussion of the shape of his sermons. Here it will be seen that his pulpit work

---

[1] Richard A. Riesen, 'The sermons of William Robertson Smith' in *William Robertson Smith; Essays in reassessment* , ed. by William Johnstone (Sheffield: Sheffield Academic Press, 1995), pp. 86-94; David N. Livingstone, 'Public Spectacle and Scientific Theory: William Robertson Smith and the reading of evolution in Victorian Scotland', *Studies in history and philosophy of biological and biomedical sciences*, 35, pp. 1-29.

[2] William Wright, 'John Oman as Minister' in F.G. Healey, *Religion and Reality: The Theology of John Oman* (Edinburgh: Oliver & Boyd, 1965), pp. 150-52 (p. 151).

was motivated by the down-to-earth desire to help his listeners grow in their experience and practice of God's love. This focus led to a form of preaching that was biblical and in which much attention was given to the careful choice of memorable phrases and telling illustrations. Finally, Oman's preached message will be summarised. A key theme is the character of faith; the vision that informs it, the demands that it makes and the life-changing influence that it exerts. Another important aspect of his preaching is the degree to which his message is Christ centred. The life and teaching of Jesus is the crucible in which the Christian finds his vision of the love of God and of the spiritual victory and duties that faith offers.

One qualification needs to be added. This essay will be limited primarily to a consideration of Oman's published sermons. A development of the work here would include attention to the archive of unpublished sermons and talks deposited at Westminster College, Cambridge. However, whilst extending the discussion would be a worthwhile scholarly task, it would not, in my view, greatly modify the understanding of Oman's preached gospel as it is presented here.

The Background to Oman's Preaching

In our own days, when preaching is not so highly regarded, it is somewhat difficult to appreciate the importance that it had in times past. Even today, in Scottish Reformed worship the sermon remains a high point of a service, but this was even more so in times past. Preachers such as Knox, Melville and Henderson had a marked influence on the convictions of believers through their preaching and what was true of the great preachers was also true of the many hundreds of other preachers who have shaped Scottish faith since the Reformation.[3] Whether what was preached was acceptable or not, the emphasis on the sermon meant that it was rarely treated as 'negligible'.

The church that Oman was reared in, the United Presbyterian Church (UPC), had a distinctive approach to preaching that sheds light on Oman's own practice. The UPC was the fruit of the Secession from the Kirk in the 18th Century, led by such as Ebenezer and Ralph Erskine and from the first preaching played a big part in the movement. Indeed, it has been argued that a particular form of 'Gospel preaching' was the raison d'etre of the Secession and subsequently of the UPC.[4] What seems to have characterised Secession preaching at its best was the focus on the relationship of the individual Christian to God; one might say the experiential focus.[5] The difference between the preaching of the Secession and that of the Kirk was not doctrinal, but in the

---

[3] David Woodside, *The Soul of a Scottish Church* (Edinburgh: United Free Church, 1917), p. 145.
[4] Woodside, *Soul*, p. 146.
[5] Woodside, *Soul*, p. 147.

former's emphasis on the subjective need of the individual to be reconciled to God.[6] Consistent with this theme was the vivid, evocative language and mannerisms of Secession preaching, meant to bring the sinner to repentance.[7] Concomitantly, preachers in the Secession tradition were encouraged to avoid reading sermons, or spend too much time in ornamenting their discourses with 'fine writing'.[8] This reflected the perceived purpose of a sermon, which was to present the Gospel unadorned. Woodside comments: 'The United Presbyterian ministry, as a whole, recognized that they were there to lead men to the deeper decisions of life, and to set before them the great facts of eternal life, judgement and the world to come.'[9]

Oman's own Christian nurture and theological education was informed by interaction with some signal exponents of Secession preaching. The growth of the Secession churches in Orkney, Oman's home, had been dramatic and, according to one commentator, was largely due to the lively preaching that was offered as against the 'cold and lifeless' offerings of the Kirk.[10] Certainly, by the time of Oman's birth (1860) the UPC was flourishing in the area where he lived. The congregation in Stromness to which the Omans went had, from small beginnings with 30 communicants meeting in a school in 1806, grown to include over 500 communicants by the time of Oman's birth. Moreover, during the short history of the congregation they had erected no fewer than two church buildings and a manse. Further, the ministers whom Oman would have known during his Orkney childhood were all men of spiritual vigour. James Nisbet (1865-74) became a travelling secretary for the National Bible Society after his ministry in Stromness, whilst his successor, Thomas Kirkwood was known as an able preacher.[11] Oman was further influenced by impressive and spiritual churchmen when he attended the UPC theological hall in Edinburgh (1872-75). Principal Caird and Dr John Ker, for instance, two prominent members of staff of the time, were exemplars of spirituality and good preaching. It is particularly important to consider Ker's influence on Oman. Of Ker, it is said that he was 'pre-eminently and above all a preacher'.[12] A forerunner of Oman's in Clayport Church, Alnwick, Ker preached sermons that have been described as a 'kind of extraordinarily elevated conversation'.[13] Careful preparation leading to a full

---

[6] Woodside, *Soul*, p. 148.

[7] Woodside, *Soul*, p. 149.

[8] Though, as Woodside notes there was some discrepancy here between the Secession and Relief churches, which were the two sides of the Secession movement which combined to form the UP. See Woodside, *The Soul*, p. 151.

[9] Woodside, *The Soul*, p. 150.

[10] John Smith, *Annals of the Church of Scotland in Orkney from 1560: History of the UP Church in Orkney until 1906; and also the Episcopal Church from 1694* (Kirkwall: W R Macintosh, 1907), p. 42.

[11] Smith, *Annals*, p. 43.

[12] Woodside, *The Soul*, p. 161.

[13] Woodside, *The Soul*, p. 161.

script, led to sermons that seemed to 'come straight from the heart' and which were conveyed with telling gestures.[14] Ker published two books of sermons, the first of which went through 14 editions. No doubt, as Oman was taught homiletics by Ker and as he witnessed him in his pulpit work he would have been hugely influenced by 'UP preaching at its best'.[15] The marks of Ker's pulpit work was variety of topic, breadth of view, intense but subdued feeling, and the setting before his congregation of the choice between life and death.[16] In this way, Ker's pulpit work was evangelical, aiming to encourage, as he put it, 'life from above', which expressed itself in a 'straight, steadfast walk' that alone offers 'deeper spiritual peace' and witnesses to the truth of the faith.[17]

A little reflection on Oman's own preaching shows how greatly he was influenced by his nurture in the UPC. His preaching was always, like Ker's, aimed at challenging people to an authentic religious life. In his sermon, 'A Dialogue with God', for instance, he argues that Christian faith is not primarily about the acceptance of a scriptural revelation given in the past, but an ongoing encounter, a dialogue with the God who speaks in Scripture and awaits an answer.[18] What is truly revelatory in scripture, he holds, is the way in which it requires answers from us about our mode of life and priorities, and in this way lays bare the soul of a person. In Oman's view, the role of preaching is to evoke this experience of the word of God. To this end, Oman eschews the histrionic; his preaching is careful and passionate in a controlled way. Whilst Oman, himself was erudite, his preaching is firmly located within the Bible and where assisted by illustrations and allusions, these tended to come from the everyday, rather than the abstruse. In all these senses Oman's pulpit work stands firmly in the UPC tradition.

It may be as well here to comment on the oft repeated charge that Oman's preaching was lacking in some important respects, particularly in clarity and oral ability. The evidence about Oman's oral skills is mixed. It seems from comments of life-long friends that he was not by temperament an orator; Alexander describes him in his student days as a 'dreamy, shy youth who addressed fellow-students of his own Church with such diffidence'.[19] The comment of Rev'd T Kirkwood (Oman's former minister in Stromness) at Oman's ordination to Alnwick that he 'never thought he would come into the ministry', may also be a gentle indication of Oman's temperamental

---

[14] Woodside, *The Soul*, pp. 161-2.

[15] Woodside, *The Soul*, p. 162.

[16] Woodside, *The Soul*, p. 162.

[17] Woodside, *The Soul*, p. 163.

[18] John Oman, *A Dialogue with God* (London: James Clarke, 1950), p. 94.

[19] George Alexander, 'Memoir of the author', in John Oman, *Honest Religion*, new edn (London: Religious Book Club, 1941), pp. xv-xxv (p. xv).

unsuitability to the task of the preacher.[20] The idea of Oman's unfitness for the pulpit is given further weight by the rumours that circulated during his time at Westminster that he had been a pulpit failure, an idea that was perhaps built upon the difficulties that students themselves had with Oman's lecturing style.[21] Again, several authors have suggested that Oman's difficulty in obtaining a charge at the beginning of his career indicates a difficulty and this point is related to Hick's suggestion that the lack of an invitation to give a Gifford Lecture series was also indicative of his difficult speaking style.[22] Finally, there are Oman's own comments in which he refers to his 'native defects' in public speaking and the damage that was done to his vocal chords early on by his following bad advice in this area.[23] He also avers that he is not a 'good example' in this matter of speaking.

Clearly, Oman was not renowned for his public speaking and could not be held up as a master of the spoken word. Through a combination of diffidence, lack of native ability and, perhaps, some physical impediments preaching was a great challenge. However, there are several reasons for thinking that his inabilities in this regard have been somewhat overstated. On the matter of his call to a charge, the UPC Synod records show that when he began training he was one of 37 new students,[24] who were part of a student body numbering 123, of whom 114 were in training for the UPC ministry.[25] This is to say, that the number of ordinands in the UPC was buoyant at this time, which inevitably made it difficult for licentiates to find a charge. Indeed, there are indications in the records that Hall and Church officials recognised this problem. The minutes of Synod from 1880 indicate that the Church was in conversation with overseas churches, as well as the Presbyterian Church of England as to how to deploy the increasing numbers of students.[26] Whilst, in 1888 Hall staff petitioned the Synod to ask that assistantships be made available to probationers, a further indication, perhaps of the intractability of the difficulty for licentiates of finding a charge.[27] The impact of too many probationers chasing too few vacant

[20] 'Ordination of the Rev J. W. Oman', *Alnwick and County Gazette*, 21st December 1889, p. 8.

[21] William Wright, 'John Oman as Minister', p. 150.

[22] Alexander, 'Memoir', p. xix.

[23] John Oman, *Concerning the Ministry* (London: SCM, 1936), pp. 110-1. See also Alexander whose comment: 'in the critical years ... great thinking strove with limitations of oral expression', might indicate that as the years progressed the physical aspects of Oman's speech became an increasing problem. Alexander, 'Memoir', p. xvi.

[24] *Proceedings of the Synod of the United Presbyterian Church 1883-85* (Edinburgh: Morrison and Gibb, 1886), p. 132

[25] *Proceedings 1883-85*, p. 139.

[26] *Proceedings of the Synod of the United Presbyterian Church 1880-82* (Edinburgh: Morrison and Gibb, 1883), p. 17.

[27] *Proceedings of the Synod of the United Presbyterian Church 1886-8* (Edinburgh: Morrison and Gibb, 1889), pp. 960-1.

charges inevitably meant that it took time to find a position. This was not only Oman's experience, but that of many others including noted preachers such as David Cairns. Cairns notes that after he was licensed to preach the gospel in 1892 (a preliminary to ordination), there followed a succession of temporary appointments and sixteen failed applications for pastorates prior to his finally being settled in the borders fishing village of Ayton in 1895.[28] Bearing in mind that Cairns was not only a good preacher, but also well connected – his uncle was Professor John Cairns, Principal of the UPC theological hall – his experience puts Oman's into perspective.[29]

Again, it may be that the effectiveness of Oman's delivery has been underestimated. Certainly the valediction of William Wright, a former parishioner in Alnwick gives a very different impression from that sometimes created by authors. Wright comments on the 'deep and lasting impression on my mind and heart' left by Oman's ministry.[30] His sermons, says Wright, were usually direct and clear, the product of 'meticulous care' and written out in full. This perhaps bears out the sentiments of Alexander, who states that Oman's friends felt that once a congregation had 'got over' the initial impression given by Oman's delivery, they would grow to appreciate the value of their minister.[31]

Finally, it is worth remarking on the theological rationale of Oman's approach to speaking. Oman's colleague, T.W. Manson comments on his 'complete disdain for all ad captandum arts'.[32] This was not an attempt at self-justification, but an aspect of Oman's utter commitment to honest religion, which is to say a living, adventurous religious faith arrived at through a rigorous search for a truth that could be lived. In this regard, Manson comments that 'The secret of Oman's hold on his students was the obvious fact that he was completely in earnest in the search.'[33] The converse of this is that Oman disdained the persuasive arts in order to enable his listeners to come to their own mind on the issues. He sought, not to overpower his listeners with rhetoric, but to enable them to glimpse the issues and push out on their own spiritual quest. In Oman's view, the task of the preacher was not to form replicas of himself, but to facilitate people in reaching 'a personal grasp of truth and a personal sense of duty' even at the cost of their taking a view quite at variance

[28] David Cairns: An autobiography', ed. by A. H Cairns & D. C. Cairns with memoir by D. M. Baillie (London: SCM, 1950), pp. 11-12.

[29] See also James Brown, The Life of a Scottish Probationer, 4th edn (Glasgow: James Maclehose, 1908) for an account of another talented UPC probationer who found it difficult to find a charge.

[30] Wright, in Healey, Religion, p. 150.

[31] Alexander, 'Memoir', p. xx.

[32] T W Manson, 'Introduction' in John Oman, Vision and Authority, 8th edn with new introduction (London: Hodder, nd), pp. 1-6 (p.1).

[33] Manson, 'Introduction', p. 3.

with that of the preacher himself.[34] In this respect, Oman's approach to speaking was consistent with his idea of how God deals with each person in a wholly personal, non-coercive manner.

The Shape of his Sermons

The Motive

According to Oman, the preacher's motive must transcend cleverness, or the mere ability to hold the attention of his listeners with well-crafted sermons. The aim of the preacher is to enable his listeners to glean insight from the Bible, through discovering it to be a divine means for spiritual growth: 'profitable for teaching, for reproof, for correction, for discipline in righteousness'.[35] Part of what is implied is that the preacher has a reasonably adequate knowledge of the scholarly lights, so that she can convey effectively and enthusiastically to her audience that 'the Bible is a library of great religious literature, each book of it a message to its own age and having a message still for ours'.[36] However, the preacher's ability to convey the excitement of the Bible is subordinate to her task of exposing her listeners to the word of God 'something which even the Bible only serves'.[37] The word of God – the essential message of the Bible and the heart of the Christian life is the perception that 'in spite of all the seeming success of violence and evil…, it is mercy and righteousness and not violence and evil which rule the world'.[38] This 'word' is not a mere external piece of information which can be gleaned from a book, but is a matter of spiritual discernment that goes against all appearances.[39] It is a matter of 'digging down to the true meaning of life and listening to the voice of God in all their conduct of it'.[40] This describes the means by which the writers of the Bible discerned the 'word' and it describes the process by which all people of faith discern the 'word' in their own time. The task of the preacher is to enable this encounter with the word to take place. The encounter takes place when men and women learn to live triumphantly through faith; it is only then that the preached word actually becomes good news in the experience of those who hear.[41] 'Every man must learn truth that is to be of value to him in life, in his own experience'.[42]

---

[34] Oman, *Dialogue with God*, p. 147.
[35] Oman, *Concerning the Ministry*, pp. 234-5.
[36] Oman, *Concerning the Ministry*, p. 235.
[37] Oman, *Concerning the Ministry*, p.236.
[38] Oman, *Concerning the Ministry*, p. 237.
[39] Oman, *Concerning the Ministry*, pp. 237-8.
[40] Oman, *Concerning the Ministry*, p. 238.
[41] Oman, *Concerning the Ministry*, p. 239.
[42] Oman, *Dialogue with God*, p. 70.

The Form

Oman's style of preaching, as alluded above, tends to be careful and perhaps sometimes wordy, but often sprinkled with pithy sayings and vivid illustrations. His sermons are typically built upon the solid ground of biblical exposition.

Taking the latter feature first, Oman's comments on preaching to his students express his own practice. In his view, the Bible 'is the most wonderful book in the world' offering the preacher 'endlessly varied inspiration and endlessly full instruction'.[43] Moreover, the Bible should not be used simply as a peg for one's own thoughts, but should ideally shape one's preaching: '...as a general habit, preaching on a text and not merely with one, and that in its exact meaning, is a great safeguard from keeping out of ruts both in matter and treatment'.[44] Indeed, since Oman values the truth as it was seen in 'life and action', he counsels that attention to the context of words in the lives of people was essential to appreciating their message.[45] Rather than dealing with ideas such as 'meekness' in abstraction from the Bible, he argued that the full sense of this idea could only be seen as it was exemplified in the life of Jesus, where it was seen as 'no passivity, but the active acceptance of God's will'.[46] In Oman's view, the setting out of abstract theological ideas should not take the place of attention to the concrete words and images of scripture. This was a homiletic principle, but also perhaps alluded to Oman's doubts about the possibility and usefulness of a system of doctrine serving as a hermeneutical key to the whole of scripture.[47] Further, attention to the range of scripture would lead the preacher to dwell on the various moods and interests of human life, and not only to those moods or attitudes to which she most easily fell.[48]

An examination of some of Oman's own published sermons indicates the extent to which he followed his own dictums on scripture based preaching. In 'God's victory and ours' (based on Psalm 146.4), for instance, he uses his text to launch into a discourse on salvation as victory over the flesh and the devil, discussing his theme in some detail through analysis of the story of Jonathan and Saul – albeit that his analysis is somewhat allegorical – and through discussing the example of Jesus.[49] In 'Faith' (based on Mark 2.1-12), Oman suggests that faith is essentially trusting in Jesus as the 'manifestation of the goodness and mercy of God', and he examines this theme through detailed

---

[43] Oman, *Concerning the Ministry*, p. 228.

[44] Oman, *Concerning the Ministry*, p. 229.

[45] Oman, *Concerning the Ministry*, pp. 229-30.

[46] Oman, *Concerning the Ministry*, p. 230.

[47] Oman, *Concerning the Ministry*, p. 233.

[48] Oman, *Concerning the Ministry*, p. 233; See also 'The Exposition of the Word' in Oman, *Dialogue with God*, pp. 145-152, for a discussion of Oman's adherence to expository preaching.

[49] In Oman, *Dialogue with God*, pp. 9-14.

scrutiny of the motives and moods of the men involved in the story of the healing of the paralytic – once again using an allegorical technique.[50]

Even where Oman doesn't proceed through detailed exposition of a particular text, he always preaches in a way that is suffused with biblical awareness. In his sermon 'The purpose of calamity' (based on Phil 3.10), he discusses the role of suffering in the Christian's life through drawing on a range of biblical allusions, sometimes metaphorical – such as his use of 'pillar of cloud' and 'pillar of fire' – and sometimes more direct, such as his reflections on Christ's sufferings as a model for our own.[51]

In his book *Preaching*, Fred Craddock identifies six possible ways in which the Bible can be used in preaching.[52] Of these, three methods seem to typify Oman's sermons: direct, thematic and typological preaching. Direct preaching is the relatively uncritical application of a passage to an audience. Craddock comments that sometimes this can be appropriate, as when the preacher comes to the conclusion, through intense study, that a passage says today what it said in the past, but this approach can also, in unskilled hands be 'pernicious and destructive'.[53] In Oman's oeuvre there are examples of good use of this technique. Thus, to give one example, in his sermon on Paul's injunction to be content in all things ('Christian contentment' based Phil 4.12) Oman very effectively applies Paul's words as a perennial lesson informing all Christian discipleship.[54] Oman holds that Paul's words teach that the Kingdom of God is spiritual and not material (the working out of God's purposes of love) and that the supreme litmus test of our lives is what Jesus thinks of us, which frees us from concerns about the material state of our lives. In this way, Oman draws out lessons that are perennial.

Thematic preaching is that which aims to interpret particular passages in the light of and as expressions of the major themes of the Bible.[55] That is, such preaching aims to present a unified body of Christian thought through a consideration of particular texts. The continuity and constant repetition in Oman's sermons of themes such as the Christian's victory over adversity through their faith and their sense of vocation, suggests how important this method was to him. An example of Oman's thematic preaching is his sermon 'A sinful heart' (Rom 1.18) in which he talks of the Bible's analysis of sin from 'Genesis to Revelation'.[56] In this sermon, Oman draws on the definition of sin in the Westminster Catechism and discusses the theme of sin on a broad canvas, drawing on a range of texts. Another example of thematic preaching is

---

[50] In Oman, *Dialogue with God*, pp. 24-9.

[51] In Oman, *Dialogue with God*, pp. 30-4.

[52] Fred B. Craddock, *Preaching* (Nashville: Abingdon, 1985), pp. 136-50.

[53] Craddock, *Preaching*, p. 138.

[54] In Oman, *Dialogue with God*, pp. 61-6.

[55] Craddock, *Preaching*, pp.145-7.

[56] Oman, *Dialogue with God*, pp. 67-73 (p. 67).

'Freedom and obligation', which is a discourse on the meaning of Christian freedom that draws on a range of ideas and is not tied to any one text or exposition thereof.[57]

Again, Craddock talks of typological preaching, which is 'a way of addressing present listeners with an ancient text by discerning in that text events or conditions having clear correspondence to those of the listeners'.[58] This mode of interpretation is based on the premise that there are analogies to be drawn between the text and contemporary life; perhaps, for example, in both, people face similar issues and encounter the same God. An interesting example of Oman's use of the typological method is found in his sermon 'The goodness of God'.[59] In this sermon, Oman considers the text Ex 33.18-19, which is concerned with Moses' request that he might see God's glory, and God's response, which is that he allows Moses to see only his goodness. The key to Oman's hermeneutic here is his comment that 'if we read this narrative with a desire to see the spiritual meaning in it, we shall find something that agrees with our own experience'.[60] According to Oman, like Moses, all humans desire to see God's glory. This is because we think we need a clear view of God's power 'for success and for hope and joy'.[61] In developing this theme, Oman gives close attention to Moses situation. As leader of a 'horde of slaves' in a precarious situation, Moses might well pray for an evidence of God's power. In the same way, in our situations we seek 'the grand manifestation of His existence, the grand manifestation of His presence'.[62] This, says Oman, is part of what natural theology is about; it is a kind of 'prayer for divine light'.[63] Likewise, our attempts to read providence off history are attempts to identify the glory of God. Like Moses, however, our attempts to see the glory of God are frustrated. We see but a glimpse of God's power and purposes in history or in nature; 'we are only flies seeing the shadows on a tiny pool'.[64] However, this is not to say that we know nothing of God's goodness. Like Moses, though we are denied a panorama of God's power, yet in the day to day encounters that we have with Him we do know Him, through the 'countless blessings of our lives'.[65] In Moses' case, in his struggles he was maintained by the daily grace of 'strength for the present burden'.[66] He knew in practice the 'response of a

[57] Oman, *Dialogue with God*, pp. 74-80.
[58] Craddock, *Preaching*, p. 141.
[59] Oman, *Dialogue with God*, pp. 35-40; See also 'The Transfiguration' for another good example of typological preaching, Oman, *A Dialogue*, pp. 128-133.
[60] Oman, *Dialogue with God*, p. 35.
[61] Oman, *Dialogue with God*, p. 36.
[62] Oman, *Dialogue with God*, p. 36.
[63] Oman, *Dialogue with God*, p. 36.
[64] Oman, *Dialogue with God*, p. 37.
[65] Oman, *Dialogue with God*, p. 38.
[66] Oman, *Dialogue with God*, p. 38.

father's heart'.[67] Likewise, in Christ what we find is not an explanation of God's being, but an articulation of God's goodness seen in His humility and suffering. Jesus reveals 'the heart which beats for all with an infinite affection'.[68] What God gives Moses and us alike is what we need for 'the immediate direction and support of our lives'; that is, the confirmation of the goodness of the Father which governs all things.[69]

Pithy and Graphic

If pithy is 'condensed, terse and forcible' then Oman often shows this quality in his preaching. His sermons show attention to the framing of memorable phrases that capture some spiritual message. Thus, to give some examples, in talking of the value of suffering he speaks of it teaching that there is 'more in life than enjoyment ... more in suffering than mere sorrow';[70] in referring to the power of the Gospel, he comments: 'it places us so securely on the bosum of the Omnipotent Love';[71] describing the misunderstanding of meekness, he talks of it being understood as 'a virtue of the jelly-fish', 'a standing apology for having the misfortune to exist'; [72] on the Christian life he comments, 'his [the Christian] is no journey to heaven by the primrose path', some days 'you smell the earth and see the worm'.[73] In discussing the Bible he says that too often it is 'treated as a gay-hearted person might treat his doctor. He is looked on as a dear old man and very careful, but a terrible alarmist'.[74]

Oman commonly uses illustrations in his sermons, but avoids allowing these to overpower his text, or the biblical content of what he is saying. The sources of his illustrations are varied. Some are drawn from his knowledge of high culture, for instance, the paintings of Rubens, Rembrandt and Tintoretto.[75] Again the writings of novelists, poets and thinkers feature regularly, see, for example his allusion to the *Tempest* in his sermon 'Turfing the grave'.[76] Also, see his discussion of John Woolman's *Journal* in 'Justice and piety'.[77] Regularly his illustrations are drawn from his early experience of life in Orkney. Ships and the seamen often feature. A particularly powerful example of this is found in his sermon 'The peacemaker and the peaceable' where he speaks of the impression made upon him of 'a fisherman whose face used to

---

[67] Oman, *Dialogue with God*, p. 38.
[68] Oman, *Dialogue with God*, p. 39.
[69] Oman, *Dialogue with God*, p. 39.
[70] Oman, *Dialogue with God*, p. 30.
[71] Oman, *Dialogue with God*, p. 34.
[72] Oman, *Dialogue with God*, p. 9.
[73] Oman, *Dialogue with God*, p. 16.
[74] Oman, *Dialogue with God*, p. 67.
[75] Oman, *Dialogue with God*, p. 41.
[76] Oman, *Dialogue with God*, pp. 45-8.
[77] Oman, *Dialogue with God*, pp. 41-4.

haunt me when I was a boy'.[78] Oman takes the old fisherman as an illustration of the way in which experience of life can be the basis for peace in adversity, but also of Christ – the one who offers us peace because of his mastering of life. Sometimes, Oman uses his own adult experiences and travels to illustrate his talks. In 'Incarnate majesty' he makes very effective use of his trip to the cathedrals at Louvain and Antwerp, utilising a detailed discussion of the ritual and images of both places to discourse on Christ's majesty.[79] Again, in 'Turfing the grave' he reflects insightfully on his experience of the dedication of a war memorial in Cambridge.[80]

His Message

Alan Sell has suggested elsewhere in this volume that Oman's sermons tend to strike 'soteriological notes which are normally muted' in his more academic works. I would frame this insight somewhat differently, saying that Oman's sermons are marked by his desire to provide practical, down-to-Earth assistance to his hearers in living the Christian life. This means that his sermons are primarily concerned to explain what the practice of the Christian faith consists of, especially how it is grounded in a view of the divine providence; and the role of Jesus as saviour. In his sermon 'Incarnate majesty' Oman indicates his fear that he will present his subject as 'abstract and unpractical as if it were not a concern of daily life'.[81] This concern drives his preaching throughout and gives it an immediacy and clarity that is sometime lacking in his other work. This means that his sermons are a good place to begin engaging with Oman's oeuvre as a whole, since they touch his key concerns in an accessible way.

The Practice of Faith

In Oman's view, faith is a way of being-in-the- world, which sees the world for what it is, but sees in the world more than the natural eye can glimpse. Faith is a way of being, in that it is a practice rather than merely a set of beliefs or a religious experience. Oman comments that the 'radical, fundamental element' in Christian piety is 'God worshipped in deed and in truth'.[82] Moreover, such faith relates, unflinchingly and sincerely to the world as it is. This is borne out for Oman by the centrality of the Cross itself to Christianity, since the Cross represents 'naked, unjust, human agony which is life's supreme mystery'. This

---

[78] In John Oman, *The Paradox of the World* (London: CUP, 1921), pp. 155-167 (p. 162). See also for other illustrative examples of Oman's use of Orkney for illustration – Oman, *Dialogue with God*, p. 15; Oman, *Paradox of the World*, p. 7.

[79] Oman, *Dialogue with God*, pp. 49-53 (pp. 51-2).

[80] Oman, *Dialogue with God*, pp. 45-49.

[81] Oman, *Dialogue with God*, p. 58.

[82] Oman, *Dialogue with God*, p. 44.

is to say that faith faces up to the harsh realities of life, its transience and sinfulness. It does not minimise 'life's darkest trials', nor does it seek to avoid the depths of human agony through the diversions of possessions, sensuous pleasures or reputation.[83] Instead, the way of faith is to look unflinchingly on the world with all its blemishes, but to find hidden depths of meaning within the suffering of the world. 'The Cross is a mystery and the actual deliverance it works is not to remove mystery but to give a new attitude towards it.'[84]

In contrast to the 'objective' character of faith – its character as the search for meaning in the world as it is – there lies human insincerity. This, for Oman, is the opposite of faith and it expresses itself in a number of modes, subtly differentiated. The heart of insincerity is the desire to substitute God's will and truth for what is humanly desirable – depicted as the truth. Ultimately the issue is what we value most, 'humble and unselfish serving', or self-serving.[85] One mode of insincerity is the use of apparently good practices to draw attention to ourselves. Another might be hatred of what one tacitly feels to be the truth. Still another might be the conscious attempt to avoid hearing what one fears to be true. Again, the attempt to merely remove the obstacles to one's preferred beliefs, allied with little concern about possible alternatives is a still more subtle form of insincerity. Oman comments: 'True sincerity is not a mere emotional response to impressions, but puts all its mind, as well as all its heart, into interpreting the signs.'[86] An illustration of sincerity that Oman gives is that of the fisherman considering the weather prior to deciding whether to venture out on the sea. Drawing on his past experience, he gives full, conscientious attention to all the various signs that bear on the life and death decision that he has to make. In contrast, the insincere are like children on the morning of a picnic who interpret the weather out of an overriding concern to 'be allowed to go'.[87]

The Cross is central to Oman's understanding of the distinctive attitude of faith. Oman has no sympathy for ways of thinking of the crucified one that make his death a symbol of 'magical ceremonies'.[88] He has little time for the transactional theories of an Anselm or other forms of 'objective' understanding of the crucifixion.[89] In Oman's view, the importance of the Cross is that it reveals the agonies of the world, yet also the faith of Christ in the loving purposes of God through these agonies. This is to say that on the Cross we glimpse, through the trust of Jesus in his heavenly Father, the possibility of seeing the whole of life as permeated with the love of God.

---

[83] Oman, *Dialogue with God*, p. 47.
[84] Oman, *Dialogue with God*, p. 46.
[85] Oman, *Paradox of the World*, pp. 2-4.
[86] Oman, *Paradox of the World*, p. 7.
[87] Oman, *Paradox of the World*, p. 7.
[88] Oman, *Dialogue with God*, p. 46.
[89] Oman, *Paradox of the World*, p. 128.

This [the Cross] for us, as for the apostle, is the true unblurred mirror of life in which we see all that is dark and distressing in life, transforming itself however partially and brokenly and dimly, into a face of divine love which knows us perfectly, however imperfectly we know it. This is the heart of the Christian faith. It does not turn all our darkness into light, or make all our paths smooth, or deliver from all sense of blindness and weariness and distress, but it enables us to trust that God's love is in them.[90]

Nor does the person and work of Christ – the Gospel – bring about a new phase in God's dealings with humankind, though it offers a clearer statement of what has ever been true of God.

God's message is the same at all times and in all things, and is not different, but only plainer and fuller and better authenticated in Jesus Christ. He is no mere incident contrary to the burden of the rest of creation and revelation, but is the consummation and supreme manifestation of all they mean.[91]

The crucified Jesus, in the first place, helps us to see the darkness of human life in all its horror.[92] The light that Christ brings is not cheery, but illuminating.[93] Since the Cross 'penetrates to the heart of all sorrow', in that there injustice, bigotry and hypocrisy triumphed, then we can be sure that in all circumstances of life God's love can be revealed and His purposes served.[94] Moreover, just as the disciples found that the experience of the Cross was most 'fruitful' in teaching them who was God and what they were, so it is that it is only as Christians focus on the suffering Son of Man that they catch a glimpse of God as He is.[95]

Faith then is understood as trust in the loving purposes of God through the vicissitudes of life. An aspect of this faith is that it is grounded in a trusting attitude to the Father, which far exceeds the believer's understanding of the 'wheres and why-fors' of life. This trust is grounded in the experience of the love of God and in the paradigmatic example of Christ. However, it does not include a full knowledge of the ways of providence. One metaphor that Oman uses to describe faith, in this regard, is that it is like trekking across rough country in the twilight towards a dimly visible horizon. The horizon – God's love – draws one on in the journey, though the ground over which one travels is

---

[90] Oman, *Dialogue with God*, p. 47.
[91] Oman, *Paradox of the World*, p. 129.
[92] Oman, *Paradox of the World*, p. 79.
[93] Oman, *Dialogue with God*, p. 78; Oman, *Paradox of the World*, p. 100.
[94] Oman, *Dialogue with God*, p. 126.
[95] Oman, *Dialogue with God*, p. 132.

only vaguely seen. In Oman's view, the partiality of our understanding of providence is to do with our inability to grasp the 'height and blessedness of God's loving purpose', he writes, 'Life is so dark a mystery just because God is love and His love is infinite and can be manifested to us blind, sinful, finite mortals only in broken glimpses'.[96]

With regard to the partiality of our grasp of providence, Oman holds that the limit on our understanding is both moral and epistemological. It is moral, in that sin gets in the way. Sin, for Oman is not just a neglect of the Ten Commandments, but is the desire to avoid the truth about God and to live independently of Him.[97] The truth about God is that concerning His love and the demands that His love place upon us. Sin, in contrast, is the insincerity that avoids the truth at all costs in the service of self-interest. The sincere seeker after truth is always hungry for the truth, ready to revise settled views, courageous in departing from the conventional opinion, always willing to listen to those who, with integrity, challenge the norm.[98] Nor is the litmus test of truth, happiness, for there can be contentment in untruth since minds can be habituated to look for that which is merely enjoyable or comfortable.[99] All this means, that perceiving the truth and being ready to live out the truth are two dimensions of the same experience.

An aspect of the moral impediment to spiritual perception is that very often people's perception of the truth is blurred by reason of their desire to avoid the challenges of the truth. Conversely, one can tell much about a person's sincerity by their actions and the reactions of others to these.[100] In this regard, Oman argues that the 'peacemaker' is often the person who lives a tempestuous life because they are habitually fighters against 'every disturbing, disruptive force', that is, they fight against selfishness in all its guises.[101] In this sense, the peacemakers are not the peaceable – that latter look for an easy life, which is the very epitome of the selfishness that the peacemaker fights against. Oman, speaking of the peaceable, comments that, so far as the Church is concerned,

> He is the most dangerous man in it … Under his shelter all abuses tend to gather, all the poisonous low vapours which only the lighting and the hurricane can purge away. The evil which corrupts the world is not fostered mainly by bad men, but by ease-loving men who will never take their stand upon principle and dare the consequences.[102]

---

[96] Oman, *Dialogue with God*, p. 47.
[97] Oman, *Dialogue with God*, p. 69.
[98] Oman, *Dialogue with God*, p. 71.
[99] Oman, *Dialogue with God*, pp. 71-2.
[100] Oman, *Paradox of the World*, p. 159.
[101] Oman, *Paradox of the World*, p. 159.
[102] Oman, *Paradox of the World*, p. 160.

The challenge of grasping the lineaments of providence are also epistemological in that our finitude prevents us grasping the breadth of the loving purposes that God has for the world. God works slowly, allowing time for humans to come to a willing understanding and obedience to the truth. However, individuals tend to judge God's ways on the basis of brief incidents or life spans.[103] The issue here is not just an inevitable consequence of the finitude of human beings, but is closely connected to the character of the faith that God wills. An assumption of Oman's is that God always deals with human beings as personal, autonomous beings and that He desires only obedience that is willing and freely offered: 'If He cannot have free service He cares for no other'.[104] This means that, for Oman, God's way of working with humankind is persuasive rather than coercive and this explains why God works slowly and through the normal messiness of life. A God who, for instance, always rewarded faith with material rewards would remove the moral space in which faith and willing obedience develops.

It's interesting to surmise that in his emphasis on the epistemic limitations of the Christian, Oman may be mirroring an aspect of Scottish thought with a provenance going back at least as far back as the eighteenth century. Fergusson comments that Thomas Reid, for one, was very aware of the boundaries of human knowledge; he continues: 'This awareness of the limits of knowledge produces a distinctive form of piety. By attending to what we can know, we are able to live wisely in the darkness.' [105]

In the passing, it is important to note that, contrary to the stereotypical view of a 'liberal' theology, Oman's theology is rooted in an awareness of the shadowside of life. He is, in fact, disparaging of a view that sees Christianity as, 'only a roundabout way of arriving at the belief that God looked after things and made it easy for sensible people'.[106] The faith that avoids dark problems and moral difficulties is fragile.[107] In contrast, Christian faith is concerned to look 'every evil straight in the face' and finding 'a way beyond it'.[108] 'The ground of our faith must ever lie on the other side of Gethsemane and Calvary.'[109] True faith is that which realises how insignificant human beings are in the context of the universe as a whole; it sees 'what sorrows and sins mar even what is granted to us of life and movement, what an unsatisfactory, dreary, wretched business life is for countless thousands'.[110] 'No word of God

[103] Oman, *Dialogue with God*, p. 56.
[104] Oman, *Dialogue with God*, p. 88.
[105] David Fergusson, 'Introduction' in *Scottish Philosophical Theology 1700-2000*, ed. by David Fergusson (Exeter & Charlottesville: Imprint, 2007), pp. 1-24 (p. 6).
[106] Oman, *Dialogue with God*, p. 123.
[107] Oman, *Dialogue with God*, p. 122.
[108] Oman, *Dialogue with God*, p. 123.
[109] Oman, *Dialogue with God*, p. 123.
[110] Oman, *Dialogue with God*, p. 123.

blinks a fact, and no one is a prophet except as he sees deeper into evil and feels more bitterly oppression and wrong than other men.'[111]

> Faith is not blindness to life's uncertainties and miseries. Until faith in providence as mere beneficence breaks down, the faith which reconciles us to God in face of every conceivable evil cannot arise. But, then, nothing whatsoever in the world is omitted from what works together for good.[112]

Such a perspective frames the belief that in all things God is working for good, which is counter intuitive, not a 'mere natural religion'.[113] Faith looks beyond surface appearances and interprets the world in terms of a 'meaning stretching far beyond' these.[114] It is the centrality of this strong doctrine of providence that explains Oman's comments in the preface to *Grace and Personality* that the experience of the First World War forced him to a 'reconsideration of my whole religious position'. He continues, 'the fact that such sorry and wickedness could happen in the world, became the crucible in which my whole view of the world had to be tested'.[115] This is not the confession of a man who previously had looked only for the best in humankind, but the sincere questioning of a theologian who, looking open eyed at human sinfulness, had always argued that there was a deeper, divine meaning to be found in human experience. Oman's published post-war sermons show a heightened awareness of human sinfulness, but do not materially change his position.[116] The war made him more acutely aware of the failure of the human trust in progress based on educational opportunity, material prosperity or the discoveries of science.[117] He traces the source of social wrongs to the human heart and the 'covetous soul'.[118] The key question is what do people value most; what do they worship. Wars, says Oman, can never be brought to an end until humans give up the worship of those things 'for which wars are made'.[119] In this sense, his reflections on the Great War confirmed him in his view of the centrality of religious questions when it came to the wrongs of life and thus reinforced his pessimism about the resolution of human problems through non-religious means.

---

[111] Oman, *Paradox of the World*, p. 66.
[112] Oman, *Paradox of the World*, p. 112.
[113] Oman, *Dialogue with God*, p. 123.
[114] Oman, *Dialogue with God*, p. 124.
[115] John Oman, *Grace and Personality*, reissue (London & Glasgow: Fontana, 1960), p. 5.
[116] See, for instance, Oman, *Paradox*, pp. 60-97.
[117] Oman, *Paradox of the World*, p. 65.
[118] Oman, *Paradox of the World*, p. 69.
[119] Oman, *Paradox of the World*, p. 69.

If faith is trust in God's purposes, then its practical outworking is obedience or submission to the will of God.[120] There seem to be two dimensions to this. First, the task of the ministry of the Church and of the Christian discipline of prayer are to enable believers to submit to the vision of God's love that we see in Christ. In the example of Jesus' self-sacrificial love of the Other, we see what it is to submit to the Father.[121] Moreover, the submission of the Christian to God's will is not in tension with, but is the fullest expression of freedom. Freedom, here is not just liberty to do what one wishes, but the use of one's liberty to pursue the highest duties – it is to be liberated, through a sincere awareness of God's will, from slavery to the pursuance of mere pleasure or reputation or ease of life.[122] In this regard, Christ sets the Christian free by offering, through his life and death, a deeper awareness of God's love and the supreme importance of our response to that love. The influence of Jesus is liberating because in the light of his devotion to the Father every other obligation is relativised.

Second, submission to the will of God includes an acceptance of the apparently contingent circumstances of one's life as the will of God.[123]This acceptance is what the Bible calls meekness, understood as a:

Glad sense of a wiser, more loving power over and around our life and all lives, wiser and greater than any foresight of man can measure, of a power to which therefore we should joyfully submit, accepting the duties it enjoins, bearing the trials it appoints, and thus march steadily onwards, our faces even in the darkest night facing the dawn.[124]

Oman carefully distinguishes meekness from fatalism by reason of the Christian's awareness that they are in the hands of a loving God, not an impersonal fate. Indeed, the salvation that Christianity offers arises within the awareness of life being in the hands of infinite wisdom and love.

As well as faith being individual, Oman also considers it corporate. In discussing the corporate character of Christianity, he emphasises that it is grounded in Christian fellowship, which is the close spiritual relationship amongst Christians rooted in the common possession of a 'common good', the Christian Gospel.[125] Underpinning this communal relationship is the fellowship that Christians have with God. The fellowship that Christians share is that arising from their individual, but shared experience of seeing the truth in Jesus, which has divine authority because it has effectively, experientially reconciled

---

[120] Oman, *Dialogue with God*, p. 56.

[121] Oman, *Dialogue with God*, p. 58.

[122] Oman, *Dialogue with God*, pp. 74-5.

[123] Oman, *Dialogue with God*, p. 13.

[124] Oman, *Dialogue with God*, p. 11.

[125] Oman, *Paradox of the World*, p. 264.

them to the world and to God.[126] Their unity therefore resided in a 'common vision of the same reality' and is constituted by their individual response to the word of the Lord.[127] It can, indeed only be constituted in this way because the sole purpose of the Gospel is to bring 'joy and emancipation' to people and this can only come about as people gladly perceive and receive the message: 'Good-news, by its very nature, cannot be forced upon the mind, but must sing its way into the heart'.[128] Moreover the unity that faith brings about challenges and breaks down the 'divisive forces of human nature and human society' – class, status and power differentials.[129] It is nothing less than the context of God's rule, which is a challenge to the order of the world and in this way the fellowship of the Church is, itself, the most effective hermeneutic of the Gospel.[130]

Jesus as Saviour

H.H. Farmer reputedly said that Oman did not have a Christology. This, I think, has been shown to be unfair. Oman may not have been very interested in the finer points of Chalcedon, but his theology, as represented in his sermons, is remarkably Christ centred in that Jesus is seen as both the supreme articulation of God's love and of the ideal pattern of human faith and obedience. Because Oman is primarily interested in nurturing faith, his Christology might be described as 'functional'. Whether or not one regards this as a 'proper' Christology is, of course, a reflection of one's theological persuasion.

At the heart of Oman's understanding of the Christ as saviour, is his perception that he is saviour as a man who faced up to 'unjust human agony which is life's supreme mystery' and who was able to achieve a personal victory over the injustice of his suffering.[131] Christ accepted the Cross through his trust in the Father that obedience to the divine will was within the His purposes of love. And through his acceptance of the Cross as the way of obedience, Jesus transfigured the mystery of suffering into the mystery of God's love. The Cross is therefore not defeat, but 'the death that brings joy into all sorrow'.[132] That is, through his ability to accept suffering and trust that there was divine meaning within it, Jesus invites the Christian to adopt a new attitude to life that penetrates to the love that permeates all experience. The harsh experiences of life are not thereby rendered transparent, but a different attitude is taken up towards them because there is trust that God's love is being worked

---

[126] Oman, *Paradox of the World*, p. 266.
[127] Oman, *Paradox of the World*, p. 267.
[128] Oman, *Paradox of the World*, p. 273.
[129] Oman, *Paradox of the World*, p. 269.
[130] Oman, *Paradox of the World*, p. 277.
[131] Oman, *Dialogue with God*, p. 46.
[132] Oman, *Dialogue with God*, p. 49.

out through and in all. There is still a mystery – the mystery of how God's love is being expressed in the vicissitudes of everyday life – and this remains a mystery because humans are sinful and finite. Yet through trusting in God as Jesus did, the Christian is delivered from the mystery of suffering.[133]

Jesus is saviour, then, not because his life and death change the facts of existence, but because through adopting his attitude we are enabled to relate in a new ways to the 'facts'.[134] Salvation is to trust that through all the duties, challenges and difficulties of life that God's love is being worked out. 'Did we always know that it fashions all our discipline and directs all our tasks, there is no life that would not be blessed.'[135] In this way of thinking, the eschatological hope is that one day the Christian will understand more fully how the love of God was being worked out in human experience.[136]

The Cross is also saving in the sense that it bears witness, from the God-ward side, to the Father's loving purpose to overcome the 'bondage of sin' and the 'chaos and ruin it works in God's world'. The Cross, in this regard is the supreme expression of God's devotion to the task of liberating humankind from sin.

> Had there been no death, what expression, what vehicle, what instrument could God have found to utter and convey the entire, the absolute devotion of His love, to maintain the majesty of His injured law and redeem the guilt of his erring children.[137]

Oman's statement of Christ's divinity is framed in terms of his understanding of Christ's victory over sin. Through his torn flesh his 'divine majesty' is shown.[138] In Christ, God shows himself as love and this is revealed through the self-surrender of Christ in service to others and through his obedience to God, which is the meaning of calling Christ one with the Father.[139] In Christ, we see that what God values above all is 'meekness and patience ... a heart receptive of His truth and responsive to His will'.[140] Christ, 'whose life was in another sphere', lived and died within our sinful world and through all the conflicts of human life that typically cause people to 'doubt God's love', Christ remained faithful to a vision of God's love permeating all of life.[141] In this way, Christ is both a revelation of God's own being, and also a model of

---

[133] Oman, *Dialogue with God*, p. 46.
[134] Oman, *Dialogue with God*, p. 47.
[135] Oman, *Dialogue with God*, p. 48.
[136] Oman, *Dialogue with God*, p. 48, p. 120.
[137] Oman, *Dialogue with God*, p. 120.
[138] Oman, *Dialogue with God*, p. 49.
[139] Oman, *Dialogue with God*, p. 11.
[140] Oman, *Dialogue with God*, p. 125.
[141] Oman, *Dialogue with God*, p. 92.

the realisation of human life.[142] Christ's life, in that sense transfigures our understanding of God and ourselves. It is in this way, that Christ is a liberator; he reveals what are our highest obligations to God and ourselves and in this way releases us from the domination of 'lower' duties and demands.[143] 'To obey God and follow Christ. This is the liberty wherewith Christ has set us free.'[144] Christ is our liberator as a man, but it is only as a unique man – the incarnate Son – that he is able to show humankind a love through which victory over sin and suffering is possible.[145] 'Reconciliation to God is just agreement with His mind about this good. What it is appears in Jesus Christ. He is the Second Adam – all God intends man to be.'[146]

Moreover Oman understands that the revelation in Christ is confirmed by the resurrection[147] and is perpetual because the ascended Christ has not changed: he is still the prince of peace in the old way of 'sacrifice and love'.[148]

In his suggestive sermon, 'A dialogue with God', Oman uses the metaphor of a dialogue to clarify the sense in which Christ reveals the Father.[149] Christ reveals God because God 'had specially to do with Jesus'. That is, Jesus is uniquely the Son of God, God's representative on earth. In this sense, Jesus is God speaking to us. However, Jesus is also uniquely a human being speaking to God. He is the one human being of whom it can be said that 'the will of the Father was the breath of life to Him', so that in his faithful response to God he shows us how we ought to live before the Father.[150] Jesus, in this way is, as human being, the word of God which both guides and judges our way of life. In relation to this latter point, Oman's argument is that Christ stands as God's eternal expression of what is of ultimate value in human life, so that his life probes and challenges our lives; in Christ, God spells out what is our 'highest good' and awaits our response. His word in Jesus is one of judgement because it includes an explanation of the consequences of our deceiving ourselves and refusing to respond positively to God's word in Christ. Oman comments, 'That, after all, is the only judgement that can matter much, the only condemnation from which love itself cannot save us, that we have seen the light and reject it because we are not of it, that we hear the appeal of love and answer it with hatred.'[151] In contrast:

---

[142] Oman, *Dialogue with God*, p. 58.
[143] Oman, *Dialogue with God*, p. 75.
[144] Oman, *Dialogue with God*, p. 77.
[145] Oman, *Dialogue with God*, p. 33.
[146] Oman, *Paradox of the World*, p. 114.
[147] Oman, *Dialogue with God*, p. 51.
[148] Oman, *Dialogue with God*, p. 88.
[149] Oman, *Dialogue with God*, pp. 94-5.
[150] Oman, *Dialogue with God*, p. 95.
[151] Oman, *Dialogue with God*, p. 116.

To awake to this folly [self-deception] is repentance and peace with God. It is simply the recognition that your replies to God are all wrong and that your dialogue with Him in life is getting quite perverted by your own answers, and a great cry in your heart to know reality at all costs and be taught by God what you are to reply to Him. It is to desire to be open and naked with God with whom you have to do, which is only possible by being naked and open to your own eyes as well.[152]

Not only is Christ's example a revelation of the divine love, his Cross is also an instantiation of God's loving relationship with humankind. It is in the sense that it has the status of an invitation to share in God's love through a free response. 'The reason why the Cross of Christ means so much is just that God beseeches us in it by every sacrifice love can offer, and tells us that He can only beseech He cannot compel.'[153] This is to say, the saving influence of the Cross is its power to evoke a free response to the love of God as shown in the life of Jesus. The space for human freedom is maintained in that the Cross reveals God's goodness, not his omnipotence.[154] Using Oman's metaphor of dialogue, we might say that God speaks through the story of the Cross, but he leaves room in this story for humans to reply. The Cross is not an articulation of an objective law that says that acceptance of the crucified one will lead to prosperity. It is rather a mode of divine 'counsel', which is only truly effective as people come to apprehend it for themselves as the truth about the 'way He has actually made the world'.[155] Moreover, the divine counsel or wisdom that is apprehended in the Cross is never exhaustive, for there is always room for the individual to make further discoveries about God's purposes for the world.

Conclusion

Oman's theology has sometimes been portrayed as opaque and one cannot dispute that some of his writings are obscure. This being so, a study of his sermons can be of great benefit in orientating oneself to his thought as a whole. His sermons reflect his rootedness in the UPC tradition with their focus on the experience of faith. They are thoughtful, sometimes inspiring and often couched in captivating phrases and imaginative illustrations. The message they convey is that faith is an attitude to life based on the perception that the whole of experience, good and bad, is held in the loving purposes of the Father. Jesus is central to faith in that he reveals the love of God the Father and also the human faith and obedience that can be victorious through all the storms of life. In Jesus, we see that faith is not a matter of prospering in a material sense, but

[152] Oman, *Dialogue with God*, p. 97.
[153] Oman, *Dialogue with God*, pp. 88-9.
[154] Oman, *Dialogue with God*, p. 39.
[155] Oman, *Paradox of the World*, p. 229.

of living obediently as he did. Moreover, the manner of God's approach to us in Jesus, shows that God wishes humans to grow into faith through a sincere search for truth. In Jesus we are not overwhelmed by the power of God, but wooed by His love and goodness. In Oman's opinion, sin holds people back from acknowledging the Gospel. Sin is essentially self-centredness and it expresses itself very often in insincerity, which is the self's attempt to evade the truth and its demands. Insincerity often involves self-delusion, as well as the attempt at self-justification. Whatever form insincerity takes it always involves a deficit of integrity, because it involves choosing what is desirable over what is true.

CHAPTER 7

A Voyage Round John Oman

John Hick

This title is intended to indicate that I shall be looking at Oman from several angles, and also that I shall be trying to look at him in the round.

First, from a personal angle. John Oman's two most widely read books are *Grace and Personality*[1] and *The Natural and the Supernatural*.[2] I first read the former during a lull in 1944 when serving in the Friends' Ambulance Unit in Italy. I read "Nat and Supernat", as we all called it, much later. So Italy 1944 was my first long distance contact with Oman. It affected me profoundly, still immersed as I was in a highly conservative Calvinist theology. It taught me that God is not primarily omnipotence and judgement but personal grace and love. The second long distance contact was when I was the minister of the Belford Presbyterian church in Northumberland from 1953-56. Oman had long before been minister of the Presbyterian church at Alnwick, fifteen miles further south. He was there for fourteen years (1889-1907), publishing three books during that period. In his time, and since, there have been several scholarly Presbyterian ministers in Northumberland, Oman being the greatest, but another being the New Testament scholar T.W. Manson, and later still, on a lower level, myself; for it was there that I wrote my first book, *Faith and Knowledge*. And then my third long distance contact with Oman was when I went to Westminster College, Cambridge, from 1950-53 to train for the ministry of the then Presbyterian Church of England (now merged into the United Reformed Church). Oman had taught there and also become the College Principal, and his influence was still strongly felt.

Oman's *The Natural and the Supernatural* ought, in my opinion, to have been delivered as Gifford Lectures, but he was never invited to do so. F.G. Healey, in *Religion and Reality: The Theology of John Oman* says that this was 'on the grounds, it was often surmised, of his disabilities as a public speaker',[3]

---

[1] John Oman, *Grace and Personality* (Cambridge: Cambridge University Press, 1st edn, 1917).

[2] John Oman, *The Natural and the Supernatural* (Cambridge: Cambridge University Press, 1931).

[3] F.G. Healey, *Religion and Reality: The Theology of John Oman* (Edinburgh: Oliver & Boyd, 1965), p. 12.

for Oman was a notoriously poor public speaker. I am not clear, from the different things I have read about him, whether this was due to some kind of physical problem in his throat, or simply to a dull and monotonous delivery. But when he was called by the congregation to the pastorate at Alnwick, this was by only one vote. Nevertheless I am inclined to doubt whether Oman's inadequacy as a public speaker explains why he was not invited to give the Giffords. The most important thing about the Gifford Lectures is not the delivery of the lectures but the book coming out of them. (In the period when I gave them, my own being in 1986-7, the audiences at Edinburgh averaged between forty and fifty) Further, there have been Gifford lecturers who have rapidly lost their audiences, the most famous being A.N. Whitehead, whose *Process and Reality* was delivered as Gifford Lectures but which practically emptied the hall after the first lecture. The problem was not Whitehead's delivery but the impenetrable nature of the material, which could not be taken in at a first hearing but had to be carefully studied in print. And there have been other major books which ought to have been Giffords: most notably F.R. Tennant's *Philosophical Theology*; one of the books by the American, Charles Hartshorne; and something by G.E. Moore – he was not a philosopher of religion, but then neither have several Gifford lecturers been, for example the Finnish philosopher, Henrik von Wright, and the Oxford philosopher H.H. Price, who was interested in religion, and who does discuss it marginally, but the bulk of whose Giffords are about, as his title suggests, *Belief*. So it seems that the Gifford electors have overlooked several important thinkers for other reasons than their public speaking abilities – probably not for any positive reason but merely because they were not sufficiently aware of them.

At Westminster College I was taught by Oman's successor, H.H. Farmer, who had been Oman's favourite pupil. Farmer was a good deal more orthodox than Oman had been for, as I shall show, Oman had virtually no theology in the sense of a systematic set of Christian doctrines. Farmer, on the other hand, had a consistent liberal theology

Oman's books are generally regarded as a difficult read. Much of his writing is straight forward enough, though always in Oman's distinctive style. But there are also sentences a paragraph long, like this from his supposedly 'popular' book, *Honest Religion*:

> Only when we thus realise the danger from life's attrition and the heart's fainting, do we know the need of Jesus Christ to affirm God's glory in life, and still more, seeing how blind and deaf we are to it, to enable us to say Amen even when the glory of life is very dim to us and of the life to come very far away, with an attitude of trust and patience, which, while giving full place in our affections to their evanescence and in our labours to their futility, will enable us to carry on to the end with ever growing

assurance that what we do not see God does.[4]

However, Oman is always well worth reading. He has a great number of memorable illustrations. For example, 'the idea that all reality is contained in the laws of motion is on the same level of intelligence as the notion that all English literature is contained in twenty-six vocables'.[5] Or, writing about the 'emergence' of mind from matter, 'This is as much as to say that a signpost turns into a policeman when the traffic becomes complex enough to need him.'[6]

He also has a number of interesting observations. For example, speaking of the child's perception, and remembering his own childhood, he says:

> is how minutely, definitely, decisively everything in it was individual. My language being an advanced Aryan tongue, I had abstract terms, and no doubt made use of some of them. But they were luxuries and not necessities. That to their owner a flock of sheep was only sheep, which he did not know one from another, seemed to show an incredible blindness. The birds were too numerous and rapid and changing for personal acquaintance, but a flock of them was an object by itself, with its qualities of flight and grouping; and when birds were nearer and few enough for separate attention, they were always particular living creatures, each with some singularity of colour or form or behaviour. Life of every kind fascinated: and there was a different quality of apprehension of it which is lost when interests are in another direction and classification has to be used to save the trouble of individual apprehension.[7]

There are also some striking pithy remarks, such as 'faith is what we act on'.[8] Or 'It is one thing to reach the middle of a ladder by climbing and another by falling',[9] or this brief but brilliant summary of Kant's epistemology, 'As grammar is already in speech, the forms of mind are already in the context of sensation.'[10] Or 'The only truly religious hope of immortality so lives with God now as to know that God is not the God of the dead but of the living.'[11] 'To be reconciled to anything is just to find it good.'[12] And some amusing ones, such as 'Wapping Quay, it used to be said, was the most religious spot in the British

---

[4] John Oman, *Honest Religion* (Cambridge: Cambridge University Press, 1941), pp. 190-91.

[5] Oman, *Natural and the Supernatural*, p. 25.

[6] Oman, *Natural and Supernatural*, p. 199.

[7] Oman, *Natural and Supernatural*, p. 133-4.

[8] Oman, *Natural and Supernatural*, p. 206.

[9] Oman, *Natural and Supernatural*, p. 143.

[10] Oman, *Natural and Supernatural*, p. 154.

[11] Oman, *Grace and Personality*, p. 304.

[12] Oman, *Grace and Personality*, p. 299.

Empire, for there the Scotsman left his religion.'[13] Another angle focuses on Oman's philosophy of religion in Natural and Supernatural. He was a pioneer in what some of us regard as the right approach to the epistemology of religion. I must have had Oman's ideas at the back of my mind when I developed in my own way the same basic ideas: that, in Oman's words, 'the Supernatural, like the Natural, being known only by direct experience ...'[14]; but at the same time that all experience is interpreted, or as I put it, is experiencing-as, and that faith is a religious interpretation of, and way of experiencing the universe. So Oman says: 'If our knowing is knowledge only as we establish securely the frontier of our minds and allow nothing to pass except as our meaning, and if knowledge is right meaning in our minds by active interpretation of a meaning that is the true reality, much judgment is embedded in all our knowing.'[15] Or again, 'Thus knowing is not knowledge as an effect of an unknown external cause, but is knowledge as we so interpret that our meaning is the actual meaning of our environment.'[16] Or again, 'From pure mechanical vibration without meaning there is no possible opening for knowing, which is all meaning.'[17]

And in its implications for confronting the problem of evil, of reconciling a good and all-powerful God with human wickedness and suffering, this epistemology suggests that in order to ensure our human freedom and responsibility, God has set us in a world apart from himself, operating according to its own laws. This is part of the approach that I much later developed in *Evil and the God of Love*. Again and again I find in re-reading Oman that I have been following in his footsteps.

Natural and Supernatural was also one of the first attempts by a major Christian theologian to take systematic account of the other world religions, with Oman's division into the primitive, the polytheistic, the mystical, the ceremonial-legal, and the prophetic. His understanding of Buddhism was, however, largely a misunderstanding. He speaks of 'Buddha's wail that all life is misery',[18] referring to the Buddhist very realistic teaching of *dukka*, corresponding to the Christian teaching that we are sinful beings in a challenging world. And he dismissed Buddhism almost contemptuously as 'merely a rationalistic sect of Hinduism, with no soul and no Supernatural'.[19] In its *anatta* teaching it denies a soul in the sense of the unchanging Hindu *atman* but it affirms it in the sense of a continuing and perfectible individual karmic project; and it does affirm a supernatural reality in the *dharmakaya*. However, less was known about Buddhism in the West in Oman's time than today. And

---

[13] Oman, *Honest Religion*, p. 15.
[14] Oman, *Natural and Supernatural*, p. 97.
[15] Oman, *Natural and Supernatural*, p. 201.
[16] Oman, *Natural and Supernatural*, p. 175.
[17] Oman, *Natural and Supernatural*, p. 158.
[18] Oman, *Natural and Supernatural*, p. 406.
[19] Oman, *Natural and Supernatural*, p. 419.

we must be grateful to him for drawing attention to the non-Christian religions. A better, but in my opinion still very inadequate, attempt was made by his successor H.H. Farmer, in his first set of Gifford lectures, *Revelation and Religion*. (The second set, with which Farmer was very dissatisfied and which he decided not to publish, ought not, in my opinion, to have been published posthumously by others, as it has been).

But coming now to Oman's theology, and starting at the traditional beginning, Oman, as a Presbyterian, inherited the Calvinist doctrine of total depravity due to the Fall of mankind and salvation by faith alone, and rejected it:

> you have, as your first difficulty, that the whole notion of total depravity is exaggerated and unreal, and confession of sin little more than a habit of professional piety; and, in the second, that, whatever the evil may be, faith alone seems an extraneous and arbitrary way of escaping it. ... . Neither in the Old Testament nor the New is mention ever made of [the Fall] in dealing with sin itself, and it is never used to explain sin. The real source of the prominence it came to have is Augustine and his views on concupiscence and the evil of matter, which were relics of his Manichaeism and not due to the teaching of Christianity.'[20]

More generally, I shall argue that he had no theology in the sense of a consistent body of doctrines – despite the fact that at Westminster College he was professor of systematic theology (and apologetics). The central Christian doctrines, when they came to be officially defined, have always been Incarnation, Trinity and Atonement. These hang together in a logical order. Incarnation means that Jesus was God incarnate, both God and man. He was the Son of God, or rather God the Son, second person of a holy trinity, living a human life. Already the Trinity is involved in this; for if Jesus was God on earth, and there was at the same time God in heaven, this creates a binity, a divine twoness, and when we add the felt divine presence in the lives of Christians, we have the Spirit, and hence a trinity. So the doctrine of the Trinity is a protective doctrine for the Incarnation. And the doctrine of the Atonement, whereby Jesus' death on the cross was an atonement for the sins of the world, presupposes his divinity, which alone makes the atonement sufficient.

All this was made official church teaching in the creeds, though the idea of atonement was not yet developed in the early creeds. Thus the Apostles' Creed (although the apostles had nothing to do with it, for it originated as the Old Roman Creed in the fourth century) affirms God almighty, and Christ Jesus, his only son, and the remission of sins – not specified further – and the Holy Ghost. The Nicene Creed, also fourth century, likewise affirms God, the Father all-sovereign, and Jesus Christ, Son of God, of one substance with the Father, and

---

[20] Oman, *Honest Religion*, pp. 10-11.

the remission of sins by baptism – but with no mention of Jesus death as an atonement. However, in fully developed Christian theology Atonement is as important as the other key doctrines.

Oman had little use for these historic Creeds of the church. He says that 'we may be allowed to feel relief when our common confession is the Church's central creed, which is the Lord's Prayer'.[21] And in general he was not sympathetic to what he saw as authorities and institutions, which he saw as generally more restricting than liberating. In a typical Oman illustration:

> What all life does say to us is that God does not conduct His rivers, like arrows, to the sea. The ruler and compass are only for finite mortals who labour, by taking thought, to overcome their limitations, and are not for the Infinite mind. The expedition demanded by man's small power and short day produces the canal, but nature, with a beneficent and picturesque circumambulancy, the work of a more spacious and less precipitate mind, produces the river. Why should we assume that in all the rest of His ways, He rejoices in the river, but, in religion, can use no adequate method save the canal? The defence of the infallible is the defence of the canal against the river.[22]

Again, concerning the churches, 'they may give us, for a time, needed shelter on man's long dangerous journey. ... Yet, as they are no more than temporary means to infinite ends, they belong to the fashions of this world and ultimately pass away...'[23] So I think we can say that, whilst accepting the inevitability of churches and rituals and confessions of faith and ecclesiastical authorities, he puts them firmly in second place.

Turning now to Christology: Farmer once told me, and has told others, that Oman had no Christology. There are however passages here and there, and most systematically in his last book, *Honest Religion*, from which we get, not so much a coherent doctrine as an attitude, an approach, an outlook. He uses traditional language, but often not in its traditional sense. His underlying concern, as it seems to me, is not so much with the exaltation of Jesus as with God's grace and human freedom. Here are some of the things he says:

> An abstract omnipotence of like substance with the Father replaces the truth Jesus taught and the life He lived, which speaking through living human intercourse to men's own minds and lives, were the way to the Father. The divinity of Jesus, set forth by itself as a metaphysical principle and apart from the humanity it inspired and sustained and the love of the Father which appeals through it, reduces the humanity to an

---

[21] Oman, *Honest Religion*, p. 160.

[22] Oman, *Grace and Personality*, pp. 14-5.

[23] Oman, *Honest Religion*, p. 35.

illusion and the divinity to an abstract symbol. A humanity which is a mere cloak for deity is no humanity at all; and, with a metaphysical deity as pure omnipotence, real religion has no concern. Faith has to do with God's mind, and only, through it, with His might, even though, if it be truly His mind, it has as much right to be regarded as significant of the quality of the universe as the understanding of motion for its quantity: and in the sense of being the supreme revelation of this mind in all and also the source of a new reconciliation to bring us into accord with it through all, Jesus has universal significance. Or we might say significance for the universe.[24]

Further, speaking of atonement,

Though of this [i.e. divine grace] our Lord's sacrifice is the supreme and most efficacious example, it is not so by being singular and different from God's rule for any of us. Its quality is in being the fullest manifestation of what works by all the saints and is for the deliverance, through the Father's appeal in it, of all sinners. So far from being to appease God, it is the supreme appeal of what His love is and always will be. ... The idea of the Crucifixion then as a compensation to a God needing to be reconciled to us, is just a harking back to the religion of fear. ... Restoration has no conditions whatsoever except just what God is and willingness to accept it.[25]

There is some ambiguity here, with the result that it can be interpreted in two different ways, one more orthodox and the other less orthodox. The general tenor of his outlook leads me to adopt the latter interpretation. For 'although our Lord's sacrifice is the supreme and most efficacious example', it is 'not by being singular and different from God's rule in any of us'. Further, 'Its quality is in being the fullest manifestation of what works by all the saints and is for the deliverance, through the Father's appeal in it, of all sinners.'

So, the traditional uniqueness of Jesus' atonement is abandoned. It is a matter of degree. And since that uniqueness depended on his unique divinity, this suggests that this also may be a matter of degree. It does not logically require this, but it suggests it. If so, Oman has a 'degree Christology', along with several other modern theologians. He would, I think, be sympathetic to the understanding of Jesus suggested by several theologians of the period, one and two generations ago when Christology was under intensive discussion and debate, namely a Degree Christology. This was advocated, primarily, by Nels Ferre in *Christ and the Christian*,[26] Norman Pittenger in *The Word Incarnate*.[27]

---

[24] Oman, *Honest Religion*, pp. 96-7.

[25] Oman, *Honest Religion*, pp. 98-9.

[26] Nels Ferré, *Christ and the Christian* (New York: Harper, 1958).

According to them, the Logos, which is God at work in relation to his creatures, is at all times seeking to influence and to become united with each human being; so that whenever we can rightly speak of God acting through humans, or of them responding affirmatively to God (as in the case, for example of great saints, or some of the ancient prophets, or the prophets of other religions, there we have an instance of the Logos becoming united in some degree with human beings. Such union, whenever it occurs, is incarnation, which is thus capable of many different degrees, from the near-zero that we see in an evil person to the one hundred per cent that we see in Jesus. The ultimate purpose of God for mankind is that one hundred per cent incarnation shall occur in us all, who will then be on the same moral and spiritual level as Jesus, the only distinction being that he was the first to attain, in cooperation with the divine.

Logos, to that status, and who being first there, help others towards it. However, so far as I know, Oman did not read these two writers, and we shall never know whether I am right in thinking that he would have approved of their ideas.

So Oman was sceptical about the doctrines that he singles out for mention. Even so, he does not spend his time offering new and more acceptable interpretations of them. He is not sufficiently interested in them, because for him they were almost irrelevant to true religion, which consists in knowing God's limitless grace and living in response to it.

In summary, then, Oman does not explicitly deny or reject the traditional Christian doctrinal system, but thinks that it can easily be misleading, and in practice he relegates it to a secondary place. In this he points to a possible future, in my opinion much to be desired, in which ideas that have become no longer seriously believable in a questioning age are filtered out by being radically reinterpreted. The religion of Jesus himself, which must surely be normative for those who seek to follow him, was a life lived in direct relationship to a gracious and loving God. There is no mediator between us and the heavenly Father, and no condition for forgiveness except that we forgive and accept one another. Christianity as a hierarchical church with a doctrinal system began with Paul and the author of the Fourth Gospel. But the Jesus of history, in so far as we can glimpse him through the fragments of memory embedded in the synoptic gospels, is prior to all that. In the Fourth Gospel Jesus is consciously divine and omnipotent. In the Lord's Prayer, on the other hand, we address God directly and we ask to be forgiven for our wrongdoings as we forgive those who have wronged us, trusting in God in all things. From this point of view, the church, the Christian community, is necessary because we are communal beings, all bound together in the bundle of life; but like the Sabbath it is made for us, not we for it.

And so, from the point of view of a 'radical' Christian of the twenty first century, John Oman was one of the comparatively few theologians of the past

---

[27] Norman Pittenger, *The Word Incarnate* (London: Nisbet, 1959).

who is still relevant today.

But of course most Christians today are far from radical. On the contrary, throughout the world there is a general drift to the right, to traditional pre-critical orthodoxy. As a result, Christianity may well split in two, the numerically larger Christianity being doctrinally oriented, ecclesiastically rooted, and culturally conservative, and a smaller second Christianity that is more liberal and progressive. The split has already happened on the ground, although both groups are still held uneasily together under the same denominational umbrellas. But they are likely sooner or later to move visibly apart into separate organisations.

But before both of these was the religion of Jesus, from which what is today's majority Christianity departed long ago and to which the minority seeks to return. And Oman stands as a signpost pointing both back to the religion of Jesus and forward to a second Christianity.

PART THREE

ISSUES AND IMPLICATIONS

CHAPTER 8

John Oman's Doctrine of a Personal God: Implications for Mission in Today's World

Stephen Bevans

Introduction

What I would like to explore in this paper brings together the two main concerns – I would even say passions – of my academic career: John Oman's doctrine of a personal God on the one hand and a theology of mission – God's mission in which the Church is privileged to participate – on the other. I believe that Oman's understanding of God can shed much light on the way our church engages in mission in today's globalized, pluralized and secularized world. Right at the beginning of *The Church and the Divine Order* Oman suggests that one's ecclesiology necessarily depends on one's doctrines of God and salvation: 'Arguments about the Church can only end in barren logomachies, so long as we are not at one about what manner of God we believe in and what manner of salvation from him we expect.'[1] What I hope this paper will demonstrate is how Oman's statement is also true of the Church's mission.

The first section of my reflections will lay out briefly what I have done more extensively in my doctoral dissertation and subsequent book, *John Oman's Doctrine of a Personal God.*[2] In the second section, I will sketch an understanding of mission that theologians of mission have developed in the last several decades. In the final section, I will reflect on how Oman's understanding of God's personal nature might help enrich the practice of mission in today's world.

John Oman's Doctrine of a Personal God

Even though he speaks here and there about God as 'a person', I do not believe

---

[1] John Oman, *The Church and the Divine Order* (London: Hodder and Stoughton, 1911), p. 3.

[2] Stephen Bevans, *John Oman's Doctrine of a Personal God* (Cambridge: Cambridge University Press, 1992).

that this phrase adequately expresses Oman's understanding of God's personal nature. God is not 'a person' like we are persons, only wiser and more powerful. God is not a person, as Oman would say, in the sense of an 'individual.'[3] In a passage from *The Natural and the Supernatural* Oman uses the term person as a kind of 'limit language' to describe God's reality.

> The idea of God as a person may be inadequate at best, an assertion only that he cannot be less than our highest way of dealing with him, and not that he is no more than we can conceive as the highest. But the least adequate form is that he is one individual, standing over against each of us as other individuals.'[4]

That God is personal, rather, has to do with the way God acts, the way God deals and relates with women and men, indeed with the entire universe, as 'A Father not a force.'[5]

Much of Oman's understanding of God's personal dealing with humanity is rooted in his critique of common understandings of divine action as direct, infallible and omnipotent. As often conceived, God's grace and will are simply irresistible, and so if God acts, human beings are little more than robots, puppets, or passive clay in God's mighty hands. The problem is, though, why in fact humanity and the world is in the terrible state that it is in. If God were omnipotent in the traditional sense, Oman argues, 'the problems of nature, society and the heart of man ... would never ... have existed from the beginning.'[6] But perhaps, he suggests, something else is the case. Perhaps God is about creating an order in which *freedom* is the goal. And so personal relationship, and not *control*, is what God is about in God's deepest self. As Oman writes at the end of Part I of *Grace and Personality*:

> ... the essence of a personal system is not to manufacture us good, but to help us to win our freedom and the right use of it together. In that case God cannot relieve us of our responsibility even when calamitous. Without it we might be the clay and He the Potter, but we should not be children and He our Father. Only with responsibility are sins real disasters, but the victory of responsible freedom is an end great enough to justify so perilous a road, for, without it, God would merely have a dull universe of perfectly manipulated marionettes.[7]

---

[3] For example, see John Oman, *Grace and Personality* (Cambridge: Cambridge University Press, Third Edition, Revised, 1925), pp. 43, 58, 64.

[4] John Oman, *The Natural and The Supernatural* (Cambridge: Cambridge University Press, 1931), p. 335.

[5] John Oman, 'A Gracious Relationship,' *The Expositor*, 3 (May, 1912), p. 471.

[6] Oman, *Grace and Personality*, p. 14.

[7] Oman, *Grace and Personality*, p. 90.

A God of Infinite Patience

Because of this, Oman reasons, God's infinity and omnipotence is expressed not in direct power but in patience. 'God's ways,' he says, 'are long, long ways.'[8] God's ways are personal, and so patient. God 'proceeds in the slow and hard way, which alone promises the highest prize,'[9] a prize so valuable – an order of free creatures – that it is 'worth an eternity of working for.'[10] God works by a method that does not impose from without, but that challenges and persuades from within human hearts. God makes only one demand, that the human response be free and personal. Oman says this over and over again in his writings. To give one more final example, he writes in *Vision and Authority* that God 'will not force his mystery on us. He will lead us up to it. Violence is the destruction, the contradiction, the absolute opposite of this mystery.'[11] God is infinite and strong in patience. God 'hasteth not and is not weary.'[12]

God as Parent

Oman's favourite image of God's personal dealing with us is that of a parent, especially that of a father. Once, in a conversation, his student and eventual successor at Westminster College, F. G. Healey, told me that Oman had a picture of his own father above his working desk, and how much Oman had revered him. If I remember Healey's words right, he thought that Oman's love for his father and his father's dealing with him had a great influence on his image of God. Oman, of course, dedicated *The Problem of Faith and Freedom* to his father, calling him 'my best teacher'.

God's parenthood/fatherhood has an 'austere and freedom-respecting purpose.'[13] Parenthood is not well exercised by providing everything for a child, without the child having to earn anything for himself or herself. It is not about 'every time the prodigal falls into the gutter, his father should be by him to pick him up and his mother to brush his clothes.'[14] This would only be a way of keeping the child within the parents' sphere of influence. The true test of

---

[8] John Oman, *The Problem of Faith and Freedom in the Last Two Centuries* (London: Hodder and Stoughton, 1906), p. 6.

[9] John Hick, Introduction to *Grace and Personality* (New York: Association Press, 1961), p. 6.

[10] D.M. Niccol, 'Philosophy of Religion. Lectures by Dr. John Oman on God in Relation to the World and Man.' Student notes in typescript, ca. 1920, p. 33.

[11] Oman, *Vision and Authority*, p. 225.

[12] Oman, *Vision and Authority*, p. 176.

[13] The phrase is H.H. Farmer's. See *God and Men* (Nashville, TN: Abingdon, 1947), p. 157. The phrase is a genuine echo of Oman's voice, however. See, for example, *Vision and Authority*, pp. 237-238.

[14] John Oman, *Honest Religion* (Cambridge: Cambridge University Press, 1941), p. 78.

parental love, says Oman, is how the mother or father allows and challenges the child to grow in responsibility and freedom. What it means that God is a Father

> is not in giving good gifts, but in knowing how to give them that they may secure us in freedom and not merely in fortune. The most liberal domination on God's side and the most indebted subjection on ours will never make us sons of God, but only puppets of his pleasure.'[15]

We see God's method exemplified in Jesus' parable of the 'Prodigal Son' or 'Loving Father.' When the son asked for his inheritance, the Father, though obviously pained, gave it to him and allowed him to leave. But then the father waited with pain and longing for the son to come to his own senses and return, when he is unconditionally accepted back into the father's love – in fact, much too easily in the eyes of the older brother! The father's love is no force that 'alters the substance of his soul or hedges in his career,' but a willingness to give his son freedom and a patience to wait in hope for his return.[16]

A God of Concrete Human Beings

As a father, God deals with women and men as *unique* persons, or with their *individuality*. To speak of God as father, wrote Oman, 'means that he does not, as a mere Ruler, deal with men in groups, but that each man has to Him the distinctiveness, the importance, the whole significance he can have to himself.' In this way is revealed 'the infinity of His care for the individual,' God's 'patient minuteness.'[17] And it is an individual care that is nevertheless exercised *indirectly*, pointing more to the interdependent, relational quality of personal life. God reveals Godself in the events and objects among which men and women live. Grace is offered not like a light passing through a window – directly, clearly, irresistibly – but in 'a curve of patient, personal wisdom, encircling and embracing us and all our concerns.'[18]

This brings me to my favourite passage in Oman's writings, which I believe is the favourite of many others as well:

> God does not conduct His rivers, like arrows, to the sea. ... Why should we assume that, in all the rest of His ways, He rejoices in the river, but, in religion, can use no adequate method save the canal? The defence of the infallible is the defence of the canal against the river, of the channel

---

[15] Oman, *Grace and Personality*, p. 176.

[16] Oman, *Grace and Personality*, p. 218.

[17] The first two of these quotes is from John Oman, 'Individual,' in *Hastings' Dictionary of Christ and the Gospels*, I (1908), p. 815. The third is from John Oman, sermon on Is. 42:3 and Mt. 12:20, April 28, 1891. Unpublished. Found in the Oman Collection at Westminster College, Cambridge.

[18] Oman, *Grace and Personality*, p. 188.

blasted through the rock against the basin dug by an element which swerves at a pebble or a firmer clay. And the question is whether God ever does override the human spirit in that direct way, and whether we ought to conceive either of His spirit or of ours after a fashion that could make it possible.[19]

A God Strong Enough To Be Gentle

Yes, insists Oman, God is omnipotent, 'the final and absolute power'.[20] The question is, however, what real power is. Is it simply the ability to 'blast through the rock', or is it the power of swerving 'at a pebble or a firmer clay'? Soon after my dissertation was completed I gave a talk on Oman to the faculty at my *alma mater*, a seminary college outside of Dubque, Iowa. One of my friends on the faculty was quite taken with Oman's understanding of power as patience, as the 'omnipotence of love',[21] and he offered me two recollections from his boyhood that he had always remembered. The first was a phrase of the science fiction writer Isaac Asimov who wrote somewhere that 'violence is the last resort of the weak.' The second was an advert for piston rings on a tractor that he had seen in the magazine *Farm Journal*–that these piston rings were 'strong enough to be gentle'. I think these two phrases capture Oman's understanding of God's power perfectly. As he wrote in another of my favourite passages,

> We must rid ourselves of the idea that we can believe in the might of goodness and not in God; and in God and not in the might of goodness. When we are reasoning about God we are considering whether, in spite of the success of wickedness, wickedness wins the final success; whether, in spite of the power of violence, violence is the final power; whether the meaning of the world is cruelty and cunning or truth and goodness. The question of God is precisely the question of the meaning and purpose of the world, and that resolves itself into the question whether truth is the last reality and goodness the one imperishable possession.[22]

This is why, even though Oman's solution to the problem of evil is not completely satisfying, God will not – cannot! – intervene in human affairs or cosmic history to avert sin, no matter how destructive its consequences, or to

---

[19] Oman, *Grace and Personality*, pp. 14-15.

[20] Oman, *Honest Religion*, p. 95.

[21] The phrase is my own, interpreting Oman. See my *John Oman and His Doctrine of God*, p. 98.

[22] John Oman, 'War,' in *The Elements of Pain and Conflict in Human Life, Considered from a Christian Point of View* (Cambridge: Cambridge University Press, 1916), pp. 171-172.

avert natural disasters. Ultimately, evil – especially moral evil but also natural evil – is to be overcome by women and men gathered together 'in some order of love and freedom, that is, in some kind of Church.'[23] Women and men, touched by and responsive to God's grace, can join God in working for a world of freedom, love and relationship – the 'Divine Order' as Oman calls the Reign of God. They do it in the same personal way that God does it, by sharing in God's mission.

God is Like Jesus

Oman is clear that it is in the ministry, life, death and resurrection of Jesus that God manifests God's self and God's method most clearly. In Jesus, 'God was not an abstraction with many strangely contradictory attributes, but a Person Whose large nature could govern a world and care for a creature, condemn for sin and love a sinner.'[24]

Jesus was the greatest religious authority because he never spoke merely *as* an authority, but appealed to what was 'deeper, more tenderer, more truly God's image' in men and women.[25] Jesus' authority was not like the scribes, but a challenge to 'author' one's own response to the truth he taught. Oman emphasizes the importance of the fact that Jesus did not leave any writings behind, but that his followers were called to constantly interpret his teachings for their own times.[26] Jesus' preferred way of teaching was in parables–not dull repetitions of truths, but colourful stories inviting engagement. When people heard Jesus' teaching, they might have gone away 'angry, perplexed, disturbed,' but they never went away with the 'mere outward acceptance of any truth'[27] and still have accepted him.

God's 'supreme revelation',[28] however, was in Jesus' death and resurrection. The death of Jesus is the 'consummation of all revelation because it displays the Divine method, not as a masterful compulsion of power, but as the condescending, patient, self-sacrificing device of an infinitely tolerant and wise love.'[29] Jesus' resurrection, Oman emphasizes, is not God going back to 'business as usual'–God as all powerful Lord. It is rather the way that God vindicates the divine freedom-respecting, radically personal method. In the final analysis, the cross, transformed by the resurrection, teaches that 'the last word of power is not human might but the Father's rule, so that we may be one

---

[23] Oman, *The Church and the Divine Order*, p. vii.

[24] John Oman, 'The Consistence and Unity of the Bible,' *Presbyterian Messenger*, 586 (February, 1895): p. 39.

[25] John Oman, *Concerning the Ministry* (London: SCM, 1936), p. 84.

[26] Oman, *Vision and Authority*, p. 217.

[27] Oman, *Vision and Authority*, p. 110.

[28] Oman, *Vision and Authority*, p. 226.

[29] Oman, *Vision and Authority*, p. 226.

with the Father even amid the hardest trials and the sternest duties.'[30]

***

This, in a very sketchy way, is Oman's marvellous, inspiring doctrine of God's personal nature – or, perhaps better, God's personal dealing with God's creation.

Mission as Sharing in the Mission of God – a reflection on contemporary understandings of God

God is a Verb

In my own development of a theology of mission, I have realized that we must begin with the understanding that God is a *verb*, not a noun. In a way similar to Oman's understanding of God–at least as I have interpreted him–God is not a 'person,' an individual Being who is 'up there' or 'out there.' God, rather, is a movement, a flow, an embrace, more personal than we can ever imagine. God's movement pervades the entire universe, and has held it in embrace since the first nanosecond of creation, and never ceases to invite creation to the fullness of its capacity. To use Oman's language, from the very beginning of creation, God has been working for creation's freedom, especially the freedom of women and men.

Such an understanding of God has some basis in the Christian tradition. Thomas Aquinas spoke of God as 'pure act.'[31] Bonaventure described God as 'self-diffusive love.'[32] The medieval mystic Mectilde of Magdeburg wrote about the 'restless Godhead,' an 'overflow … which never stands still and always flows effortlessly and without ceasing … .'[33]

Tradition also teaches that God is not even static within God's self. As Brazilian theologian Leonardo Boff expresses it, 'in the remotest beginning, communion prevails.'[34] This communion spills over into creation, calling all creation into that communion, calling women and men into a life of freedom, relationship, full personhood. I like to imagine this overflowing communion as a dance–a great conga line that moves through the world, gathering dancers as

---

[30] John Oman, *The Church and the Divine Order*, p. 57.

[31] See Thomas Aquinas, *Summa Theologiae*, Part I, Question 3, article 1.

[32] Bonaventure, *De Trinitate*, 3.16. See Ilia Delio, 'Bonaventure's Metaphysics of the Good,' *Theological Studies*, 60, 2 (1999): p. 232.

[33] Mechtilde of Magdeburg, *The Flowing Light of the Godhead*, Book VII, Chapter 55, in *Classics of Western Spirituality*, Vol. 92, Frank Tobin, trans. (New York: Paulist Press, 1998. See Oliver Davies, 'Late Medieval Theology,' in G. R. Evans, ed., *The Medieval Theologians: An Introduction to Theology in the Medieval Period* (Oxford: Blackwell, 2001), p. 228.

[34] Leonardo Boff, 'Trinity,' in *Mysterium Liberationis: Fundamental Concepts of Liberation Theology* (Maryknoll, NY: Orbis Books, 1993), p. 389.

it goes. And the more that join the more attractive the joining becomes.

Another way to describe this movement, this embrace, this flow, this dance is to speak about God as *mission*. Not God *having* a mission, but the mission itself. From the very beginning God has been active in the world. In the biblical tradition, the way God's pervasive, saving presence was described, is the word *ruach*: wind, breath, spirit. The Spirit is the breath of life, as we read in Genesis and Psalm 104. She is the inspiration for prophecy, as in the great passage in Chapter 61 of Isaiah. She is the source of healing and new life, as in Ezekiel's marvellous visions of the valley of the dry bones and the water flowing out of the temple.

God Revealed in Jesus

'In the fullness of time' (Gal 4:4), the Word of God became flesh and gave God's all-pervasive yet elusive Spirit a human face. As Oman put it beautifully,

> the entire singular place Jesus occupies in the revelation of God is not so much through the new light He brought into the world, as through combining into the pure white beam which men can see, the rays already there.[35]

By the way he taught, especially, as we have said, in his parables; by the way he healed the sick and exorcised the power of evil; by the way he included in table fellowship and friendship those who were normally excluded, Jesus demonstrated that the Spirit that had been in the world since the beginning was now poured out upon him. He had been anointed with that Spirit to bring good news to the poor, to proclaim liberty to captives, recovery of sight to the blind, freedom for the oppressed (see Lk 4:18). It was because of what he did and how he did it that he was executed on the cross, 'the supreme revelation,' says Oman, 'of the mystery of God, the supreme assurance that it awaits the perfect solution of love.'[36]

The Mission Has a Church

But, as we know, the cross was not the end. The disciples soon experienced that Jesus was alive, gathering them back together into community. And even more, they gradually began to realize, through the inspiration and perhaps even the push of the Spirit, that Jesus' mission of proclaiming God's love, forgiveness and salvation was now their mission. As Paul was to describe it years afterward, the community began to realize that it was to be the body of Christ in the world, the temple of God's Spirit. And, perhaps even more than Jesus

---

[35] Oman, 'The Consistency and Unity of the Bible,' p. 39.
[36] Oman, *Vision and Authority*, p. 226.

himself realized, they were to proclaim Jesus' message beyond the boundaries of Judaism, to peoples of all cultures, of all times, to the ends of the earth.

It was, I believe, in this gradual realization of this mission that the disciples realized that they were no longer simply a part of Judaism – although strongly rooted in it. They were something different – a new community, an *ecclesia*, a church. Seen in this light, it is much more appropriate to say that the church doesn't so much *have* a mission as that the *mission* has a church. The church comes to be, and continues to exist, only insofar as it actively participates in the great movement, the strong embrace, the joyful dance of God. Mission has its roots in the mission of God as such. The church is 'missionary by its very nature' as the Second Vatican Council says, because it participates in the very life of God as such.

A Single, Complex Reality

This one mission of God in which the church participates has been aptly described by Pope John Paul II as 'a single but complex reality.'[37] While direct proclamation is described by the pope as mission's 'permanent priority,'[38] 'the witness of a Christian life is the first and irreplaceable form of mission.'[39] My colleague Eleanor Doidge and I have suggested that Roman documents, official Protestant, Evangelical and Pentecostal documents and contemporary missiologists propose five additional elements.[40] Constitutive of mission as well is (perhaps surprisingly) engagement in Liturgy, Prayer and Contemplation; commitment to Justice, Peace and the Integrity of Creation; participation in Interreligious and Secular Dialogue; efforts of Inculturation; and working for Reconciliation.

Mission today, in other words, is much more than efforts to make converts to Christianity and/or to expand the church. As a participation in the overflowing and all-embracing life of the Trinity, it is about preaching, serving and witnessing to the Reign of God, or as Oman would call it, the Divine Order. What Oman wrote in 'Vision and Authority' in 1902 has a very contemporary ring: 'The visible Church is therefore not to be regarded as an end in itself, but only as a means for the final Kingdom of God.'[41]

---

[37] John Paul II, *Redemptoris Missio* (RM), 41. In William R. Burrows, ed., *Redemption and Dialogue: Reading Redemptoris Missio and Dialogue and Proclamation* (Maryknoll, NY: Orbis Books, 1993), p. 27.

[38] RM 44. In Burrows, ed., *Redemption and Dialogue*, p. 28.

[39] RM 42. In Burrows, ed., *Redemption and Dialogue*, p. 28..

[40] Stephen Bevans and Eleanor Doidge, 'Theological Reflection,' in Barbara Kraemer, ed., *Reflection and Dialogue: What MISSION Confronts Religious Life Today?* (Chicago: Center for the Study of Religious Life, 2000), pp. 37-48.

[41] Oman, *Vision and Authority*, p. 283.

Mission As Prophetic Dialogue

Roger Schroeder and I, borrowing from the official documents of our religious congregation, the Society of the Divine Word, have characterized the way the church does mission as 'prophetic dialogue.'[42] On the one hand, mission must be done in 'dialogue': with real respect for those among whom we minister, with an understanding of their context and cultures, with reverence for the holiness of their religious traditions (acknowledging the 'rays already there'). On the other hand, mission must be done as 'prophecy': clearly proclaiming the person and message of Jesus, witnessing to the life that the gospel can give, opposing any injustice, offering a vision of the world as it could be transformed by the gospel. Prophecy is another theme that is quite prominent in Oman's writings.[43] It is in order to understand this method of 'prophetic dialogue' more deeply that, I believe, we can profit from an understanding of Oman's doctrine of a personal God. It is to this that our third section will attend to.

Sharing in the Mission of a Personal God

Because the church's mission is a result of its participation in the mission of God, we must engage in mission in the way God does mission. We need to follow what Oman speaks of as God's 'method,' and do mission 'in Christ's way.'[44] This is a way of doing mission – witnessing, proclaiming, praying, working for justice, etc. – which practices patience, which is indirect, which is never violent and overbearing, which is persuasive, which is not discouraged, which acknowledges the 'otherness' of the other.

Mission as Patient and Non-Coercive

Mission done in the light of God's personal dealing with God's world is patient and not coercive. It is the opposite of a pushy proselytism. Mission has often been about numbers and results: so many baptisms performed, so many churches planted, 'the evangelization of the world in this generation,' as John

---

[42] See Stephen Bevans and Roger Schroeder, *Constants in Context: A Theology of Mission for Today* (Maryknoll, NY: Orbis Books, 2004).

[43] For example, see Oman, 'The Prophetic,' *The Natural and the Supernatural*, pp. 446-471; 'Prophetic Revelation,' *Honest Religion*, pp. 52-63.

[44] See, for example, Oman, *Grace and Personality*, p. 17; *Vision and Authority*, p. 270. See also Lesslie Newbigin, *Mission in Christ's Way: A Gift, A Command, An Assurance* (New York: Friendship Press, 1987). Oman uses the phrase 'in Christ's way' in a relatively casual way. The phrase was the theme of the 1989 meeting of the World Council of Churches' Committee on World Mission and Evangelism in San Antonio, Texas in 1989. Newbigin, however, was Oman's student and, at least in his younger days, was strongly influenced by him, especially in regard to his understanding of God.

R. Mott famously proclaimed.[45] We speak of 'target areas' and 'people groups' to be converted. This is all well and good, but many of the ways that these results were achieved have not been in accord with God's way of mission. Mission has often used force, as did Charlemagne against the Saxons in the ninth century or as in the evangelization of the Americas in the sixteenth. God certainly wishes and hopes for results, but never at the cost of compromising God's personal dealing with women and men. God persuades, God puts up with evil, and above all God respects the freedom of women and men to accept or reject God's efforts. 'Mission,' writes U. S. theologian Darrell Guder, 'must be characterized by freedom. ... Love does not coerce; it woos.'[46] What is ultimately important are not the results, but the way the gospel is witnessed to and proclaimed. Mission according to God's method, mission done 'in Christ's way' lives out the gospel and proclaims it every day, year in year out. Charles de Foucauld, the hermit who lived in Algeria for years without making one convert, might exemplify this. His was a mission of patient presence, and has become one of the great exemplars of mission today. 'We are not called to be successful,' Mother Teresa is credited with saying, 'but we are called to be faithful.'

One of my favourite chapters in *Vision and Authority* is entitled 'A Forgotten Sacrament,' and in it Oman deals with what he calls the 'Sacrament of Failure.' This is a sacrament that can help those who might be discouraged in their preaching of the gospel, and who might be tempted to use other, more unworthy means to convince people, such as lowering the truth of Christ to a more human level. The sacramental action is that of the disciples shaking the dust from their sandals outside a town that had not received their message, and then moving on to another place. As Oman explains it:

> They were not to adapt their message to make it more acceptable, nor to resort to any other device to win success, but simply to deliver their message and leave the responsibility for accepting it with men's own souls, and for the final success with God. Thus they were no more to waste their energy and sacrifice their peace in making good victorious than in opposing evil. This is the significance of what we have called the sacrament of failure.[47]

Oman talks of a certain vulnerability. What is important is simply to

---

[45] J.R. Mott, *The Evangelization of the World in This Generation* (New York: Student Volunteer Movement for Foreign Missions, 1905 [originally published 1900]).

[46] Darrell L. Guder, 'The *missio dei*: A Mission Theology after Christendom,' in Max L. Stackhouse and Lalsangkima Pachuau, eds., *News of Boundless Riches: Interrogating, Comparing, and Reconstructing Mission in a Global Era* (Delhi, Bangalore and Princeton, NJ: ISPCK, United Theological College and Center of Theological Inquiry, 2007), p. 18.

[47] Oman, *Vision and Authority*, p. 310.

proclaim the message, 'to manifest the truth in plainness and humility, not striving, but being gentle to all men.'[48] If the message is not received, 'the true significance of a plain, God-inspired messenger of the truth is then to be made manifest.'[49] In recognizing failure and leaving success to God, the church is only imitating God's way of acting. Oman's last sentence in the chapter has a very contemporary ring, and is worth pondering as we struggle with the church's growing eclipse in especially Western cultures today:

> Instead of mourning over the present loss of privilege, should she not rather recognize the dispensation of a wise Providence, appointed to teach her the wealth of her own resources, to give her a higher idea of the patience of God, and to show her a truer view of the Kingdom and his children, whom, by the sole method of truth and obedience, He has set free?[50]

Perhaps, as the late Japanese theologian Kosuke Koyama urges, we Christians in mission have to lay aside our 'crusading minds' and put on a 'crucified mind.'[51]

Mission and Witness

Like the God who surrounds the world with grace rather than forcing it upon the world like a thunderbolt, Christian mission is always indirect. This does not mean that the message of the gospel is not clearly articulated, but it does mean that Christian witness and example become major vehicles in the communication of the gospel. The church, as Oman expresses it at the beginning of 'The Church and the Divine Order', needs to be an 'order of love and freedom' in the world.[52] It cannot force the world to join it, but it can be a witness to what the gospel is most deeply about. People should be able to look at the church – look at its vital community, its respect for diversity, even its honest struggles with deep differences of opinion – and see what the world could be like if people accept the gospel message of love and freedom. In this way the church can appeal to what is the most noble in women and men, what is the deepest yearning of their hearts. It convinces not by threats or external rules, but by persuasion and demonstration. Oman's student Lesslie Newbigin wrote significantly of the individual Christian community as a 'hermeneutic of

---

[48] Oman, *Vision and Authority*, p. 311.

[49] Oman, *Vision and Authority*, pp. 311-312.

[50] Oman, *Vision and Authority*, p. 317.

[51] Kosuke Koyama, 'What Makes a Missionary? Toward Crucified Mind Not Crusading Mind,' in Gerald H. Anderson and Thomas F. Stransky, eds., *Mission Trends, No. 1* (Grand Rapids, MI: William B. Eerdmans Publishing Company, 1974), pp. 73-86.

[52] Oman, *The Church and the Divine Order*, vii.

the gospel.'[53]

Such an indirect approach to mission also brings to mind a phrase used first by my friends William Burrows and Jonathan Tan, and consequently developed recently by Terrence Tilley. We have often in the past, as had Pope John Paul II, spoken of mission *ad gentes* or mission *to* those to whom the gospel had not been fully proclaimed or accepted. Burrows suggested that, as we conceive mission today more in dialogical terms (he was responding to a talk by Indian theologian Michael Amaladoss on interreligious dialogue), we might better describe such mission as mission *inter gentes* or *among* those who have not heard nor accepted the gospel. The new preposition is significant. It points to the fact that we, like God, do not *target* people, but live among them, share their lives, get to know them, share with them. Tilley writes, quoting Burrows:

> To have a *missio inter gentes* is to witness to the *basilea tou theou* in a minority situation – a situation that characterizes not only Asia but Europe and North America as well. If all the world are to be disciples, then discipleship cannot be a foreign import that people will resist as colonialist and hegemonic or a Trojan horse that will destroy what is good in indigenous traditions. Rather, such traditions can be seen not as enemies but as 'potential allies against real, *mutual* enemies –' the structural power of evil and Mammon as selfish attachment to wealth and pleasure.[54]

Mission and The Other

The personal God is a God who cares for persons in their individuality. God, Oman says, does not deal with human beings generally, but in a way that each person 'has to Him the distinctiveness, the importance, the whole significance he can have to himself.'[55] In mission today this understanding of God's personal care for each person might have two resonances.

First, there is a concern in thinking about mission today to recognize the genuine 'otherness' of persons, not imposing our own agenda on their needs, not presuming that we have the answers to their questions–not even presuming

[53] Lesslie Newbigin, 'The Congregation as Hermeneutic of the Gospel,' *The Gospel in a Pluralist Society* (Grand Rapids, MI: William B. Eerdmans Publishing Company, 1989), pp. 222-33.

[54] Terrence W. Tilley, *The Disciples' Jesus: Christology as Reconciling Practice* (Maryknoll, NY: Orbis Books, 2009), p. 256. Quoting William R. Burrows, 'A Response to Michael Amaladoss,' *Proceedings of the Catholic Theological Society of America*, 56 (2001), pp. 15-20. See also Jonathan Y. Tan, '*Missio Inter Gentes*: Towards a New Paradigm in the Mission Theology of the Federation of Asian Bishops' Conferences (FABC),' *Mission Studies*, 21, 1 (2004): pp. 65-95.

[55] Oman, 'Individual,' p. 815.

we understand their questions. Lutheran pastoral theologian Herbert Anderson speaks of the need to 'see the other whole,' the first step of which is to treat the individual persons among whom we minister with a sense of wonder. As Anderson writes:

> ... wonder presupposes simultaneously knowing and not knowing. To make room for wonder we need to suspend judgement. Wonder presumes being in uncertainties without being irritated or need[ing] to establish fact and reason. Such receptivity toward the Other demands the capacity to tolerate uncertainty and ambiguity. It also limits arrogance.[56]

In the same way, my colleague Claude-Marie Barbour speaks of the importance of doing mission 'in reverse.' Rather than thinking first about one's own work of evangelizing, Barbour insists on the prior necessity of the *missionary* being evangelized by the people among whom she or he works. Unless we are willing to allow people to be our teachers, to learn from them and learn to respect their world, we can never really develop the trust or the understanding by which we can make the gospel intelligible to them.[57]

Second, God's 'patient minuteness'[58] in regard to persons anchors the need for respect and knowledge of contexts as the church does mission. We do not need 'universal theologies;' we need contextual theologies. Our preaching, our education, our counselling, our healthcare services, our church structures need to take individual circumstances and particular cultures into account. Inculturation, in other words, is not ultimately a strategy. It is rooted in the very method of God as such. In dealing with the world, God respects and loves people in their concrete circumstances, their social locations, their cultural identity. As we participate in God's mission, we are challenged to do the same.

A Prophetic Community

Oman's understanding of God's personal nature does not understand God as intervening to avert sin, its dire consequences, or natural disasters like cancer in persons or floods and tsunamis. God rather works through those who have caught the vision of the Divine Order, and so the solution to the problem of evil is for him a group of women and men who will spend their lives witnessing to the truth, opposing evil, and, where necessary, helping to relieve it. Part of

---

[56] Herbert Anderson, 'Seeing the Other Whole: A Habitus for Globalization,' *Mission Studies* XIV, 1 & 2 (1997): p. 51.

[57] Claude-Marie Barbour, Kathleen Billman, Peggy Desjarlait, Eleanor Doidge, 'Mission on the Boundaries: Cooperation without Exploitation,' in Susan B. Thistlethwaite and George F. Cairns, eds., *Beyond Theological Tourism: Mentoring as a Grassroots Approach to Theological Education* (Maryknoll, NY: Orbis Books, 1995), pp. 72-91.

[58] Oman, Sermon on Is 42:3 and Mt 12:20.

participating in God's mission, therefore, is the taking on of a prophetic stance against sin, oppression and evil, working for human and for creation's liberation.

However, it is important to note how Oman describes how one denounces as God does. One may speak about 'divine wrath,' but he insists that it is always 'the work of love and not of anger.'[59] He gives two examples. The first is of Jesus weeping over Jerusalem and speaking in the tenderest terms to Israel – but only after Matthew records one of Jesus' most ferocious condemnations of the Jewish leaders' intransigence.[60] Like the prophets in Israel's history, denunciation was a result of love – like the anger of a parent. Oman's second example is from the life of the eighteenth century American Puritan, John Woolman. Before preaching to slave owners to denounce the practice, Woolman used to bring the matter before God until his heart was 'tendered.' Only then was he able to deliver his stern and challenging message. Even against perpetrators of evil, mission in the name of the personal God still sees them as persons. Participating in the mission of a personal God calls us to a prophetic dialogue.

Conclusion

We have come a long way in the past century in our understanding of the church's mission. We no longer speak about mission as a crusade, working for Christ's victory in the world, fighting for justice, developing tactics for conversion. We no longer glorify, as does the American hymn, 'an army of youth flying the standards of truth ... heads lifted high, Catholic Action our cry.' Mission today is understood much more in terms of dialogue–prophetic dialogue, yes, but dialogue nonetheless. The hymn quoted above goes on to say that it is the *cross* that is 'our only sword.' In working on this paper I have come to realize how much my study of and love for the work of John Oman has influenced my own missiological thinking, and I hope my missiological practice. My conviction is that Oman's work can further help us be worthy of the amazing grace of being called to share God's mission. This paper has been only a modest start.

---

[59] Oman, *Grace and Personality*, p. 287.
[60] John Oman, 'Tenderness and Judgement,' in *A Dialogue with God* (London: James Clarke, 1950). The text is Mt 23:37. The verse quoted on p. 111 (v. 34) is incorrect.

CHAPTER 9

Patterns of Response to Darwinism: the Case of John Oman

Adam Hood

The reading of post-Darwinian debates, about the theological implications of Darwin's ideas, has been beset and misdirected by the metaphor of conflict. The idea that theology and science were, in the 19th and 20th centuries, locked in an ideological war has been as prevalent, as it has been misleading.

James Moore, in his influential book, *The Post-Darwinian Controversies* has argued that it was in fact, only in the late 19th Century, through the work of American historians John Draper and Andrew White, that the military metaphor came to dominate interpretations.[1] The effect of this has been significant: prejudicing historical understanding and, in Moore's words, perpetuating a 'false conceptualisation' of the relationship between theology and science.[2]

Moore goes on to argue that the force of the metaphor of conflict was 'enriched by the vocabulary of Victorian politics, the polemics of T.H. Huxley, and the tactics of American Fundamentalism in the twentieth century', so that a particular, ideologically driven interpretation of the 19th Century – Draper, for instance, presented a history guided by Comte's ideas of an ineluctable movement from religion to science – became the standard way to understand the relationship between religion and science and religion and Darwinism in particular. Moore, fascinatingly, comments on how the military metaphors prevalent in the evangelical hymnology of the mid-19th century – see, for instance, hymns such as 'Fight the good fight' and 'Onward Christian Soldiers' – reinforced the tendency to view the intellectual encounter between Christianity and science as conflictual. Moreover, the popular tendency on the part of some to see the world in terms of conflict influenced both Christians and non-Christians alike; Huxley's approach was shaped somewhat by the enthusiasm of Christians for the metaphors of warfare,[3] just, as in our own day, Richard Dawkin's aggressive atheism may be a response to the aggression

---

[1] James R. Moore, *The Post-Darwinian Controversies: a study of the Protestant struggle to come to terms with Darwin in Great Britain and America 1870-1900* (Cambridge: Cambridge University Press, 1979), pp. 12-13.

[2] Moore, *Post-Darwinian*, p. 13.

[3] Moore, *Post-Darwinian*, chp. 2.

shown by some theists. Of course, there were thinkers who saw the issues between Darwin and Christianity in terms of opposites, but, as Moore suggests, merely reading Huxley or Wilberforce or Tyndall does not establish the case that there was a generalised conflict between Christianity and Darwin. Indeed the evidence is that the response to Darwin amongst Christian thinkers was far more complex and multi-faceted than is often thought. Moore claims, for instance, that with a few exceptions 'the leading thinkers in Great Britain and America came to terms quite readily with Darwinism and evolution'.[4] No doubt he is thinking here, so far as Scotland is concerned, of people such as Professor John Tulloch of St Andrews, Professor Robert Flint of Edinburgh and Henry Drummond, the great populariser of evolutionary theism.

If, in trying to describe the early relationship between Darwin and Christianity, we move away from the metaphors of conflict, there remains the task of accurately mapping the religious responses and trying, as far as possible, to show what patterns there might have been amongst these. This I take to be of intrinsic interest, requiring no further justification. However, if a justification is required, it can be pointed out that in historical theology we rehearse theological strategies that are still around today, which is to say that we can make theological progress by observing the strengths and weaknesses of the approaches adopted in the past.

It is with this goal in mind that I wish in this paper to review John Oman's ideas on the challenges and opportunities offered by Darwinism. This task will be approached by firstly, discussing the context within which Oman encountered Darwinism; and secondly, by outlining Oman's ideas as these are found in some key texts.

I begin with some shading of Oman's context, since, like all thinkers, his work was nurtured and informed by those who reared, taught and conversed with him, both directly and indirectly.

The broad background to his work was the Scotland, which in the second half of the 19th Century was going through a period of intense, even revolutionary, change across the spectrum of economy, society, politics and the intellectual life. The extent to which contemporaries felt this to be a revolutionary age is shown in the words of the prominent Scottish churchman, Marcus Dods, who commented, in 1889: 'It might be difficult to lay one's finger on any half-century in the worlds history during which changes so rapid, so profound, so fruitful, and so permanent have taken place as those which the past generation has seen.'[5]

Such far-reaching adaptations of context had inevitably drawn a variety of responses from the churches. Many, according to Vidler, were unwilling to change, but others responded more positively and, indeed, it is arguable that

---

[4] Moore, *Post-Darwinian*, p. 92.
[5] Marcus Dods, quoted by A.C. Cheyne, *The Transforming of the Kirk* (Edinburgh: St Andrews, 1983), p. 1.

without some willingness to adapt belief and practice to the new circumstances the Late-Victorian churches might have been far more marginalised than they were.[6] Certainly amongst the Scottish churches, and particularly the various branches of the dominant religious form, Presbyterianism: The Church of Scotland, The Free Church of Scotland and the United Presbyterian Church, the 50 years following the publication of the *Origin of the Species* saw, in Cheyne's words 'a vigorous and thoroughgoing reappraisal of the entire range of inherited faith and practice'.[7]

Many Presbyterian churchmen recognised the profound changes taking place around them; some sought to respond positively and this is reflected in the energetic and sometimes rancorous debates around the twin pillars of Presbyterianism, the Bible and the Westminster Confession of Faith. On the Bible, controversy gathered around the attempt to read the Scriptures as historical documents. Teachers such as Andrew Davidson and William Robertson Smith argued that historical methods showed the process by which God makes himself known through history.[8] On the Westminster Confession; by the 1870s, under the influence of German and English theological, philosophical and scientific thought, a mood had developed which brought about a decisive change in the relationship with the 'historic statement of belief'. In this regard, the decision in 1879 of the United Presbyterian Church Synod to allow 'liberty of opinion' to ministers and elders on those teachings of the Confession which were not of the 'substance of the faith' is a threshold moment. The example of the United Presbyterians was subsequently followed by the other, main Presbyterian churches, effectively loosening the ties of Westminster orthodoxy for good or ill.[9]

Cheyne and Calum Brown have argued that the ebb and flow of debate around these foci overshadowed evolution for much of the 19th Century, such that significant public discussion in Scotland of Darwinism, only began in the 1880s, though the historical emphasis of prior debates prepared the way for a positive treatment of Darwin. However, it can be argued that this understates the degree to which Christian intellectuals in Scotland had already, in the 1860s and 1870s, engaged with Darwinism. As early as 1860 John Duns, a Free Church minister and later teacher of natural science at New College, had argued that unless a tapir could be 'caught in the act of becoming a horse', then

[6] Alex R. Vidler, *The Church in an age of Revolution* (Harmondsworth: Penguin, 1961), p. 270.

[7] Cheyne, *Transforming the Kirk*, p. 3.

[8] Cheyne, *Transforming the Kirk*, p. 42.

[9] One author who regards the introduction of the 'conscience clause' as a 'decline' is Ian Hamilton, *The Erosion of Calvinist Orthodoxy* (Edinburgh: Rutherford House, 1990).

Darwin's theory of the transmutation of species would be unsubstantiated.[10] Whilst in 1862, David Brewster, Principal of the University of Edinburgh and experimental physicist as well as a Free Church elder, suggested that there was too much "wild speculation" in the *Origin of the Species*.[11] Also in 1862, T.H. Huxley gave two lectures at a well filled Queen's Hall in Edinburgh, which cast doubt on the *Genesis* account of creation, arguing that humans were descended from the same stock as apes.[12] This threw the Free Church *Witness* newspaper into paroxysms of rage, claiming that Huxley had put forward the "'vilest and beastliest"'of ideas.[13]

Jon Roberts, in his book, *Darwinism and the divine in America,* has argued that there were broadly two stages in the reception of evolution in the American churches. His approach may arguably help us to understand the Scottish situation.

Prior to the publication of the *Origin of the Species* in 1859, Christian intellectuals had been amongst the most vociferous advocates of natural science. Many scientists were clergymen, but, more importantly, the churches saw science as an ally underpinning the design argument, which was a primary tool in the battle with unbelief.[14] The argument was that God's existence, just like any other fact, could be proved. The compelling evidence of design in creation suggested the existence of a divine architect and it was in this sense that the study of nature was seen as a kind of theology and the scientific enterprise gained status from the backing of the churches.

The publication of the *Origin of the Species* did not initially challenge the churches' attachment to science, for, according to Roberts, the first, general response, lasting up until the mid-1870s, was to challenge the scientific legitimacy of the theory. The churches' attack on Darwinism drew on its inconsistency with the Bible, its perceived ideological bias to naturalism, but, most importantly, on the scepticism of the scientific community itself. One critical factor here was that Darwinism represented a move away from the Baconian ideal of inductive science to a more speculative model.

From 1875 onward the American churches were forced into a new mode of response to Darwinism. The catalyst was the growing perception that the broad scientific community had come to accept Darwin's thesis. Protestant theologians responding to this new consensus, looked to one of three options:

---

[10] Quoted in D.N. Livingstone, 'Public spectacle and scientific theory: William Robertson Smith and the reading of evolution in Victorian Scotland', *Studies in history and philosophy of biological and biomedical sciences* 35 (2004), pp. 1-29 (p. 6).

[11] Quoted in Livingstone, 'Public spectacle', p. 6.

[12] Quoted in Livingstone, 'Public spectacle, p. 6.

[13] Quoted in Livingstone, 'Public spectacle', p. 6.

[14] Jon H. Roberts, *Darwinism and the divine in America: Protestant intellectuals and organic evolution 1859-1900* (Madison & London: University of Wisconsin, 1988), pp. 8-9.

some thought Darwinism could be accommodated with minimal theological change; others saw more radical changes were needed if evolution was to be successfully integrated in Christian doctrine, some even coming to view evolution as a motif for God's total dealings with the world; some rejected any accommodation with Darwin, largely on the question of maintaining the authority of the Bible.[15]

Roberts' analysis of developments in America helps in the interpretation of the Scottish experience, since there seems to be correspondence between the two situations. Certainly pre-1859 Scottish thinkers such as Thomas Chalmers[16] championed the consonance of scientific enquiry and the design argument, Fergusson comments: 'So much of the natural world was inexplicable without appeal to the God-hypothesis that it was assumed that a greater understanding of its workings would only confirm the intuitive impression of design.'[17]

Again, the initial reaction of Scottish thinkers to Darwinism, was one of scientific scepticism, which was able to draw on the work of renowned scientists such as Lord Kelvin, whose estimate of the age of the Earth, based on the cooling of the planet, was at variance with the Darwinian hypothesis.

Finally, from the 1870s onwards there is evidence of a more diverse range of religious responses amongst Scottish Christians. Some, such as Duns, continued to doubt the scientific and theological credentials of Darwinism. Well into the 1880s, Duns was still arguing that evolution and theology were at loggerheads.

Others, of whom Principal Rainy is perhaps the best example, gave a cautious welcome to Darwinism. In his 1874 inaugural lecture as Principal of New College, entitled 'Evolution and Theology', he continues to harbour doubts as to the scientific credentials of Darwin's theory – not least because he judges that it has been associated with 'atheistic and infidel tendencies'.[18] However, if the theory is true, it would not, he argues, pose insuperable difficulties to the doctrine of creation; it would simply push the creative act of God back in the process. Having said that, Rainy is insistent that theology is at variance with any theory of evolution that would offer a purely naturalistic account of the world and humankind, trying to exclude direct 'divine interposition' in the creation of the world, in the inspiration of the scriptures, and in the origin of 'mind'.[19] Fergusson, commenting on Rainy's approach, suggests that it contains 'the best response today to creation science and

---

[15] Roberts, *Darwinism*, pp. x-xi.

[16] Thomas Chalmers, *On the power, wisdom, and goodness of God as manifested in the adaptation of external nature to the moral and intellectual constitution of man*, 2 vols (London, 1933).

[17] David Fergusson, 'Darwin and Providence', unpublished paper, p. 3.

[18] Robert Rainy, *Evolution and Theology* (Edinburgh: Maclaren and Macniven, 1874), p. 11.

[19] Rainy, *Evolution*, p. 18.

intelligent design theory'. He continues, 'An evolving world, as described by the natural sciences, can equally well be viewed as the outcome of divine design.'[20]

Henry Drummond was chief amongst those who exhibited 'whole-hearted enthusiasm' for Darwinism, particularly in his best sellers *Natural law in the spiritual world*[21] and *The ascent of man*.[22] Drummond came to re-interpret Christianity through the prism of evolution, though he combined this with 'deep devotion to the person of Jesus Christ'.[23] Drummond's attempt to fuse biblical and evolutionary thought has not weathered well; some see an unfortunate obeisance to Spenser's 'social Darwinism', whilst others judge he advocated 'the naturalisation of the spiritual world'. Owen Chadwick, however, suggests more positively that Drummond was able to articulate some of the questions that dogged thinking people at the time.[24]

Allowing that Duns, Rainy and Drummond represent the spectrum of Scottish responses to Darwinism in the period, the question can now be posed: 'Where might Oman fit?' In my view, Oman sits somewhere between Rainy and Drummond. Like Rainy, Oman was chary of Darwinian naturalism if it excluded God from the world. Like Drummond, Oman saw that the implications of evolutionary thinking went far further than Rainy and others perceived. Oman acknowledged the scientific validity of Darwin; he was cautious about the claims of naturalistic Darwinism to explain the mind; he offered an innovative evolutionary and theistic explanation of the mind; and he advocated an evolutionary view of religious development.

Before pressing on to develop the analysis of Oman's position, it is as well to offer a general qualification to what follows. Oman's writing no where includes a detailed account of Darwin's writings. In interpreting his views on evolution it is not always clear whether he is responding to the general idea of evolution that pre-dates Darwin, or to Darwin himself or his interpreters. For all that, there is a case that where Oman discussed evolution he is attending to some of the issues that had been raised by Darwin – specifically the development of humankind through adaptation to context – albeit that Oman appears to be relating primarily to Huxley's writings and not to those of Darwin himself.

Oman's own personal heritage and training guided him towards valuing new discoveries. Brought up within the most theologically liberal of major Scottish churches, the United Presbyterian Church, Oman's ecclesial culture encouraged tolerance of diverse views and constructive engagement with new movements

---

[20] Fergusson, 'Darwin', p. 4.

[21] Henry Drummond, *Natural law in the spiritual world* (London: Hodder, 1885).

[22] Henry Drummond, *The ascent of man* (London: Hodder, 1894).

[23] A.C. Cheyne, 'Religious World of Henry Drummond' in *Studies in Scottish Church History* (Edinburgh: T&T Clark, 1999), pp. 185-98 (p. 191).

[24] Cheyne, 'Religious World', pp. 192-3.

of thought, though only within limits. When, during his education in Edinburgh, he witnessed a heresy trial in a sister church, this spurred him to a vocation to become a minister of religion, with the express aim of engaging in a 'search for a truth, which would shine in its own light in face of all inquiry'.[25] Oman's vocation was fired by a desire to articulate a way of believing that was consonant with all inquiry and yet distinctively religious. Underlying this were the convictions that, since God was a God of Truth obscurantism was unbelief; that only a courageous facing of the issues could yield a religion that was 'virile and stable'; and that an attempt to argue for religion on the basis of its practical functionality was unlikely to convince.[26] This approach dovetailed with the dominant tenor of the theology of the time, as expressed by thinkers such as Caird and Tulloch, who eschewed dogmatic for apologetic theology.

One might also reflect that the theological register that Oman chose expressed a personal quest that he shared with many of the finest minds of his generation. A number of authors comment on the tensions that many in the period felt between an inherited theology and wider, cultural knowledge.[27] In some cases, such as that of Robert Louis Stevenson, intellectual tensions led away from the Church.[28] In others, such as that of Oman, the tensions defined a life-long search for integrity.

Oman's writing career ran from 1902 through to 1939, and 'evolution' is a theme that recurs time and again. Here, though, the concentration will be on just three of his books, which will serve to illustrate something of his approach.

In 1902, whilst a church minister, he published *Vision and Authority*, which he described as the fruit of 'long years of reading and thinking' about a situation that was contemporary and challenging'. One of the interesting features of *Vision and Authority* is that it is directed towards a general audience and, indeed the fact that it was reissued many times, suggests its success in capturing a public. Oman's interest in a general audience arose from his view that the whole purpose of religious thought was to nurture and inspire the practice of the Christian faith.[29] It is in this light that we can understand why much of his thinking on evolution is directed towards countering, what he perceives to be, the detrimental effects of the ways in which Darwin's theory

---

[25] John Oman, *Vision and Authority*, 2nd edn (London: Hodder and Stoughton, 1928), p. 12.

[26] John Oman, *Vision and Authority*, 1st edn (London: Hodder and Stoughton, 1902), pp. 4-5; 2nd edn, pp. 23-4.

[27] See T.W. Mansion, 'Introduction', in John Oman, *Vision and Authority*, 8th edn with new introduction (London: Hodder and Stoughton), pp. 1-6 (pp. 1-2); *David Cairns: an autobiography*, ed. by A.H. Cairns & D.C. Cairns (London: SCM, 1950), p. 125.

[28] Claire Harman, *Robert Louis Stevenson: a biography* (London: Harper, 2006), especially chp.3.

[29] John Oman, *The Problem of Faith and Freedom in the Last Two Centuries* (London: Hodder and Stoughton, 1906), p. 3.

has been interpreted, particularly with regards to the potentialities of human beings.

In none of his writings did Oman dispute the scientific correctness of Darwin's theory. Indeed, he regularly affirms the accuracy and necessity of Darwin.[30] Oman's primary concern was to counter and correct some inadequate interpretations of Darwin, not least because he believes that bad ideas may have baleful consequences.

A fundamental building block of Oman's thought is that human beings are able to interpret their environment for themselves and to modify their actions in line with their interpretations. These ideas form the basis of his criticism of the way in which the personal and moral implications of evolution had been understood. Oman perceived that certain ways of seeing 'evolution' had led to a diminished understanding of the human being. If humans were a product of evolution, if their consciousness and conscience were a matter of adaptation[31], then what did the claim to uniqueness consist of, what could be said of human dignity, and what were the human potentialities. Oman argues that this incipient lowering of the human gaze had given rise to moral dissipation. Where people thought of themselves only as the product of a material process driven by the needs of survival, this tended to undermine their sense of their own potential for moral and spiritual development. The fruit of this diminished perspective was the tendency to moral chaos as[32] people indulged 'selfish impulse'.[33] It's against this analytical background that Oman offered his reflections on the implications of evolution; his aim being to show that evolution was consistent with a religious and moral vision of reality.[34]

In criticising popular interpretation of evolution, Oman pinpointed the assumption that the temporal origins of a phenomenon, in this case the human species, wholly determined its nature – a view which more recently has been called the 'genetic fallacy'. That is, Oman criticised the idea that natural selection wholly defines what humans were and could become, he writes: 'Only on this account has the theory of Evolution had any hurtful effect on our adoration for the high and holy, or weakened the authority of the true and right.'[35]

Part of the problem here, of course, was that if the human species was wholly shaped by a material process, it was more difficult, though not impossible, to identify a role for the divine.

A further problem was that this account did not adequately make sense of those human capacities, such as moral discernment and unconditional love,

---

[30] Oman, *Vision and Authority*, 1st edn, p. 9.
[31] Oman, *Vision and Authority*, p. 2.
[32] Oman, *Vision and Authority*, p. 4.
[33] Oman, *Vision and Authority*, p. 5.
[34] Oman, *Vision and Authority*, p. 4.
[35] Oman, *Vision and Authority*, p. 14.

which went far beyond any needs specified by survival. In this regard Oman points out that there is a qualitative difference between patterns of behaviour driven by desire and self-interest, and patterns of behaviour shaped by ideas of duty and conscience.[36] Again, the difference in kind between the mutual commitments involved in 'physical love' and those involved in 'selfless' love cannot be explained by a focus only on a material process of evolution.[37]

As against the emphasis on origins, Oman held that a more 'scientific' way to explain the development of humankind is to begin from what human beings actually are in the present. Arguing that the basic premises of evolutionary thinking were that human development was to be explained through a process of adaptation to the environment, and that all distinctive human capacities had a function in relation to environment, Oman held that one must conclude that human development is only explainable by postulating an interaction with a material and a supra-natural, or divine environment.[38] It is for this reason that Oman strikingly comments that: 'Religion, instead of fearing Evolution, should rather welcome it as essentially a religious conception of the world.'[39] In Oman's view if one seeks a developmental understanding of the range of human capacities, physical, moral and intellectual, one is led to infer a divine environment as an explanation as to how human beings have evolved far beyond their 'base' or 'carnal' beginnings.[40]

Just as physical sight evolves in response to light, so spiritual sight evolves in response to the divine environment; and just as sight is an evidence of light, so religion, which is universal, is an evidence of the divine: 'In both cases the very fact of Evolution must be a guarantee of correspondence to reality.'[41] In this sense religious sensibilities are part of the 'natural development of man'.[42] Moreover the striking movement from carnal beginnings to the spiritual, for instance from sexual desire to the unconditional love of Christ, may suggest the possibility of further spiritual growth in the future: 'If the spiritual has been a growth from the carnal, why should we doubt that our highest aspirations are forerunners of a fulfilment beyond our anticipation.'[43]

In his second book, *The Problem of Faith and Freedom* published in 1906, Oman reiterated a central theme of *Vision and Authority*, that of the inadequacy of a genealogical approach to explaining the 'vast and wonderful' world in which we live. The appropriate method was to take stock of our experience in all its variety, and ask how such might have evolved. Oman's answer was that

---

[36] Oman, *Vision and Authority*, p. 16.
[37] Oman, *Vision and Authority*, p. 17.
[38] Oman, *Vision and Authority*, p. 13.
[39] Oman, *Vision and Authority*, p. 12.
[40] Oman, *Vision and Authority*, p. 15.
[41] Oman, *Vision and Authority*, p. 11.
[42] Oman, *Vision and Authority*, p. 13.
[43] Oman, *Vision and Authority*, p. 15.

the wonders of the world could only be explained by assuming that there was an overarching goal or purpose that guided the evolution of the world and humankind. Perhaps one might use painting as a metaphor to explain Oman's point. The material elements of the painter's work are integrated into the creation of a work of art, and, in a similar way, physical evolution is an integrated part of a larger and more creative process.

On this occasion Oman did not develop his idea in terms of a divine environment, so that there is here the potential for arguing that the divine plan is brought to fruition through evolution in the natural sphere alone. However, since the idea of the supra-natural sphere is developed in later books, it would be problematic to think that there is discontinuity between *Faith and Freedom* and *Vision and Authority* on this point.

A new concern of *Faith and Freedom* was to counter the view that evolution diminishes the role of the individual and free-will. Oman agreed with William James that Darwinian evolution depends on, admittedly involuntary, improvements in the individual as the motor of change and, when free-will emerges, 'Then man's will becomes the supreme force for a higher development.'[44] That is, the individual and free-will plays a key role in the evolution of the material and spiritual world as we know it. The early material phase of evolution is characterised by all creatures being vehicles for the 'forces of the world'.[45] The emergence of human freedom, which is the immediate goal of the evolutionary process, gives rise to creatures who are able to interpret the purpose of the world and to agree or disagree with it.[46]

A third concern of *Faith and Freedom* was to argue that though moral ideas and, more broadly, the idea of divine purpose had evolved out of more 'base' emotions and desires, this did not diminish their significance and value. We are here back to Oman's point in *Vision and Authority* that the origin of human values does not define their nature, since there is a qualitative difference between the evolutionary origins and the character of emotions such as the sacrificial love of Christ.

Oman's magnum opus, *The Natural and the Supernatural*, published in 1931, set out to explore a religious view of the relationship between the physical world and the divine. Within this context, it was inevitable that he would give attention to evolution. He turns to the theme directly in Part III of the work, which is entitled 'Necessity and Freedom': evolution is to be dealt with in the context of a discussion of the relationship between natural, material processes, the emergent properties of mind, and the action of God. The discussion here can be characterised as the consolidation and elaboration of the themes that were already present in his earlier books.

Oman's overall goal is to show the scientific and philosophic implausibility

---

[44] Oman, *Faith and Freedom in the Last Two Centuries*, p. 405.

[45] Oman, *Faith and Freedom*, p. 408.

[46] Oman, *Faith and Freedom*, p. 408.

of a purely naturalistic account of the evolution of life, and human life in particular. Following the axiom that theory must explain experience, not force experience into a procrustean bed; Oman holds that a purely naturalistic, evolutionary account of human life, as found in Huxley and Weismann, but not in Darwin, inadequately accounts for the role of intention, meaning and value in human experience. Moreover it misrepresents the necessary character of the environment within which life evolves.

Oman's intellectual target here is the view, put forward by Huxley, that evolutionary science aims to give a comprehensive explanation of human life in terms of 'matter and causation'.[47] The implication is that science will banish ideas of 'spirit' and 'spontaneity' as explanatory categories. Oman holds that this view, as a scientific theory, is inadequate because it fails to explain significant features of human life, namely the role of intentionality and the character of the environment that gives rise to human beings such as we are. All organic life, for Oman, is marked by mind and the capacity to form purpose and act with intention.[48] It follows that organic life is qualitatively different from the non-organic. Since this is intuitively recognised, it is scientifically wrong to attempt the reduction of mind to matter. This is to confuse origins with nature – the genetic fallacy. 'Why not', Oman asks, 'Understand the character of matter with reference to mind, rather than the other way around?'

Again, the neglect of the mind by some evolutionists obscures the role of mind and purpose in the evolutionary process. Here, Oman follows William James in arguing that evolutionary change depends upon the purpose of creatures:

> The living creature does not first develop a lung and then get out of the water on to the land, but, having an object to gain on the land which it is ever striving after, it develops the means of attaining its purpose.[49]

As a minimum, at a sub-conscious level, mind and purpose are the creative elements at work in any organism and evolution cannot take place without them. One thing that this implies is the place of learning in the evolutionary process.[50] A connected point is that the growth of self-interest or even selfishness seems to be predicated on a relatively high level of self-awareness and self-determination. It is in this sense that, according to James, the individual has a key role for Darwinism as the '"ferment in the race"'.[51]

A final flaw of naturalistic Darwinism is the inability to explain the richness

---

[47] John Oman, *The Natural and the Supernatural* (London & New York: Cambridge University Press, 1931), p. 259.

[48] Oman, *Natural and Supernatural*, pp. 263-4.

[49] Oman, *Natural and Supernatural*, p. 265.

[50] Oman, *Natural and Supernatural*, p. 267.

[51] Quoted in Oman, *Natural and Supernatural*, p. 273.

of the 'evolution of life'.[52] The evolution of humankind is marked by growing self-awareness, linked with an expanding desire for ways of responding to the environment that are based on truth and goodness. 'The evolution of life', writes Oman, 'is like the evolution of a house, which grows in hospitality as it becomes increasingly wind and water proof'.[53] The point is that the postulation of a purely material world provides no grounds for explaining how human beings evolve as moral beings. Only the postulation of a supernatural or divine environment explains this development: 'If progress is by reaching forward to fuller meaning, the environment must be such that the value is there waiting to be realised.'[54] Evolution on this model involves the individual adapting themselves to both the material and the divine environments, which are, in practice, indivisible.[55] In fact, the fullest account of evolution is that it involves organic beings reaching out for meaning, and discovering their environment 'challenges and rewards life's adventure'.[56] Evolution literally involves a meeting of minds, human and divine, and it is in that sense that it is a thoroughly religious conception for Oman.

In conclusion, we have seen that Scottish theology, in the Late Victorian period, offered a context in which Darwin could be positively evaluated by some theologians. Important here was the fact that many educated Scots were already familiar with the concept of evolution through exposure to the art, literature and philosophy of the Romantic movement.[57]

John Oman's approach to evolution is that of a churchman who wishes to integrate Darwin into a broader understanding of world development. His most salient methodological point is that our explanations need to do justice to the full range of human experience. Theory should express experience, not corrupt it. It is on this point that he charges that some interpretations of Darwin were deficient, yielding a desiccated view of the world.

In Oman's view, when we assume what we intuit namely, human freedom and the reality of our moral and spiritual values, this leads to an explanation of human development which integrates natural selection into a broader conception of evolution. Material evolution is the substructure upon which spiritual evolution takes place. If material evolution is driven by natural selection, then evolution in its spiritual phase is driven by the freedom of human beings to discover and to act upon the purpose of God for creation. The goal that underlies the whole process is that of 'man's advance towards God's purpose'.[58]

---

[52] Oman, *Natural and Supernatural*, p. 274.
[53] Oman, *Natural and Supernatural*, p. 274.
[54] Oman, *Natural and Supernatural*, p. 277.
[55] Oman, *Natural and Supernatural*, p. 278.
[56] Oman, *Natural and Supernatural*, p. 279.
[57] Oman, *Natural and Supernatural*, p. 258.
[58] Oman, *Faith and Freedom*, p. 409.

Finally, how plausible is Oman's work on evolution? In evaluating his work it is helpful to distinguish between his comments on the ill-effects of naturalism; and his idea that evolution includes adaptation to a divine environment. On the first point, there is much to commend in Oman's writings. His attack on the genetic fallacy appears sound, in that there is an important distinction between human origins and what human beings are and can become. Mind cannot be reduced to matter. One dimension of this is that, if humans perceive themselves as purely material beings, there may be the temptation to think of human possibilities wholly in terms of the fulfilment of personal or communal desires. Some might see contemporary moral discourse as reflecting such a development. Oman's argument that the finer human qualities cannot be reduced to 'matter and causality' is a powerful argument against a diminished view of the human being. It is also a plea against the application of naturalism in a way that erodes the place of purpose and meaning in evolutionary theory. In this respect, Oman's approach could be an important corrective to the overweening ambitions of some evolutionary psychologists.

An interesting aspect of Oman's discussion of 'mind' is the way in which he extends this quality to all organisms. It is often said that 'evolution' integrates human beings into the natural world. Oman's point is the somewhat different one, that all organisms are related through their common capacity for purposeful action. It is difficult to assess the plausibility of this generalised point, but it does concur with work done on primates, which suggests the close relationships between humans and the great apes.[59]

A distinctive contribution of Oman to the evolutionary debate is his contention that evolution includes adaptation to the divine. Two drawbacks of this idea may be highlighted. Oman presents this idea as a way of explaining what naturalism is unable to explain. In this sense, his theological strategy is a throw-back to the early 19th century when, as has been seen, theologians sought to present God as a complement to scientific explanation. However, as Roberts argues, this strategy is fundamentally ill-conceived, in that its success is dependent upon the failure of scientists to offer convincing naturalistic accounts.[60] Theologies in this situation can quickly lose credibility once scientists fill in the explanatory gaps. Indeed, Roberts suggests that the decline in the public status of theology in 19th century America was driven by the fact that it was seen as an unsuccessful competitor to science. This highlights the dangers inherent in Oman's approach. For instance, recent work on the evolutionary background to altruism, suggests that there is a plausible naturalistic account of the origins of morality that renders Oman's theory

---

[59] See for instance Frans De Waal, *Primates and Philosophers* (New Jersey: Princeton, 2006).

[60] Roberts, *Darwinism*, p. 19.

redundant.[61] In mitigation it must be said that Oman's work always aimed at integrating current knowledge with the lived experience of faith, thus his willingness to see humans, and perhaps animals as having an on-going concourse with the divine. The potential deficiency of other approaches, such as that advocated by Fergusson, is that, in relegating the divine to setting the conditions of evolution, God becomes a more distant being altogether.

A second limitation of Oman's postulation of a divine environment is that it tends to transpose all of Christian theology into an evolutionary key. Oman, in taking this tact, was identifying himself with a common approach of the time, that underlying, for instance, the higher criticism of Robertson Smith.[62] The dangers of this approach are legion. It certainly suggests a hierarchy of religions and religious forms. Robertson Smith, for instance, thought of Protestantism and even Presbyterianism as at the top of the evolutionary tree. Again, this approach tends to a linear view of religious and social development. In terms of Oman's own emphasis on human free will as including the potential for sin, it seems difficult to justify a view that suggests we move from glory to glory. Utopias can't be constructed from the crooked timber of humanity.

Oman's comments on evolution are both stimulating and reflective of his own place and time. They touch on issues which are still current, though they have the deficiency of being targeted towards Darwin's advocates rather than Darwin himself. Whilst some aspects of Oman's work look dated, yet his conviction that the findings of evolutionary theory must be faced with honesty and humility remains an acid test of theological integrity.

---

[61] See Adam Hood, 'An evolutionary account of goodness', *Theology* 112 (2009), pp. 100-110.

[62] Livingstone, 'Public spectacle', p. 18.

CHAPTER 10

"Probing the Pastoral Cycle" – An Application of the Thought of John Oman to an aspect of Christian Adult Education Today

John Nightingale

Introduction

Let me begin by explaining why I have chosen this topic and then describe what I mean by it. In 2007 I retired from full-time Anglican ministry and felt that I wanted to think further about some of the theological issues which had emerged in my work over the years. Since the 1960s when I obtained first degrees in Social Studies and Theology and was trained for social work and the Anglican ministry, I have worked in two main settings, sometimes separately and sometimes together. The one setting has been the local congregation, whether in countryside, housing estate or town; the other has been Christian adult education and training in England or overseas. During this time I have become conscious of using a variety of theories and insights which do not entirely fit together and lack an overall intellectual framework. Some seem to treat learners as little more than laboratory animals whose nervous systems and behaviour can simply be explained in terms of stimulus and response. Others allow a much greater place for human creativity and freedom, both among those being educated as well as the educator, but they may or may not have a place for religion, let alone Christianity. Finally, even where there is an appreciation of religion, it may have an uneasy relationship with adult education – absorbing it, dominating it, ignoring it, or being absorbed or dominated by it. It is important to have an approach to theology and learning which holds these things creatively together and in this I have found the writings of John Oman most helpful.

This paper discusses a key term used in Christian Adult Education, 'the Pastoral Cycle'. It is the name given to a cyclical model for understanding the process of learning, which is widely used to help people understand how well their own ministry, or that of others, is developing.

The Pastoral Cycle has recently been examined in some detail in the *SCM*

Studyguide to Theological Reflection. One well known version of it is the *See, Judge, Act* method developed by Cardinal Henry Cardijn for the Young Christian Workers; it is widely used in the Roman Catholic Church and adapted in Liberation Theology. Another version of it is more secular, stemming from the thought of John Dewey and developed in the widely used learning cycle of David Kolb; it begins with *Concrete Experience*, goes on to *Reflective Observation*, then *Abstract Conceptualization* and finally *Active Experimentation*. In both cases the theories start from concrete *experience* – for example life in a particular setting – say that of a local community in the recession. There follows *reflection* on the thoughts and feelings involved and an attempt to set them in their social context, for example what is going on economically or sociologically. There is then an attempt to *judge* the situation in terms of the beliefs and values of participants and finally to make a deliberate *change*; this leads to further experience which can be reflected on it turn.

The Pastoral Cycle is often used as a tool in the education of ministerial students and other leaders for their work with congregations; for example a key text at the Queen's Foundation, Birmingham is *Doing Theology* by Laurie Green; he uses the headings *Experience, Exploration, Reflection* and *Response*. Furthermore, many people have used the idea in their professional work, or have been urged to do so, in preparation for their annual assessments – teachers, health workers, social workers, counsellors, managers or ministers of religion, when, with the help of a colleague or consultant, each is encouraged to reflect on their work experience, evaluate it in relation to their understanding and values and, as a result, to plan.

One may well ask: why does the cycle have to go round in the direction indicated, and not in the reverse direction? For example, are there not times when someone *sees* first, *acts* second and *judges* afterwards? Certainly this can happen; for example, in times of danger people tend to react instinctively *without reflection* – to run away from a shape and colour which seems to indicate a snake or to respond immediately to a threat from another human being. Our nervous systems may respond automatically very fast but that usually makes them erratic; we may mistake a snakeskin belt for a snake, or a member of the armed forces may in haste shoot an innocent person. That is why important decisions are often best made *after reflection* on all the data, hence the good advice to "sleep on it" before posting a contentious letter – a wise practice sometimes forgotten because on the computer it is so easy to click 'reply'!

The data requiring reflection include the emotions of the participants. It is true that emotions can be misleading; especially if uncorroborated they can express pure prejudice. On the other hand they may point to realities of which we are only dimly aware. The mariner may be troubled about tomorrow's weather even though it is hard to point to definite evidence or reasons; but we shall be more inclined to believe his or her hunches if there is a previous record of predictive skill. Our hunches may be worth checking out; after all the Dr Fell I find it so hard to love may turn out to be a Dr Shipman!

How may Theology and the Pastoral Cycle relate to one another? Do they have any connection at all? Some would say no. The term 'theology' has been used by critics as a catch-phrase for an abstract speculation that has nothing to do with practical decisions. Furthermore, some theologians have wanted to concentrate on the fundamental relationships between God and humanity rather than anything too contemporary; for example the entry on the Barmen Declaration of 1934 in the Oxford Dictionary of the Christian Church indicates that it was drawn up,

> to define the belief and mission of the Church in the face of the liberal tendencies of the Nazi German Christians. The foundation of the Church was held to be in the Revelation of God in Jesus Christ and not in any subordinate revelation in nature or history, and her primary mission was defined as to preach the Gospel of the free Grace of God.[1]

Others, on the other hand, both believers and critics, see the implications of theology for social action; in relation to that same historical dilemma, the subsequent life and thought of Bonhoeffer is an example of theological connections that were made and acted upon. What connections are appropriate and, if the model of the pastoral cycle is to be used, where on the cycle may they feature? These have been some of the questions in my mind as I have been trying to study Oman's thought.

The Contribution of John Oman

Let me start with a disclaimer. Oman would not have heard of the Pastoral Cycle as the term is used today, so the comments I make have to be based on my interpretation of his thought. Nonetheless he did reflect quite a bit on the nature of our experience, how we learn from it, and the place of both religion and theology in the process – and in particular on the contributions of his predecessors, Kant and Hegel, Schleiermacher and Ritschl. So let me pick out a few themes from his writings which seem to be relevant.

The Importance of Experience

Oman's creative thinking stemmed to a large extent from reflection on his experience in his long pastoral ministry in Alnwick and growth into faith as a boy in the Orkneys. He wrote:

---

[1] F.L. Cross (ed.), *The Oxford Dictionary of the Christian Church* (London: Oxford University Press, 1958), p. 132.

Experience is a dialogue, whereby we learn as we ask the right questions and appreciate the right answers. This means being both humble and alert: and there is no worse preparation for profitable dialogue than a mind school-mastering everything by dialectic. And is the product of much that we call culture anything else?[2]

Oman's sermons show a considerable awareness of the natural world and also of the situation and feelings of the people he was addressing. On the other hand he took to the interpretation of such experience the rigour and erudition of a well-stocked, aesthetic, theological and philosophical mind. He gives the example of visiting Flatford Mill; the mill itself he considered a relatively ordinary scene, but, when he looked at Constable's painting of it in "The Hay Wain" he appreciated the beauty which the artist's sensibility had detected and graphically expressed.[3]

Theology, however rigorous – and Oman was rigorous himself, involves *reflection* on experience and has consequences for life:

... so far as theologies ever were alive, they were not intellectual inferences, but the outcome of the greatest of all experiments, which is the endeavour to live rightly in our whole environment... Whether this was at any time rightly endeavoured is not to be judged by speculative consistency but by consistency in dealing with the world's problems and hazards.[4]

Consciousness and Freedom

The Pastoral Cycle is about *reflective*, not automatic response to experience. Oman gives an example from a walk along a country road, indicating that there are certain levels of knowing, from a general *awareness* of what is there (the sights and sounds and smells), to an *apprehension* of something particular coming along (a man on a bicycle), to a *comprehension* of what it is (a machine for getting along), to an *explanation* of the singular problem that 'it seems to have no support from its breadth, yet keeps upright while travelling along a line'.[5] Oman is describing a process of increasing reflection in terms not unlike those used by John Dewey.[6]

Reflection on experience involves hard thought and the presumption of the possibility of freedom in formulating judgements and making decisions. Oman

---

[2] John Oman, *Honest Religion* (London: Religious Book Club, 1941), p. 30.
[3] Oman, *Honest Religion*, p. 194.
[4] John Oman, *The Natural and the Supernatural* (London: Cambridge University Press, 1931), p. 356.
[5] Oman, *Natural and Supernatural*, pp. 120-4.
[6] John Dewey, *How We Think* (New York: Heath & Company, 1933), pp. 106-115.

is critical of behaviourists and determinists for taking what is only part of our experience (causation understood in purely physical terms and free of any implications of value) to apply to the whole. It is using causation, the construct of the active mind searching for the truth, as a Procrustean bed to cut off the very mental processes which gave rise to the idea of causation in the first place. Oman prefers to use the analogy of a spade to refer to mental activity.[7] Techniques of thought and experiment have to be used, as a spade, to dig out reality gradually, bit by bit. They may be rigid and controlled but the minds that devise them, use them and reflect on their results are not. One such tool is Science.

> Its justification is that it extends a process of arresting and stereotyping which has already begun in perception; that it enlarges man's practical management of his world by isolating quantity from all else, both the mind that knows and the varied meaning by which it knows; and that it goes behind all meaning the world manifests to find the means whereby we can make the world speak our meaning. Thus it is an effective instrument precisely because it is not fitted to provide a cosmology.[8]

In short, the scientific method should not subvert consciousness and freedom because it presupposes them.

The Developmental Nature of Freedom

To be free is not simply to kick against artistic conventions, as in Dadaism, or against moral ones as in a Sartrian *acte gratuit*. To be free is to be able to go over past thinking and to experiment for oneself, collate evidence, draw one's own conclusions and argue for them rationally, so that those who come after can draw theirs. Oman takes from the Romantics who came after Kant, and in particular from Hegel, the notion of freedom expressed through history, by a cumulative rational process, in the development of arts and sciences, of civil and political society. Here there is a family resemblance between some key thinkers who introduced the Pastoral Cycle. Dewey was initially influenced by Hegel; Cardinal Cardijn, the founder of the 'See, Judge, Act' method of the Young Christian Workers, Paulo Freire and the South American liberation theologians were all influenced by Hegel and/or the early Marx: they shared the notion that human beings, by together becoming conscious of their situations, could exercise their freedom; in the words of the Communist Manifesto 'Workers of the world unite; you have nothing to lose but your chains.' Judith Thompson writes of liberation theologians: 'Crucial in this process was the Marxist notion of *praxis* which means not simply "practice" but action

---

[7] Oman, *Honest Religion*, pp. 45-48.
[8] Oman, *Natural and Supernatural*, p. 257.

informed by a correct analysis of the situation... Theology, they argued, is not
in the business of dispensing timeless certainties but of informing and inspiring
faithful praxis.'[9] The offer of knowledge of whatever sort, if it is not going to
lead to choice, is unlikely to prove attractive or effective, and is likely to leave
uneducated people in the 'culture of silence' in which they have begun.[10]

For Oman the increasing independence of an autonomous person goes with
an increasing dependence upon:

> situations, values, wisdom, other persons, and a world that is not to be
> identified with him or her... It is in this experience of the beckoning
> quality of reality where Oman finds the reality of God as upholding both
> autonomy's need for independence and religion's call to absolute
> dependence... And in this gracious, personal relationship of God to men
> and women, through the whole of our human environment, God in God's
> self is experienced and met as personal as well.[11] 'Only by being true to
> ourselves can we find the reality we must absolutely follow; yet, only by
> the sense of a reality we must absolutely follow, can we be true to
> ourselves.'[12]

The Permanent Possibility of Error

Oman's thinking too is positive and world-affirming. However he also has a
sense of the tragic. He criticises Hegel, for example, for being insufficiently
concerned with the reality of moral struggle, for in real life human reason does
not automatically work out, and moral choices may conflict with the notion of
progress. Here, against Hegel and Marx, Oman follows Kant and Ritschl in the
thought that the unqualified love of God indicates what is possible for men and
women, not necessarily what they will achieve, as conscience may be
disobeyed or mistaken. 'Yet so far is this absolute duty of conscientiousness
from depending on infallibility of conscience that no one who is infallibly
certain that he is right is quite conscientious.'[13]

The pastoral cycle then is not spiralling inevitably upwards. Even with the
best will in the world we may still be at the mercy of events. Experience itself
may be blighted; in the words of Garrison Keillor as relayed by Bevans,

---

[9] J. Thompson, S. Pattison and R. Thompson, *SCM Studyguide to Theological
Reflection* (London: SCM Press, 2008), p. 23.

[10] See Paulo Freire, *Cultural Action for Freedom* (Middlesex, England: Penguin
Books, 1972), p. 30.

[11] Stephen Bevans, *John Oman and His Doctrine of God* (Cambridge: Cambridge
University Press, 1992), pp. 73-5.

[12] John Oman, *Grace and Personality* (4th ed. Cambridge: Cambridge University
Press, 1931), p. 66.

[13] Oman, *Natural and Supernatural*, p. 316.

experience is what you get when you don't get what you want![14] Oman might then accept one of the criticisms made by Vatican thinkers both of Cardijn pastoral cycle and of liberation theology: that they tend to underplay the fallibility of those taking part in them. (But, since he believed God valued people taking responsibility, he would surely have rejected another of the criticisms made of these thinkers that, by putting so much emphasis on human responsibility, they had diminished the role of God.)

The Right and Duty of Choice

Oman was adamant about the right and duty of human beings to make moral choices and reach intellectual conclusions out of their own convictions. He was a strong supporter of the Enlightenment in the sense understood by Kant that it was humanity's coming of age. But he preferred the term 'Illuminism' which he thought indicated that the light sought was to come from within rather than always to be accepted uncritically from without. As much as humans should use their freedom rationally and morally he realised that they might fail to do so. They should not neglect *the wisdom of the past* any more than *the experience of their own lives* or *the universal light of abstract thought*; each of the three sources is referred to in the Preface to the Second Edition of Oman's *Vision and Authority*, in his illustration of a traveller trying to find his way over an expanse of wild moorland in the dark. But in the end people have to decide for themselves. Oman realised that this coming of age was becoming a fact, in that traditional structures of authority did not have the power they once had, and he rejoiced in it. For him it was a risk worth taking. Men and women were being challenged to be mature and he thought that was part of God's plan. Oman is robust in his advice to Christians; they should do what they think is right and say what they think is true. This is not licence but basic integrity. As William Temple is reputed to have replied to Ronald Knox: I am not seeking to find what Jones will swallow; I am Jones looking for what there is to eat.

Oman did not regard human responsibility and God's activity as contrary to each other. For him each in its perfection required the other, and here his model was that of the relationship between parent and child. It is the aim of the parent that the child shall become free to take responsible decisions on his or her own; in that way true parenthood is fulfilled. Similarly, it is the mark of a mature child that he or she thanks, cares for and respects, though not uncritically, the parent. (Oman may well have approved the saying of Irenaeus: '*gloria enim Dei vivens homo; vita autem hominis visio Dei*' (Adversus Haereses IV.20.7)). Taking part in the pastoral cycle, then, would be a mark of mature discipleship, not only because it was important to make up one's own mind, but also because the theological wisdom, which he saw as an important resource for decision-making, was not so much a set of propositional truth-claims or rules for

---

[14] Bevans, *Oman and God*, pp. 57-8.

behaviour but itself an attempt to put into words the experience shared with other generations of the reality of God. If God is real then we can attend to God first and morality is likely to flow more naturally than from an initial gritting of the teeth in heroic endeavour... 'absolute moral independence and absolute religious dependence are not opposites but necessarily one and indivisible'.[15]

The Common Participation of Believers and Non-believers

What might one ask of Oman is the difference between the way in which a believer and a non-believer might be involved in the pastoral cycle? After all, atheists too can claim to act responsibly and even to take seriously the wisdom of religion, however sceptical about it they may be. Oman's response, as a realist, is to hold that a subjective claim involves a presumed objective reality (about truth, goodness or beauty). Furthermore he follows Schleiermacher in holding that humans also have a basic feeling about their relationship with the universe as a whole: 'The contemplation of the pious is the immediate consciousness of the universal existence of all finite things, in and through the Infinite, and of all temporal things in and through the Eternal.'[16] 'As used here, the Supernatural means the world which manifests more than natural values, the world which has values which stir the sense of the holy and demand to be esteemed as sacred.'[17] For Oman this feeling is the more linked to morality as society develops. It is for him the Supernatural, more than organised religion, maybe Spirituality in the broad sense of that word today. He illustrates the development of that consciousness in childhood through Wordsworth's account of it in the Prelude.[18] In fairness, it does, I think, correspond to most historical human experience as recorded today. However it is hard to see how it fits those without religion, and those who, like Richard Dawkins, profess an awe of nature (and a liking for the poetry of Wordsworth) together with a trenchant atheism. Here one has to speculate. I fancy Oman would want to distinguish between non-believers who were simply putting their own needs at the centre of everything and those who also appreciate the existence, qualities and claims of persons other than themselves. Oman would then argue outward in space as he does from time, from part to whole. For example he says that the consciousness that we are aware of among ourselves cannot be assumed simply to have appeared out of nothing; it must have had an earlier history; elements of purposiveness or at least the capacity for producing them must have been there before.[19] In the same way the totality of the universe cannot be less in quality or

---

[15] Oman, *Grace and Personality*, p. 21.

[16] Friederich Schleiermacher, *On Religion – Speeches to its Cultured Despisers* (New York: Harper & Row, 1958), p. 3.

[17] Oman, *Natural and Supernatural*, p. 71.

[18] Oman, *Natural and Supernatural*, pp. 138-40.

[19] Oman, *Natural and Supernatural*, p. 261.

quantity than what is contained in its constituent parts; the ultimate reality must be personal. Oman commends T.H. Huxley for, in spite of his description of an evolutionary process savage in tooth and claw, persisting in thinking kindness, consideration and respect for others as virtues. 'Yet by what saving conversion man turned his ape and tiger career to affection, friendship, loyalty, uprightness, reverence, humility, we are left to guess. The most extreme Methodist form of it would seem necessary.'[20]

What then is the implication for the pastoral cycle in Christian adult education? Maybe it is that the cycle can be engaged in by all who are seeking after truth and the common good, who indeed are opening themselves up to realities, to new experiences and understandings, whether or not their interpretation is in line with explicitly Christian doctrine. Those who, at the other extreme, are simply centred upon themselves, may, like Scrooge, see, judge and act, but be no more fit for an afterlife of sharing than for sharing in the present.

The Role of Partners and the Stimulus they bring

One of the features of the recent use of the Pastoral Cycle has been the attention given to the experience of persons other than those who are the subjects of the process. This may be something for the subjects themselves to think about; for example health workers may be asked to reflect on the experience of their patients. Or they may be asked to look at data from other people, eg questionnaires filled in by their patients. Or other persons may be involved in the process itself, for example consultants who help the subjects in their reflection. In the 'Partners in Mission' model used among provinces and dioceses in the Anglican Communion from the 1980s onwards, part of the rationale was a view attributed to Lesslie Newbigin: that the church in a particular place was responsible for its own mission but to be faithful and effective it needed the insights of other parts of the Christian community; hence the introduction of 'external partners' from other places and denominations than those of the subjects themselves. Oman's thinking strikes me as supporting this approach. His sympathies are broad and he commends learning from others as required of seekers after truth. On the other hand he vigorously asserts the right and duty of individual Christians to make up their own minds and not to accept beliefs or alliances out of convenience or a sense of duty if they do not really believe in them. '[F]urthering the good news means actually getting people to live in the joy and emancipation and freedom of God's own ever present, ever active, ever blessed Rule, and that it is not furthered at all by merely imposing upon others statements about it which alter nothing in either

---

[20] Oman, *Natural and Supernatural*, p. 333.

themselves or their world'.[21] This gives to the world an impression of stupidity or dishonesty, for which we have given cause 'by concerning ourselves anxiously about the body of our fellowship and failing to show glad trust in the creative power of its spirit'.[22] In *Vision and Authority* Oman contrasts such an externally imposed unity with that sought from motives of truth and love,[23] when we may be reminded through disagreement of our liability to err and may be enabled to correct our judgments. As an ecumenist he may seem hypercritical but it is the criticism born of passionate commitment; 'faithful are the wounds of a friend'. Creative disagreement is to be welcomed in the search for deeper truth.

Theological Reflection as involving the Whole People of God

One of the attractive features of much of Oman's writing is that it can apply to all Christians, not just those who are academically educated, trained to be ministers or blessed with profound spiritual experiences. The experience, and the reflection on it which he writes about, is that common to the majority of human beings, even if it is deserving of stringent philosophical and theological analysis. In *Concerning the Ministry*,

> Oman says that one's preaching should be from 'experience', but that does not mean it should be a sharing of 'experiences' of gushy emotional moments of 'mysticism'. Rather, if one is faithful and reflective in living one's life, one will truly experience what life is – and that is the matter for preaching. That is the way of the Bible as well...[24]

In a human sense people need to begin with their own conscience and understanding and go on to learn from others. In a Christian sense they start with their own relationship with Jesus of Nazareth and his followers and go on to try to put his teachings into practice. Oman was attracted by those who did, even if their actions differed from his own.

> Many years ago I read the *Journal of John Woolman the Quaker*. I do not know that I ever read a book so hastily which impressed me so deeply... he would wear no article that was dyed, because of the unhealthiness of the trade and the unnecessary nature of the labour... His example in such details as the use of dyed clothes I am not setting up. But his regard for

---

[21] John Oman, *The Paradox of the World* (Cambridge: Cambridge University Press, 1921), p. 273.

[22] Oman, *Paradox of World*, p. 275.

[23] John Oman, *Vision and Authority: Or the Throne of St. Peter* (2nd ed., London: Hodder & Stoughton, 1928), pp. 175-6.

[24] John Oman, *Concerning the Ministry* (London: SCM Press, 1936), p. 147 quoted in Bevans, *Oman and God*, p. 60.

his fellow men, his determination not to be blinded by usage, his sense of responsibility for his whole life and not merely for what he saw of it, is surely not more than Christ requires of us.[25]

Oman does not comment much on contemporary events but he does lay down principles for social action which are challenging. For example, though he was not a pacifist he was unhappy about some of the unthinking jingoism which marked the contribution of many ministers and theologians on both sides in the First World War. For him patriotism was not enough. 'Not till we worship God by reverence for man made in His image, and believe that the final might in the world is truth and character and service and the spirit of love, can war be a struggle for peace or anything more than a blotting out of humanity for material policies.'[26]

The Confirmation of the Reflection Process in the Doctrines of the Cross and Resurrection

Both doctrines fill out but do not contradict the search for truth, freedom and morality, to be found by those taking part in the Pastoral Cycle, whether they claim explicit Christian commitment or not.

The Cross shows that God's love is without limits, God's forgiveness absolute.

> The Cross itself is life's darkest mystery. It is of such supreme human significance, because it was so for our Lord himself. It was the cup that did not pass, scorn and agony and the shadow of unspeakable loneliness. But, in trust though not in understanding, it was accepted as the will of the Father, and so by forgiveness of enemies, by a life given as a ransom for many, by dying to sin once for all, it manifested a life lived forever unto God.[27]

What difference does the Resurrection make? Oman points to a change of expectation. 'Death is no longer a dark cave into the depths of the earth. It is only an overshadowed pass through the mountains. Christ has appeared to us as one who has passed through and who has again show Himself to us upon the sunny mountain-top to signal to us that all is peace and glory beyond.' Secondly there is the transformation of death into 'the supreme act of fulfilling the will of the Father'.[28] Without the Cross what other equivalent instrument would have there been for the Father to have shown his love. And furthermore,

---

[25] John Oman, *A Dialogue with God* (London: James Clarke, 1950), p. 43.
[26] Oman, *Paradox of World*, p. 69.
[27] Oman, *Dialogue with God*, p. 47.
[28] Oman, *Dialogue with God*, p. 120.

without the death on the Cross, 'in what language could He have spoken to us of the guilt and folly of sin, and of the love of God?'[29] For what Christ has gained through the Resurrection has now been made available to those who follow him. Hence for the Christian adult educator the death and resurrection of Jesus should be helping Christians in practical action, in the transformation of the world.

Where does the Pastoral Cycle lead to? The end of the world? The kingdom of God? Heaven? Oman does not deny any of these realities. But he also says we are not ready for any of them unless we are giving ourselves up to God in whatever we are doing now. '...if the love of God is the assurance that we cannot fall out of an endless purpose, and that neither life nor death can separate from it, it must also give a life so large that we can never exhaust its wonder'.[30] The guarantee is given in the Cross of Christ.

> Not till we see in this perfect service the glory of a love unconquerable in the power of which we too may live victoriously, can we rest on it a hope for another life, in the assurance that neither life nor death can separate us from the love of God which is in Jesus Christ. Nor without it can we attach any definite meaning to appearing with him in glory.[31]

Conclusion

Oman's thinking supports a Pastoral Cycle which does justice both to Christian Theology and Adult Education practice, provided that the following conditions are fulfilled:

It is important that people attend to their experience rather than evade it in abstract speculation; also that they reflect upon it critically with the help of others, in the hope of greater understanding and improvement, but with an awareness of human weakness and capacity for self-deception. There needs to be an acceptance of freedom of choice in a categorical sense and a conviction that it is desired by God even at the risk of it being abused. Such a freedom is exercised in a response to one's apprehension of what is true and good and thereby of God. Such a discipline needs partners within and outside the Christian community, lay people and ordained ministers alike. The process provides an opportunity for growth in the knowledge and love of God, in this life and beyond.

In that sense Oman's thinking comes clearly within the Transcendental Model as classified by Stephen Bevans in *Models of Contextual Theology* according to which 'What is important is not so much that a particular theology is produced but that the theologian who is producing it operates as an authentic,

---

[29] Oman, *Dialogue with God*, p. 118.
[30] Oman, *Honest Religion*, p. 125.
[31] Oman, *Paradox of World*, p. 234.

converted subject.'[32]

What difference does a study of John Oman make? In my own work as a consultant I now find myself paying less attention to external standards, those for good ministry laid down by my denomination or the precise ways in which ministerial performance can be measured. But I am paying more attention to the minister's own self-understanding of the gospel and its expression, and of the way this self-understanding features in their assessment of their performance. Constructive criticism by myself or others is in place, but the end is different; it is less to help ministers fit better into some pre-existing mould but rather to help them respond more creatively to their own understandings of the Spirit of God within.

---

[32] Stephen Bevans, *Models of Contextual Theology* (Revised and Expanded Edition) (New York: Orbis, 2002), p. 103.

CHAPTER 11

The Wide Air of Heaven: John Oman's View of Pastoral Authority[1]

Ashok Chaudhari

In George Alexander's Memoir of John Oman, found in the posthumous publication of Oman's book *Honest Religion*, it is written that '[Oman] must have had [his congregation's] leave to give three courses of lectures, one at, I think, Auburn University, in the United States, followed by the offer of a Chair...'[2] Indeed Oman did give lectures at Auburn, though it is not a university as Alexander calls it but a Presbyterian seminary founded in 1818 in Auburn, NY, West of Syracuse.[3] According to the records of Auburn Theological Seminary, the Reverend John Oman gave two courses of lectures at Auburn from February to March, 1907.[4] One of his courses consisted of twelve lectures on the 'problem of faith and freedom in the last two centuries'[5] (which corresponded to his book published one year earlier with the same title),[6] and the second course consisted of four lectures on 'the foundations of

---

[1] This is a hypothesis based on the study of the subjects of four lectures delivered at Auburn Seminary by John Oman in the Winter/Spring of 1907.

[2] John Oman, *Honest Religion* (Cambridge; Cambridge University Press, 1941) p. xxi.

[3] According to the Post-Standard Syracuse, NY, Saturday Morning, 23 February 1907, Oman was invited to give the lectures at Auburn by President George B. Stewart. The two travelled to Buffalo and Niagara Falls during Oman's stay at Auburn, according to the Auburn Citizen, Thursday, 28 February, 1907. The same newspaper reported on 10 May, 1907 that Oman's stay at the Seminary was made possible through "the generosity of friends."

[4] Auburn Seminary Record, Volume III, 1906-1907.

[5] There does not appear to have been any newspaper coverage of these twelve lectures. Perhaps they were not open to the public like the lectures on authority. The titles of these lectures are however listed in the Auburn Seminary Record for that year.

[6] The lectures given at Auburn have the same exact titles as the lectures which comprise the book, and were first given at Westminster College, Cambridge, and then Glasgow College of the United Free Church of Scotland. Lectures 7 and 9 ('The Theory of Development and Baur's First Three Centuries' and 'Methods and Results') were apparently not given at Auburn.

belief' (which presumably are based on his book *Vision and Authority'* which had been published five years earlier, in 1902). The titles of the four lectures in this second course were 'the authority of the church', 'the authority of the Bible', 'the authority of Christ', and 'the authority of experience.'[7] The subjects of these four lectures will constitute the basis for my investigation of Oman's view of authority, and most importantly, given my own personal interest, his view of pastoral authority. A brief word on the method of my investigation: since copies of these lectures are not to be found in the Auburn Seminary Archives, nor to my knowledge anywhere else, and given the fact that Oman never writes specifically about pastoral authority, the hypothesis of this essay is based on his two books published prior to the lectures, i.e., *Faith and Freedom* and *Vision and Authority*, all the relevant books published after his lectures, but also newspaper articles which reported on the lectures at the time they were given. The newspaper articles are from newspapers in both Auburn and Syracuse, where Oman gave the same lectures at Syracuse University.

In this essay there is extensive quotation directly from Oman's writings. This is intentional because, as anyone familiar with Oman's writings knows, his books are filled with many gems and also lesser stones in between. I like to think I have gathered the gems relevant to the topic at hand, and left the other stones behind. These gems speak for themselves, and there is no need to re-word them, as they are clear and reveal his insights better than I could, while at the same time giving the reader a first-hand experience of Oman's style and thought. The same holds of the newspaper articles. Quoting directly from the articles seemed the most effective way of relaying what Oman is reported to have said.

The essay begins with the first subject of his four lectures on authority, 'The Authority of the Church.'

The Authority of the Church

On 28 February, 1907, an article was published in the Post Standard, Syracuse, NY, titled 'Rev. John Oman Begins Series of Lectures.' According to the article, the exact title of his first lecture was 'The Questioning of the Old

---

[7] According to the Post-Standard Syracuse, NY, Saturday Morning, 23 February, 1907, and several other newspapers the same four courses were given by Oman at Syracuse University during this same period of time. One newspaper also reported that the course of lectures at Syracuse University was arranged by Professor Ismar J. Peritz of Syracuse University, who 'made an effort to have Oman give a course of five lectures in the Assembly Hall [at Syracuse University].' During his residence at Auburn, Oman also gave lectures on other topics on a one-off basis. These lectures included 'Ritschl and his school', 'Barnabas a Good Man', and 'the religious situation in England.' In the last of these lecture[s], he stated that '...no really great preacher remained [in England] except Dr. Alexander MacLaren, who is a very old man.'

Authorities and the Authority of the Church.'[8] The article quotes Oman as having said 'The history of the church has proved that its members are very human, and its fallibility has been shown. Nevertheless the church is an important part of the foundation of our belief.' Furthermore, he said that 'The real church provides no theologies nor creeds, and its standard is to live in purity and love, making the kingdom of God the environment of our life.'[9]

In stating that the 'real church provides no theologies or creeds', it would seem that Oman is doing away with church tradition, since what is commonly meant by tradition includes both theology and creeds. Yet, in his book *Vision and Authority*, which of all his publications deals the most with authority, Oman writes, 'We must all build on the foundations of the apostles and prophets on the foundation of those who have obeyed the Divine call and recognized the divine teaching. To be faithful to our own spiritual insight, it must be our constant endeavour to be faithful to our spiritual ancestry.'[10] This is one of many pieces of evidence supporting the view that Oman, in fact, respected church tradition. Another such piece is found in his treatment of confessions in *Honest Religion*, where he writes: 'Confessions are a part of our external heredity, which, like our personal heredity, we can neither utterly reject nor simply accept, but we have to travel through as well as go beyond.'[11]

How does one, then, make sense of the reporting in the newspaper article? One possible answer is that Oman is reacting to what in 'Vision and Authority' he calls the 'old external dogmatic attitude of the church.'[12] This attitude is perhaps best summarized when Oman writes 'Truth which is … lacking the imperious authority of Bible or Church and [is] not backed by a very material heaven and hell, is thought to be weak, and the cause of all the Church's weakness, and in particular to make its preaching uncertain and of no authority.'[13] Oman would be critical of this attitude because the 'insistence on the need of an authority from without, not to agree with the authority within, but to dominate it, is at bottom a disbelief in the possibility or even the gain of freedom.'[14] He writes that 'If it had been [Christ's] first purpose to set all dubiety for ever aside, He might have made every word be continued to man as a royal proclamation, with an *imperative authority* (emphasis added) behind it which none might doubt and few disobey. But this enslaving authority over man's mind and will He ever shunned; and to find a reason why He put no

---

[8] Oman apparently combined 'the old authorities' with 'the church' to make one lecture, which is why there are four lectures and not five, as Professor Peritz had requested.

[9] The Post Standard, Syracuse, NY, Thursday morning, 28 February, 1907.

[10] John Oman, *Vision and Authority* (London: Hodder and Stoughton, 1902), p. 90.

[11] Oman, *Honest Religion*, p. 161.

[12] Oman, *Vision and Authority*, p. 94.

[13] Oman, *Vision and Authority*, p. 94.

[14] Oman, *Vision and Authority*, p. 95.

word into writing, we only need to recall how He dealt with the men among whom He lived.'[15] For Oman the church as an authority has failed when:

> [It] has endeavoured to combine the method of the world with the method of Christ, and too often she has had the legitimate success of neither. She must make her choice between them, for the two methods are incompatible, and Christ's method of freedom departs as the world's method of compulsion enters. Either her prayer for her members must be that their awe should increase in submission, or that their love should increase in knowledge and practical discernment. She must make her choice, and by her choice she determines which with authority she would be clothed.[16]

Oman writes '…[if] either truth or liberty be infringed, the most absolute external unity, though it might silence, would not convince the world.'[17] And 'the question to be asked is, what authority would she require, if she followed exclusively Christ's method?'[18]

The answer to this question is: not any human authority. For in his book *The Problem of Faith and Freedom in the Last Two Centuries* he writes:

> An authoritative faith authoritatively announced, claiming one part of our life for God and leaving the rest as a concession to ourselves, might preclude many dangers, but it would also preclude the highest moral spiritual success. Instead of arguing with Schanz, a Roman Catholic apologist, that faith presupposes authority, that there must be an infallible authority if there is to be any revelation or any faith in the world, it might rather be argued that we have, in no right sense, either revelation or faith, so long as any human voice comes between us and God.[19]

Clearly the Catholic Church is in the background of Oman's thinking here, as it is in much of his writing and the lectures he presented at Auburn. But what of the mainline Protestant Churches of the time, with their 'theologies and creeds'? Oman writes that 'With right sowing the [mainline] church will reap true authority in the loyal heartfelt submission of her own children, who have learned to agree with her teaching and who acknowledge a debt of gratitude to her influence',[20] and 'Then the church will have no need to inquire what is the source of her authority, for her life will be a continual demonstration that it is

---

[15] Oman, *Vision and Authority*, p. 126.

[16] Oman, *Vision and Authority*, p. 158.

[17] Oman, *Vision and Authority*, p. 161.

[18] Oman, *Vision and Authority*, p. 274.

[19] John Oman, *The Problem of Faith and Freedom in the Last Two Centuries* (London: Kessinger Publishing, 1906), p. 23.

[20] Oman, *Faith and Freedom*, p. 283.

derived from the Kingdom for which she labours.'[21]

In sum, for Oman the church must base its authority not on an external dogmatic attitude built on creeds and theology, but primarily on the personal insights of its members whose faith comes not from compulsion, and always works towards increased freedom for their fellow man. Nonetheless, the true church is one which also respects and incorporates the insights of its spiritual ancestry, thereby respecting tradition. Perhaps Oman's view of church tradition is best summed up in the chapter titled 'History and Experience' in *The Natural and the Supernatural*, where he writes:

> Though tradition is the first necessity for progress, it can also be an enslavement to the past which arrests progress. And naturally religion, being the greatest power for conserving the past, is the greatest also for making it conservative. Yet this is only one side, for the greatest power for maintaining tradition as sacred may also be the greatest for assailing it in the name of the sacredness of truth and righteousness.[22]

The Authority of the Bible

On 2 March, 1907, The Post-Standard, Syracuse, NY reported that Rev, John Oman gave his second lecture titled 'The Authority of Scripture.' In this article he is reported to have 'denied that the Scriptures were *inspired* (emphasis added) as the word is generally used.' This surprising, if not startling, statement may seem inconsistent with his overall body of thought. But for Oman the word 'inspired' as commonly used connotes revelation that carries with it 'accurate information, assured authorship, and exact transmission.'[23] True inspiration, however, according to Oman, 'is not submission to a possession, but is for knowing God's order by our own insight and being sure of it by our own consecration: and only such knowing God is for salvation. To be inspired is not to cease to think, but to help to think to right purpose.'[24] Scripture then is not inspired, although it does inspire. Perhaps this reported statement 'den[ying] that the Scriptures are inspired' can best be made sense of in light of Oman's general concern for the potentially dangerous effect Scripture can be made to have on the spiritual well-being of individuals. In other words, Oman's statement comes perhaps from his concern that the words of Scripture not be taken literally. This is consistent with the following passage in *Vision and Authority*:

---

[21] Oman, *Faith and Freedom,* p. 283.
[22] John Oman, *The Natural and the Supernatural* (Cambridge: Cambridge University Press, 1950), p. 346.
[23] Oman, *Honest Religion,* p. 64.
[24] Oman, *Honest Religion,* p. 65.

Yet the use to which [Christ] did *not* [emphasis added] put the ancient
Scriptures is equally noteworthy. As a final warrant for belief, as a reason
for accepting what man has no other evidence for, He never employed a
word of it. His resort to its authority was in great, and evidently
conscious, contrast to the habits of His contemporaries.... His appeal was
never in the last resort to Scripture but to the hearts of living men, and the
true use of the Scripture was only to aid Him in his final appeal.'[25]

For Oman, Scripture 'counsels' men and women,[26] but it has no authority
beyond this counsel and the inspiration it may have on the reader. In the same
newspaper article, he is quoted as saying that 'We do not take for granted that
the Bible is a legal document laying down rules of conduct. The idea of the
infallibility of the scriptures came from the Catholic Church, and was once
stronger than the tales of the infallibility of the Pope.' While clearly
Catholicism is on Oman's mind here, I think he would make the same
statement to those Protestants who see the Scripture as infallible, for in *Vision
and Authority*, Oman writes that:

The danger [Christ] would guard against is the old danger. It is man's
readiness to consent to the form, and deny the substance. Written words
might not have been the banner of conquering souls, but an ensign on the
bosom of the dishonourably dead. With ever deepening lack of
understanding, they might have been repeated as a code of salvation.
Then the Messiah would have been changed into the great Rabbi. The end
of such a security of literal infallibility would have been to set up a
merely external authority, to which men would have conformed their
words but not their thoughts, their deeds but not their hearts.'[27]

How many fundamentalist Protestant churches today pose this threat to their
congregations? Oman writes 'No other authority than God's direct word to the
heart of His children endures for ever.'[28]
In *The Natural and the Supernatural* there is further evidence that Oman
challenged church authority that is based on a literal understanding of the Bible.
Oman writes that:

[A] great deal of dust has been raised by confusing authority as a
secondary means of knowing truth with authority as the basis of it....The
Pope or the Fundamentalist Bible, let us say, professes to be the primary
authority, with nothing behind to which anyone could dream of

[25] Oman, *Vision and Authority*, p. 103.
[26] Oman, *Honest Religion*, p. 103.
[27] Oman, *Honest Religion*, pp. 126-127.
[28] Oman, *Honest Religion*, p. 349.

appealing.[29]

Two further clues about the authority of Scripture are found in the same newspaper article. The first is that Oman stated that:

It might be that the very humanness of the Bible is a mark of God's graciousness in his divine plan. When we look at the Apostles they do not impress us as men who never made mistakes. Inspiration enlarges human individuality.[30]

Thus, while for Oman Scripture may not be inspired, the characters talked about certainly are. And perhaps Oman read the Bible with this emphasis. The second clue is that for Oman the Bible was literature. Oman is reported to have said,

No one denies that the Bible is literature and to it can be applied the ordinary tests. We may seek to discover to whom the writings were addressed and the time to which it applies. The prophets wrote for their own time and not for those yet born.[31]

In sum, for Oman the Bible must not be read literally, but rather as literature, and is not the primary source of church authority. Scripture, in fact, is not even inspired in the common use of the word. Nonetheless, to say that it has little or no authority for Oman would be an exaggeration. The Bible counsels and inspires, and his belief in the inspired characters of the Bible, combined with his overall reverence for the book, seems to indicate that the Bible was an authority for Oman, but a relativised one. Perhaps Oman's view of Scripture can best be summed up in the following statement from *Honest Religion*: '…Scripture in particular will ever be more fully revelation as it ceases to be dictation of beliefs and code of directions and becomes the *counsel of God, to be received and proved only as we make it our own*' (emphasis added).[32]

The Authority of Christ:

On 8 March, 1907, in the Auburn Semi-Weekly Journal, it is reported that Oman's manuscript (for his lecture on 'The Authority of Christ') was stolen just prior to his lecture.[33] However, this does not seem to have bothered Oman greatly, as the article asserts:

---

[29] Oman, *Natural and Supernatural*. p. 100.
[30] 'First of a Series of Lectures by Oman in Syracuse'. The Auburn Citizen, Thursday, 28 February, 1907.
[31] The Auburn Citizen, Thursday, 28 February, 1907.
[32] Oman, *Honest Religion*, p. 158.
[33] Auburn Semi-Weekly Journal, 8 March, 1907.

Before beginning his address Dr. Oman apologized for the fact that what he said would be from his own head because his notes had been stolen. While Dr. Oman was watching the beauties of New York from the ferryboat on Saturday, someone else was watching his bag. However, as Dr. Oman put it, they got chiefly sermons, which was most disappointing to them. He said "The one consolation is that my address is in the place where it is most needed."[34]

The article further reported that Oman asked:

In what way is Jesus an authority in religion? [I]t is not primarily by being a perfect teacher in theology. He is an authority because in the midst of sufferings, weaknesses and struggles, He, himself, was perfectly the subject of religion. He showed perfect fidelity through every trial that might shake Him. He not merely shows us about the father. He shows us the father. It is this that lifts the authority of Christ above all other authorities.

In *Vision and Authority* Oman writes that 'Christ speaks with authority just because He speaks straight to the heart and the experience. For this very reason He has no need to be an authority; and much less has He need to rely on others as authorities.'[35] Moreover, 'Jesus is the supreme authority in religion precisely because He never spoke merely as an authority, but always said, "You will see this to be true, unless you blind your eyes by hypocrisy."'[36] And 'He encourages his disciples to rise above the rule of authorities and to investigate till each is his own authority.'[37]

In the same book Oman writes:

The great demonstration of the Christ is just that He never sets Himself, as the absolute external authority of the perfect truth, in opposition to the imperfect authority of the finite and sinful spirit within, but that He has only one appeal, which is to the likeness of God and the teaching of God within. Jesus speaks indeed with authority. He is not as the Scribes. They had authorities, but no authority. They had nothing to speak from direct, and nothing to appeal to direct. Jesus, on the other hand, speaks from man to man the truth He has seen and to which his hearers cannot be blind, unless they close their eyes. Exclusively, he addresses Himself to the

---

[34] There is a conflicting report in the Auburn Citizen, Wednesday, 6 March, 1907, which reported that 'Dr. Oman was obliged to present his discourse without notes, his grip containing the manuscript and other belongings having been stolen from the train on which he left Jersey.'

[35] Oman, *Vision and Authority* p. 189.

[36] Oman, *Vision and Authority*, p. 84.

[37] Oman, *Vision and Authority*, p. 188.

primal spiritual authority in man – the spiritual vision which discerns things spiritual. He is not as the Scribes, precisely because when He failed there, He fell back on no other authority. On the contrary, He was able to exclude every other appeal except the appeal to the spiritual in man. No man accepted the truth from Him for any lower reason than because it had appealed to his heart as true. He had no dignity of place or office with which to impose and no material possession with which to attract. Stripped of all extraneous aid, the truth was left to be its own authority and its own appeal for the hearts made in the image of Him who is true.[38]

Perhaps the most explicit statement on the authority of Christ is made in *Honest Religion*, where he writes, 'Jesus is the ultimate authority because the truth is so manifested in Him that he needs no other appeal, and not because we should set Him among outward authorities, even if it be over them.'[39]

While Jesus is the ultimate authority, in the Post Standard, Syracuse, NY, Wednesday Morning, 6 March, 1907, Oman is reported to have said that 'Christ was limited in knowledge as well as in power.' And furthermore:

The essential point is how is Christ a religious authority? Is it because He was a perfect instructor in theology? Can we quote Him on those matters just as we quote Livingstone as an authority on central Africa? Is not He an authority because in the midst of sufferings, weaknesses, and struggles, He himself was perfectly the subject of religion?

It is worth quoting the following exchange, reported in the Auburn Citizen, on Thursday, 7 March, 1907, in its entirety:

At the close yesterday afternoon of the series of lectures which Rev. John Oman has been giving at the Assembly hall in the University building the speaker said he would be glad to answer any questions, says the Post-Standard. "What I would like to know", said a man in the front, "is whether Christ was divine or not?" "I have tried to convey the impression", said Oman, "that He was divine, but accepted human limitations to better carry on His work." "Was He a member of the trinity or not?" persisted the questioner. "I am not here to be questioned as to my theology," said Dr. Oman. "It don't make any difference what you are here for," said the inquisitor. "I am glad you have left us a personal God anyway, you have taken away almost everything else."

"If there are mistakes in the Bible how can we trust it?" was the question

---

[38] Oman, *Vision and Authority*, p. 108.
[39] Oman, *Honest Religion*, p. 157.

of an elderly woman. "What I want is something to go by. I can't study these things as scholars do." The speaker explained that it was the Spirit of the Bible that was true and that the Bible was not necessarily a text to be followed literally as a guide to right conduct."

In sum, Christ is the ultimate spiritual authority. But, at least while on Earth, he was limited in knowledge and power. Nonetheless He is the ultimate authority because he showed us God and because he speaks straight to the heart and experience.

The Authority of Experience:

On 7 March, 1907, the Auburn Citizen reported that Oman delivered the last in a series of lectures.[40] The article starts off by reporting that 'Quite a houseful greeted Doctor Oman last evening at the seminary to listen to his lecture on the Authority of Experience.' Oman is quoted as saying that:

In the old days people felt that there was a thing, at least certain, and that was feeling. But in modern times we are told that heredity and environment have altered things so much that we are like an iceberg – one eighth above and seven eighths below. Nothing has influenced Modern thought so much as evolution.

This statement points to a central concern of Oman's in this lecture and throughout his work, namely, the relationship between Christianity and science. Oman's use of the word 'feeling' here also suggests the influence of Schleiermacher on his thought, which is well known. More specifically, perhaps what Oman meant by this statement is that personal experience has become diminished in importance as a result of the influence of science, namely, Darwin's theory of evolution. The authority of Darwin is contrasted with the authority of the church. Oman is further quoted as saying 'Faith in God is as vital as faith in the world.' At first a puzzling report, it makes sense if by 'world' is understood 'nature.' Similarly, when Oman is reported to have said that:

The relations between the infinite and the finite is just what is beyond our comprehension. In the end we shall have to affirm the omnipotent God and man's freedom as well. No theory can reconcile perfect responsibility with perfect freedom, but what a theory cannot do intellectually, love can do practically.[41]

He has in mind the relation between science and Christianity. In the article

---

[40] The Auburn Citizen, Thursday, 7 March, 1907.
[41] The Auburn Citizen, Thursday, 7 March, 1907.

he is reported to have said, in the context of his discussion of science, that 'Life is the greatest reality; laws are intellectual, but not spiritual.' Again, the 'laws' he is referring to here must be scientific laws. Oman is further reported to have said in this lecture that someone said 'the words "the world, the flesh and the devil" are too strong to use, but in modern times we say "society, heredity and environment."' Here he seems to be questioning the value of the new Darwinian language versus the old Biblical language. Finally, 'We test our feelings and experiences by the relation they bear to will and freedom, not any theory of their origin. Feelings are things wrought out to life and must be tested by life.' This is to say that for Oman, feelings and experience must be grounded in life, not science. That Oman devoted so much of this final lecture on Authority and Experience to addressing Darwin's influence shows the degree to which the church's authority was being challenged. Why it should be the experiential aspect of authority that Oman sees to be challenged by Darwin is not obvious. And one can only surmise, based on the same newspaper article, that it was the Darwinian view that human life is mechanistic and predetermined that sparked a refutation by Oman who wanted to keep separate the meaning of religious and life experience from that of nature.

Perhaps Oman's view of authority and experience is best exemplified by the following statement he made in *Vision and Authority,* 'Nothing is ours, however it may be presented to us, except we discover its truth and except it prove itself again in our experience.'[42] Spiritual views, spiritual insight, and any spiritual authority, must in the end be grounded in experience.

In sum, for Oman Authority must come from our own personal experience. And the primary word for spiritual experience for Oman is the rather common and not particularly religious sounding word 'insight.' This word appears numerous times throughout his writings. Oman writes that 'After all possible demonstration, nothing is truth for us till it flash upon our inward sight, and something goes out of us to meet it, which makes it, when we find it, the native country of our spirits.'[43]

Oman's View of Pastoral Authority – A Hypothesis

Based on the subjects of these four lectures, and other publications, what would John Oman have said about Pastoral Authority?

First, for Oman, pastoral authority must come from within, from each person's own insight, and realization, and from the Spirit of Christ, who is the absolute authority. Authority does not come primarily from Scripture, although for Oman Scripture counsels and inspires and a pastor may gain authority from Scripture if he makes the Scripture 'his own'. Knowledge of the Scriptures is 'the true qualification of the minister.'[44] Nor does authority come primarily

[42] Oman, *Vision and Authority,* p. 58.
[43] Oman, *Vision and Authority,* p. 110.
[44] 'The Exposition of the Word' in *A Dialogue with God and Other Sermons and Addresses* (London: James Clarke and Co., Ltd., 1950). p. 146.

from the church organization. It is not given from some external church authority based on human agreement.

Secondly, true pastoral authority must have certain characteristics. It must be loving, without compulsion, and lead others to freedom. Thirdly, Oman writes that:

> Like the Apostle you ought to be able to say "My Gospel," for unless it is good news to you, it is not likely to be anyone else. You will only speak with authorities, and not with authority, unless the truth has already exercised dominion over your own soul.[45]

Pastoral authority, therefore, must be based on personal experience, and each pastor must be his or her own authority.

And similarly, in *Concerning the Ministry*, Oman writes that there is a difference between

> speaking with authorities and speaking with authority. The former speaks from what God has said and done in the past; the latter, even if from the revealed, is from it as the revealing, as valid for us now as it ever was in the past. The only true authority is God's truth itself and its own witness to itself; and you speak with its authority only when you speak that which you know and testify that which you have seen.[46]

Fourthly, true pastoral authority must also be the result of a process that takes place in a person. Oman offers a fascinating description of the process of claiming one's authority:

> The authority of the Church was not rejected for its own sake, but in the interest of the responsibility of personal freedom, as when a young person has to reject the authority of a parent under the constraint of a higher authority in his own heart. Outwardly, there may be little difference, but a new principle has entered, carrying with it necessarily a different type of development. Under the old view, life was divided into two compartments, one in which a man obeyed the guidance of another, and one in which he was free to follow his own devices. Responsibility and freedom divided the life between them – the idea of freedom being liberty to please oneself. But, if the *authority rises up within*, a man never escapes it, and he must then make both responsibility and independence cover the whole of life. The result may be much disturbance and sad failure, yet we recognize in the individual life that, till this task of finding our freedom not outside of our duty but in it has been undertaken, the true

---

[45] John Oman, *Concerning the Ministry* (Richmond, Va: John Knox Press, 1936), p. 68.

[46] Oman, *Concerning the Ministry*, p. 83.

moral life has not begun.[47]

To grasp Oman's view of Pastoral Authority it makes sense to look at who he believed to be the model or ideal person (besides Jesus) who best embodies and exemplifies this authority. And that person was Peter. But he was – as Oman puts it – the Peter of 'common life.' Oman writes that

The immovable rock of all authority, nevertheless, is the Peter of the common life, whose endowment is insight to perceive every revelation of God, as the ceaseless unfolding of the everlasting order in freedom through holiness and union through love.[48]

Furthermore, 'Thus we must see him [Peter], if we would discover how he wore so high a dignity and wielded so absolute an authority.'[49]

In conclusion: John Oman's understanding of authority provides a place – a space – for those who are neither content with the mainline church's blind adherence to church doctrine and tradition and which often seems lacking in insight and inspiration, nor with the fundamentalist churches which claim to have inspiration and yet are often authoritatively domineering and reject the value of tradition and education thereby ignoring a whole dimension of reality and Christian experience. Oman has showed us a place in between – a place where there is spirituality based on experience and insight, where each is his own authority, where there is no compulsion – on the contrary, personal growth and freedom are encouraged – and yet a place where tradition and education are still valued. The right leadership based on true pastoral authority is needed in such a space, and Oman sheds precious light on what this would look like, all with the aim of enabling us to 'breath[e] the wide air of heaven.'

---

[47] Oman, *Faith and Freedom*, p. 21 (emphasis added).
[48] Oman, *Vision and Authority*, p. 348.
[49] Oman, *Vision and Authority*, p. 132.

Bibliography

Works of John Oman
Books

Vision and Authority, or The Throne of St. Peter (London: Hodder and Stoughton, 1902; second edition, 1928; eighth edition with Introduction by T. W. Manson, 1948).

The Problem of Faith and Freedom in the Last Two Centuries (London: Hodder and Stoughton, 1906).

The Church and the Divine Order (London: Hodder and Stoughton, 1911).

The War and its Issues (Cambridge University Press, 1915).

Grace and Personality (Cambridge University Press, 1917; second edition, 1919; third edition, 1925; reissued by Fontana Books, 1960, 1961; with an introduction by John Hick, New York: Association Press, 1961; Japanese translation by Y. Kami, 1982).

The Paradox of the World (Cambridge University Press, 1921).

The Book of Revelation: Theory of the Text, Rearrangement, Commentary (Cambridge University Press, 1923).

Revelation: A Revised Theory of the Text (Cambridge University Press, 1928).

The Natural and the Supernatural (Cambridge University Press, 1931; reprinted 1950).

Concerning the Ministry (London: SCM, 1936; reprinted 1953; also published as a booklet, *The Office of Ministry*, SCM, 1928; second edition, 1929).

Honest Religion (Cambridge University Press, 1941).

A Dialogue with God (London: James Clarke, 1950; reprinted 1963).

Translation

Schleiermacher: On Religion. Speeches to its Cultured Despisers (London: Kegan Paul, 1893), Introduction by John Oman; reissued with introduction by Rudolf Otto, (New York: Harper, 1958).

Articles and Essays

'Preparation for the Gospel', *The Presbyterian Messenger* 586 (January 1895), pp. 15-16.

'The Consistency and Unity of the Bible', *The Presbyterian Messenger* 586 (February 1895), 39-40; 587 (March 1895), p. 64.

'Individualism', 'Individual', and 'Individuality', *Hastings' Dictionary of Christ and Gospels* I (1908), pp. 814-21.

'Boasting', *Hastings Encyclopedia of Religion and Ethics* II (1909), pp. 735-9.

'The Needs of Our College', *The Presbyterian Messenger* 764 (November 1909), pp. 378-9.

'The Beam and the Mote', in R. Scott and W.C. Stiles (eds.), *Modern Sermons by World*

232

Scholars III (New York: Funk and Wagnalls, 1909), pp. 45-59.

'Church', *Hastings' Encyclopedia of Religion and Ethics* III (1910), pp. 617-24.

'The Presbyterian Churches', in W.B. Selbie (ed.), *Evangelical Christianity: Its History and Witness* (London: Hodder and Stoughton, 1911).

'Personality and System', *The Expositor* 2 (October 1911), pp. 358-67.

'Grace', *The Expositor* 2 (November 1911), pp. 456-63.

'Autonomy', *The Expositor* 3 (February 1912), pp. 171-8.

'Dependence and Interdependence', *The Expositor* 3 (March 1912), pp. 236-42.

'A Gracious Relationship', *The Expositor* 3 (May 1912), pp. 468-75.

'Faith', *The Expositor* 3 (June 1912), pp. 528-34.

'Jesus Christ', *The Expositor* 4 (July 1912), pp. 57-60.

'Repentance', *The Expositor* 4 (August 1912), pp. 138-42.

'Justification', *The Expositor* 4 (September 1912), pp. 252-62.

'Reconciliation', *The Expositor* 4 (October 1912), pp. 354-62.

'Eternal Life', *The Expositor* 4 (November 1912), pp. 414-23.

'The Will of God', *The Expositor* 4 (December 1912), pp. 526-38.

'Methods and Problems of Evangelism. IV. Evangelism and the Gospel', *The Presbyterian Messenger* 810 (September 1913), pp. 282-3.

'The Rev. W. Rogerson', *The Presbyterian Messenger* 848 (November 1915), p. 396.

'Human Freedom' and 'War', *The Elements of Pain and Conflict in Human Life, Considered from a Christian Point of View* (Cambridge University Press, 1916), pp. 56-73, 157-72.

'Religion and its Systems', *Harmsworth's Universal Encyclopedia* X (1920).

'Looking Round Our Position', *The Student Movement* 24 (February 1922), pp. 98-100.

'The Mathematical Mechanical Order', *The Student Movement* 24 (March 1922), pp. 124-5.

'The Evolutionary Historical Process', *The Student Movement* 24 (April 1922), pp. 153-5.

'Mind as the Measure of the Universe', *The Student Movement* 24 (May 1922), pp. 171-3.

'The Sacred as the Measure of Man', *The Student Movement* 24 (June 1922), pp. 194-5.

'Our College and its Problems', *The Presbyterian Messenger* 934 (January 1923), pp. 300-301.

'Method in Theology, An Inaugural Lecture', *The Expositor* 26 (August 1923), pp. 81-93.

'The Apocalypse', *The Expositor*, ninth series, 4 (December 1925), pp. 437-52.

'The Sphere of Religion', in J. Needham (ed.), *Science, Religion and Reality* (London: Sheldon Press; New York: Macmillan, 1925), pp. 259-99.

'Christianity in a New Age', in A.S. Peake and R.G. Parsons (eds.), *An Outline of Christianity* III (London: Waverly Book Company, 1926), pp. xiii-xxii.

'The Ministry of the Non-Conformist Churches', in T.A.R. Cairns (compiler), *The Problem of a Career Solved by Thirty-six Men of Distinction* (Bristol: Arrowsmith, 1926), pp. 127-32.

'Christianity', *Encyclopedia Britannica*, 13th edn, supplementary volumes I (1926), pp. 632-5.

'Mysticism and its Expositors', *The Hibbert Journal* 26 (April 1928), pp. 445-58.

'The Moderator's Address. The Westminster Confession of Faith', *The Presbyterian Messenger* 1035 (June 1931), pp. 48-50.

'The Roman Sacerdotal Hierarchy', *Why I Am and Why I Am Not a Catholic* (London: Cassell, 1931), pp. 155-80.

'The Moderator's New Year Message', *The Presbyterian Messenger* 1042 (January 1932), pp. 234-5.

'Are We Too Academic?', *The Presbyterian Messenger* 1047 (June 1932), p. 56.

'Westminster College. Gift of Historical Portraits', *The Presbyterian Messenger* 1058 (May 1933), p. 14.

'The Abiding Significance of Apocalyptic', in G.A. Yates (ed.), *In Spirit and Truth. Aspects of Judaism and Christianity* (London: Hodder and Stoughton, 1934), pp. 276-93.

'In Memoriam: William Fearon Halliday', in J.R. Coates (ed.), *Personal Freedom Through Personal Faith* (London: Hodder and Stoughton, 1934), pp. 39-46.

'Elocution in the College', *The Presbyterian Messenger* 1084 (July 1935), p. 200.

'The Book of Proverbs', *Religion in Life* 4 (Summer 1935), pp. 330-6.

Book Reviews

Book Review of *Faith and its Psychology* by W.R. Inge, and *Ritschlianism* by J.K. Mozley, *The Presbyterian Messenger* 767 (February 1910), pp. 47-8.

'Ritschlianism', *The Journal of Theological Studies* 11 (July 1910), pp. 594-6.

'Principles of Religious Development', *The Journal of Theological Studies* 11 (July 1910), pp. 594-6.

Book Review of *Group Theories of Religion and Religion of the Individual* by Clement C.J. Webb, *The Journal of Theological Studies* 18 (January and April 1917), p. 224.

Book Review of *Nature, Miracle and Sin: A Study of St. Augustine's Conception of the Natural Order* by T.A. Lacey, *The Journal of Theological Studies* 18 (January and April 1917), pp. 246-7.

Book Review of *Essays in Orthodoxy* by O.C. Quick, *The Journal of Theological Studies* 18 (January and April 1917), pp. 246-7.

Book Review of *The Idea of God in the Light of Recent Philosophy* by S. Pringle-Pattison, *The Journal of Theological Studies* 19 (January and April 1918), pp. 278-9.

Book Review of *The Idea of Atonement in Christian Theology* by H. Rashdall, *The Journal of Theological Studies* 21 (April 1920), pp. 267-75.

Book Review of *A Short History of the Doctrine of Atonement* by L.W. Grensted, *The Journal of Theological Studies* 21 (April 1920), pp. 275-6.

Book Review of *The Ministry of Reconciliation* by J.R. Gillies, *The Journal of Theological Studies* 21 (April 1920), p. 277.

Book Review of *L'Evolution religieuse de Luther jusqu'en 1515* by H. Strohl, and *La Liberté Chrétienne* by R. Will, *The Journal of Theological Studies* 24 (January 1923), pp. 211-14.

Book Review of *A Faith that Enquires* by H. Jones, *The Journal of Theological Studies* 24 (January 1923), pp. 214-17.

Book Review of *Philosophy and the Christian Experience* by N. Richmond, *The Journal of Theological Studies* 24 (January 1923), pp. 214-17.

Book Review of *Religion and Modern Thought* by G. Galloway, *The Journal of Theological Studies* 24 (July 1923), pp. 446-9.

Book Review of *An Introduction to the Psychology of Religion* by R.H. Thouless, *The*

Journal of Theological Studies 24 (July 1923), pp. 449-50.

'The Idea of the Holy', *The Journal of Theological Studies* 25 (April 1924), pp. 275-86.

Book Review of *The Design Argument Reconsidered* by C.J. Shebbeare and J. McCabe, *The Journal of Theological Studies* 26 (October 1924), pp. 87-8.

Book Review of *Religion et Realité* by C. Hauter, *The Journal of Theological Studies* 26 (October 1924), pp. 88-91.

Book Review of *L'épanòuissement de la pensée religieuse de Luther de 1515 à 1520* by H. Strohl, *The Journal of Theological Studies* 26 (October 1924), pp. 91-2.

Book Review of *Lehrbuch der Symbolik* by W. Walther; *The Place of Reason in Christian Apologetic* by L. Hodgson; *L'humanité et son chef* by P. Bridel; *Grundlegung Christlicher Dogmatik* by H. Ludemann; *Erlebnis, Erkenntnis und Glaube* by E. Brunner; and *Organische Grundlagen der Religion* by H. Adolph, *The Journal of Theological Studies* 26 (July 1925), pp. 409-20.

Book Review of *Le Culte* by R. Will, *The Journal of Theological Studies* 27 (January 1926), pp. 183-4.

Book Review of *Miracle and its Philosophical Presuppositions* by F.R. Tennant, *The Journal of Theological Studies* 27 (January 1926), pp. 184-5.

Book Review of *Traité de philosophie* by G. Sortais, SJ, *The Journal of Theological Studies* 28 (January 1927), pp. 187-8.

Book Review of *De Kant à Ritschl* by H. Dubois, *The Journal of Theological Studies* 28 (January 1927), pp. 188-9.

Book Review of *Les contradictions de la pensée religieuse* by Jean de Saussure, *The Journal of Theological Studies* 28 (January 1927), pp. 190-2.

Book Review of *Religion in the Making* by A.N. Whitehead, *The Journal of Theological Studies* 28 (April 1927), pp. 296-304.

Book Review of *The Oldest Biography of Spinoza* by A. Wolf, *The Journal of Theological Studies* 28 (July 1927), pp. 425-6.

Book Review of *The Philosophy of the Abbé Beautin* by W.H. Horton, *The Journal of Theological Studies* 28 (July 1927), pp. 426-7.

Book Review of *Notes on St. John and the Apocalypse* by A. Pallis, *The Journal of Theological Studies* 28 (July 1927), p. 427.

Book Review of *The Nature and Right of Religion* by W. Morgan, *The Journal of Theological Studies* 28 (July 1927), pp. 428-30.

Book Review of *Adventure, The Faith of Science and the Science of Faith* by B.H. Streeter, C.M. Chilcott, John Macmurray and A.S. Russell, *The Journal of Theological Studies* 29 (April 1928), pp. 290-6.

Book Review of *The Christian Experience of Forgiveness* by H.R. Mackintosh, *The Journal of Theological Studies* 29 (April 1928), pp. 296-9.

Book Review of *Systematic Theology* by W. Herrmann, *The Journal of Theological Studies* 29 (April 1928), pp. 299-300.

Book Review of *Studies of the Psychology of the Mystics* by J. Marechal, *The Journal of Theological Studies* 29 (April 1928), pp. 300-2.

Book Review of *Rationalism and Orthodoxy To-Day* by J.H. Bleibitz, *The Journal of Theological Studies* 29 (April 1928), pp. 302-3.

Book Review of *Philosophical Theology*, vol. 1 by F.R. Tennant, *The Journal of Theological Studies* 31 (July 1930), pp. 403-7.

Book Review of *Sämtliche Werke*, Bände XII–XIV, Philosophie der Religion by G.W. Hegel, *The Journal of Theological Studies* 32 (January 1931), pp. 211-17.

Book Review of *Le problème de Dieu* by E. Le Roy, *The Journal of Theological Studies* 32 (January 1931), pp. 217-19.

Book Review of *Process and Reality* by A.N. Whitehead, *The Journal of Theological Studies* 33 (October 1931), pp. 48-52.

Book Review of *Le Culte* by R. Will, *The Journal of Theological Studies* 33 (October 1931), pp. 52-4.

Book Review of *The Philosophical Basis of Biology* by J.S. Haldane, *The Journal of Theological Studies* 33 (January 1932), pp. 216-18.

Book Review of *Philosophical Theology*, vol. II by F.R. Tennant, *The Journal of Theological Studies* 33 (April 1932), pp. 281-3.

Book Review of *The Philosophy of Religion Based on Kant and Fries* by R. Otto, *The Journal of Theological Studies* 33 (April 1932), pp. 283-6.

Book Review of *Religious Essays, A Supplement to "The Idea of the Holy"* by Rudolf Otto, *The Journal of Theological Studies* 33 (April 1932), pp. 286-8.

Book Review of *Schopenhauer: His Life and Philosophy* by H. Zimmern, *The Journal of Theological Studies* 34 (January 1933), pp. 98-101.

Book Review of *An Introduction to Schleiermacher* by A. Chapman, *The Journal of Theological Studies* 34 (April 1933), pp. 213-14.

Book Review of *Das Kommende: Untersuchungen zu Entstehungsgeschichte des messianischen Glaubens* by Martin Buber, *The Journal of Theological Studies* 34 (April 1933), pp. 214-16.

Book Review of *An Idealist View of life* by S. Radha-krishnan, *The Journal of Theological Studies* 34 (April 1933), pp. 216-18.

Book Review of *The Logic of Religious Thought* by R. Gordon Milburn, *The Journal of Theological Studies* 35 (April 1934), pp. 197-9.

Book Review of *Imago Christi* by H. Bornkamm, *The Journal of Theological Studies* 35 (April 1934), pp. 199-200.

Book Review of *Experience and its Modes* by M. Oakeshott, *The Journal of Theological Studies* 35 (July 1934), pp. 314-16.

Book Review of *The Idealistic Conception of Religion* by A. Lion, *The Journal of Theological Studies* 35 (October 1934), pp. 404-5.

Book Review of *La pensée intuitive* II by E. Le Roy, *The Journal of Theological Studies* 35 (October 1934), pp. 405-7.

Unpublished Material

Oman's sermons from 1899 until 1905, as well as unpublished talks, occasional papers, and a small book of prayers and notes for prayer are found in the special collection of Oman's unpublished works at Westminster College, Cambridge. One box found in the stacks of Westminster College library contains a report Oman wrote to the General Assembly of the Presbyterian Church of England. This manuscript answers several questions put to Principal Oman about theological education in the College.

A handwritten essay from Oman's undergraduate days at Edinburgh can be found in the library of New College at the University of Edinburgh. It is in the volume entitled 'United Presbyterian Student's (sic) University Magazine', 1882, vol. III, pp. 13-26.

Oman, John Wood, 'Rationalism and Romanticism: A Study of Kant's "Religion within the Limits of Reason Alone" and Schleiermacher's "Speeches on Religion"'

236

(unpublished doctoral thesis: University of Edinburgh, 1904).

Works About John Oman
Book

Bevans, Stephen. *John Oman and his Doctrine of God* (Cambridge: Cambridge University Press, 1992).

Elmslie, W.A.L. *Westminster College Cambridge 1899-1949* (London: Presbyterian Church of England [1949]).

Healey, F.G. *Religion and Reality: The Theology of John Oman* (Edinburgh: Oliver and Boyd, 1965).

Hood, Adam. *Ballie, Oman and Macmurray: experience and religious belief* (Aldershot, England; Burlington, VT: Ashgate, 2003).

Robson, R.S. *Our Professors. Brief notes on men who after occupying English Presbyterian pulpits have been appointed to chairs* (London: Presbyterian Historical Society of England, 1956).

Articles, Journals and Collections

An old student, 'Principal Oman's Great Book', *The Presbyterian Messenger* 1042 (January 1932), p. 249.

Bezzant, J.S., 'The Theology of John Oman', *Modern Churchman* 9 (January 1966), pp. 135-40.

Cottle, T.L. and A.S. Cooper, 'Westminster College Bulletin', *The Presbyterian Messenger* 1085 (August 1935), p. 230.

Eastwood, J.H., 'Westminster College, Cambridge. Commonwealth Day, June 7th, 1933', *The Presbyterian Messenger* 1060 (July 1933), pp. 68-9.

Farmer, H.H., 'Monotheism and the Doctrine of the Trinity', *Religion in Life* XXIX (winter 1959-60), pp. 32-41.

— 'John Wood Oman', *Expository Times* 74, no. 5 (February 1963), pp. 132-35.

Halliday, W.F., Book Review of *The Church and the Divine Order*, by J. Oman, *The Presbyterian Messenger* 789 (December 1911), pp. 379-83.

Harvey, V.A., 'On the New Edition of Scheiermacher's Addresses on Religion', *Journal of the American Academy of Religion* 39 (December 1971), pp. 488-512.

Healey, F.G., 'The Theology of John Oman', *Theology* 67 (December 1964), pp. 543-46.

Hick, J., 'Theological Table Talk. The Neglected Theologian of Your Choice', *Theology Today* 19, no. 3 (October 1962), pp. 405-6.

Jeffrey, G.J., 'Oman's Concerning the ministry: a revaluation', *Expository Times* 69, no. 2 (November 1957), pp. 36-7.

Knox, R.B., 'The Bible in English Presbyterianism', *Expository Times* 94 (March 1983), pp. 166-70.

Knox, T.M., Book Review of *Religion and Reality: The Theology of John Oman* by F.G. Healey, *The Journal of Theological Studies*, N.S., XVII (1966), pp. 546-50.

Langford, T.A., 'The concept of the person: a comparison of C.C.J Webb and John Oman', *Religion in Life* 33, no 3 (summer 1964), pp. 407-20.

— 'The Theological Methodology of John Oman and H.H. Farmer', *Religious Studies* (winter 1966), pp. 229-40.

Lindsay, A.D., review of John Oman, *The Natural and the Supernatural*, *The Journal of Theological Studies*, XXXIII, 1932.

McBean, E.K., 'Appreciation', *The Modern Churchman* (February 1932), pp. 596-604.

MacLeod, J., 'John Oman, as Theologian', *Hibbert Journal* 48 (July 1950), pp. 348-53.

Manson, T.W., 'Dr. John Oman', *The Presbyterian Messenger* 1084 (July 1935), pp. 199-200.

Mews, S.P., 'Neo-Orthodoxy, Liberalism and War: Karl Barth, P.T. Forsyth and John Oman, 1914–18', *Renaissance and Renewal in Christian History*. D. Baker, ed. (Oxford: Blackwell, 1977), pp. 361-75.

'Monthly Notes', Book Review of *Vision and Authority* by J. Oman, *The Presbyterian Messenger*, New Series (July 1902).

Morris, J.S., 'Oman's Conception of the Personal God in *The Natural and the Supernatural*', *The Journal of Theological Studies* 73 (April 1972), pp. 82-94.

Nichol, F.W.R., 'John Oman's Theology', *The Reformed Theological Review*, XVI (June 1957), pp. 33-44.

P., E.W., 'The new Principal. An Appreciation of Dr. Oman', *The Presbyterian Messenger* 928 (July 1922), pp. 154-5.

R., 'The War and Its Issues. Professor Oman's View', *The Presbyterian Messenger* 844 (July 1915), pp. 255-6.

— Book Review of *The Paradox of the World* by J. Oman, *The Presbyterian Messenger* 914 (May 1921), p. 105.

R., N.L., 'The Moderator Designate', *The Presbyterian Messenger* 1034 (May 1931), pp. 2-3.

Richards, E., 'John Oman's Doctrine of the Christian Ministry', *Expository Times* 82 (December 1970), pp. 71-4.

Tennant, F.R., Book review of *The Natural and the Supernatural* by J. Oman, *Mind* 41 (April 1932), pp. 212-18.

Wilson, M.W., 'The Theology of John Oman', *New Zealand Journal of Theology* I.

Woods, G.F., 'Revised reviews: John Oman's The natural and the supernatural', *Theology* 64 (June 1961), pp. 233-37.

Articles: Encyclopaedias

Brandt, R.B., 'Oman, John Wood', *Encyclopaedia of Religion* (1945), p. 545.

Clark, R.E.D., 'Oman, John Wood', *The New International Dictionary of the Christian Church* (1974), p. 730.

Hick, J., 'Oman, John Wood', *Encyclopaedia of Philosophy* (1967), p. 538.

Hanna, W., 'Oman, John Wood', *New Catholic Encyclopaedia* (1967), p. 686.

Litz, R.J., 'Oman, John Wood', *Encyclopaedic Dictionary of Religion* (1979), p. 2599.

'Oman, John Wood', *Oxford Dictionary of the Christian Church* (1957), p. 983.

Biographies

Alexander, G.W., 'Memoir of the Author', Introduction to *Honest Religion* (Cambridge University press, 1941), pp. xv-xxv.

238

Ballard, F.H. 'Introduction', *Honest Religion* (Cambridge University Press, 1941), pp. xi-xiv.

Best, N.R., 'Introduction', *Grace and Personality* (1925 edition; New York: The Macmillan Company, 1925), pp. vi-xvi.

Farmer, H.H., 'Death of Dr. John Oman. An Appreciation', *The Christian World* (May 25 1939).

— 'Memoir of the Author', Introduction to *Honest Religion* (Cambridge University Press, 1941), pp. xxvi-xxxii.

— 'Theologians of Our time. III. John Wood Oman', *The Expository Times*, LXXIV (February 1963), 132-5.

— 'Oman, John Wood', *Dictionary of National Biography 1931–40* (Oxford University Press; London: Geoffrey Cumberlege, 1949), pp.657-9.

Hick, J., 'Introduction,' *Grace and Personality* (1961 edition; New York: Association Press, 1961), pp. 5-10.

Simpson, P.C., 'Dr. John Oman', *The Presbyterian Messenger* 1132 (July 1939), 197-8.

Tennant, F.R., 'John Wood Oman, 1860–1939', *Proceedings of the British Academy*, vol. XXV, 1939 (London: Humphrey Milford, Oxford University Press, 1939), pp. 332-8.

Whitehorn, R.D., 'Obituary, The Rev. John Oman', *Cambridge Review* (May 26, 1939).

Who Was Who, 1929–1940 (London: Adam and Charles Black, 1941).

Doctoral Dissertations

Gross, H.H., 'The Relationship Between Religion and Morality in Immanuel Kant and John Wood Oman' (unpublished doctoral dissertation: University of Iowa, 1946).

Hjelm, R.O., 'An Examination of the Religious Thought of John Wood Oman' (unpublished doctoral dissertation: Harvard University, 1954).

Hood, A., 'The Ground and Nature of Religious Belief in the Work of John Macmurray, John Baillie and John Oman' (unpublished doctoral dissertation: University of Oxford, 1999).

Molnar, C., 'The Concept of Sincerity in John Oman's Thought' (unpublished doctoral dissertation: University of Southern California, 1970).

Morris, J.S., 'An Examination of John Oman's Theory of Religious Knowledge' (unpublished doctoral dissertation: Columbia University, 1961).

Richardson, N.E., 'The Concept of Immanence in the Works of John W. Oman and F.R. Tennant' (unpublished doctoral dissertation: Yale University, 1940).

Weaver, H.R., 'The Significance of John Wood Oman for the Problem of Religious Knowledge' (unpublished doctoral dissertation: Drew University, 1950).

Wills, J.R., 'The Understanding of Man in the Writings of Baron von Huegel, Nicolas Berdyaev, John Wood Oman, with a Concluding Critical and Constructive Statement "Toward the Christian Understanding of Man"' (unpublished doctoral dissertation: Union Thelogical Seminary, 1948).

Wilson, R.A., 'The Problem of Religious Authority in Contemporary Theological Thought with Particular Reference to the Interpretations of John Oman, P.T. Forsyth and A.E.J. Rawlinson' (unpublished doctoral dissertation: Columbia University, 1960).

Master's Thesis

Sutcliffe, H.G., 'John Oman as Theologian for Today' (unpublished Master's thesis: Manchester University, 1975).

Unpublished Material on Oman

Healey, F.G., 'The Theology of John Oman', typescript.
'Reminiscences of John Oman', typescript.
Niccol, D.M., 'Philosophy of Religion. Lectures by Dr. John Oman on God in Relation to the World and Man' (1920?).

Index

ND - #0084 - 090625 - C0 - 229/152/14 - PB - 9781842277317 - Gloss Lamination